HOMEW🍎RK HELPERS

U.S. History
(1492–1865)

From the Discovery of America Through the Civil War

RON OLSON

B CAREER PRESS
Franklin Lakes, NJ

HOMEWORK HELPERS: U.S. HISTORY (1492–1865)
EDITED BY ASTRID DERIDDER
TYPESET BY EILEEN DOW MUNSON
Cover design by Lu Rossman/Digi Dog Design NYC
Printed in the U.S.A. by Book-mart Press

Interior images provided on:
pages 20, 24, 28, 29, 64, 70, 73, 87, 213; by Clipart.com.
pages 33, 42, 62, 85, 86, 96, 97, 127, 132, 142, 145,
162, 188, 189, 203, 204, 208; by Maps.com.
pages 182, 193; by the National Park Service.
pages 43, 45, 47, 52, 226; copyright NYSTROM
Herff Jones Education Division. Used by Permission.

To order this title, please call toll-free 1-800-CAREER-1 (NJ and Canada: 201-848-0310) to order using VISA or MasterCard, or for further information on books from Career Press.

CAREER PRESS

The Career Press, Inc., 3 Tice Road, PO Box 687,
Franklin Lakes, NJ 07417
www.careerpress.com

Library of Congress Cataloging-in-Publication Data

Olson, Ron, 1959-
    Homework helpers. U.S. history (1492-1865) : from the discovery of America through the Civil War / by Ron Olson.
        p. cm.
    Includes bibliographical references and index.
    ISBN-13: 978-1-56414-917-6
    ISBN-10: 1-56414-917-X
        1. United States—History—Study and teaching. 2. United States—History—Colonial period, ca. 1600-1175—Problems, exercises, etc. 3. United States—History—Revolution, 1775-1783—Problems, exercises, etc. 4. United States—History—1783-1865—Problems, exercises, etc. I. Title. II. Title: U.S. History (1492-1865).

E175.8.O45 2006
973.076—dc22

                                                                    2006022075

Dedication

I wish to dedicate this book to two unique teachers. First of all, I would like to acknowledge my ninth-grade German teacher, Frau Hollinger, who took an active interest in "Wolfgang" and instilled in me the joy and love of learning. Secondly, I would like to acknowledge my history professor, Monroe Billington, whose love of history and dedication to teaching still inspires me in my job as a teacher today.

Acknowledgments

To my wife, Lynne, for her support during this long process.

To several of my friends who have been a great safety net of encouragement throughout this process: Brian and Colleen Redpath, Ray and Mary Armstrong, Scott and Patti Barringer, Scott and Diane Holz, Dana Roth, Steve and Gail Capatch, and Dana and Donya White.

To three of my fellow AP teachers who have also been a great safety net of encouragement and friendship throughout this process: Nancy Potter, Steve Armstrong, and Carolyn Callaghan.

To Grace Freedson for her support in arranging the opportunity for me to work on this project. It is good to see this book published!

And, last but not least, my two "guard dogs" who kept watch over me as I spent countless hours in my office typing and researching. Madison, my Springer Spaniel, and Sparky, my Cocker Spaniel, followed me everywhere and stayed close by my side during the entire process. (It's too bad they can't read!)

Contents

Introduction 11

Chapter 1: The Age of Exploration 15
    Lesson 1-1: Europe Experiences Change   16
    Lesson 1-2: Religious Challenges in Europe   16
    Lesson 1-3: Beyond the Boundaries of Europe   17

Chapter 2: The Colonial Period 23
    Lesson 2-1: The Colony of Jamestown   24
    Lesson 2-2: Puritan New England   27
    Lesson 2-3: The Middle and Southern Colonies   32

Chapter 3: Colonial Society Comes of Age 39
    Lesson 3-1: The Colonial Economy of Mercantilism   40
    Lesson 3-2: Life in Colonial America   42
    Lesson 3-3: Colonial Culture in the Age of Reason   48
    Lesson 3-4: The First Great Awakening   49
    Lesson 3-5: The Slave Trade   50

Chapter 4: The Road to Revolution 59
    Lesson 4-1: Crisis in the Colonies   60
    Lesson 4-2: The French and Indian War   61
    Lesson 4-3: British Demands and Colonial Resistance   63

Lesson 4-4: "If This Be Treason..."   69

Lesson 4-5: Independence Declared   74

Chapter 5: The Revolutionary War 81

Lesson 5-1: The Continental Army versus the Redcoats   82

Lesson 5-2: Fighting the War for Independence   84

Lesson 5-3: Surrender and Victory   87

Lesson 5-4: The Impact of the War on American Society   88

Chapter 6: Governing the New Nation 93

Lesson 6-1: Governing the New States   94

Lesson 6-2: The Articles of Confederation   94

Lesson 6-3: The Convention in Philadelphia   98

Lesson 6-4: The Ratification Debate   102

Chapter 7: The Federalist Era 107

Lesson 7-1: Washington's Vision of Leadership   108

Lesson 7-2: Federalists versus Anti-Federalists   110

Lesson 7-3: The Rise of Political Parties   112

Lesson 7-4: The Whiskey Rebellion   113

Lesson 7-5: Westward Expansion   114

Lesson 7-6: France and U.S. Neutrality   114

Lesson 7-7: Washington's Farewell Address   115

Lesson 7-8: Continuing the Federalist Legacy   116

Lesson 7-9: Silencing the Opposition   117

Lesson 7-10: Changing of the Guard   118

Chapter 8: Jeffersonian Democracy 125

Lesson 8-1: Jefferson and the Democratic-Republicans   126

Lesson 8-2: The Louisiana Purchase   127

Lesson 8-3: Westward Exploration   128

Lesson 8-4: The Aaron Burr Controversy   129

Lesson 8-5: Tension Overseas and American Trade   129

Lesson 8-6: Madison and Preparations for War   130

Lesson 8-7: The War of 1812   131

Chapter 9: The Era of Good Feelings......................... 139

Lesson 9-1: American Nationalism Takes Shape   140

Lesson 9-2: Growth of the Market Economy   141

Lesson 9-3: Economic Boom and Bust   143

Lesson 9-4: Geographical Boundaries   144

Lesson 9-5: The Marshall Court   147

Chapter 10: Jacksonian Democracy 153

Lesson 10-1: A Two-Party System of Politics   154

Lesson 10-2: The Election of 1824 and John Quincy Adams   157

Lesson 10-3: Jackson and the Era of the Common Man   158

Lesson 10-4: The Nullification Crisis   160

Lesson 10-5: The Indian Removal Act   161

Lesson 10-6: Opposition to the Bank   163

Lesson 10-7: Martin Van "Ruin" and Economic Crisis   164

Chapter 11: The Era of Reform............................ 171

Lesson 11-1: The Abolitionist Movement   172

Lesson 11-2: Women's Issues   174

Lesson 11-3: American Literature   175

Lesson 11-4: Education   176

Lesson 11-5: Crime and Criminals   177

Lesson 11-6: Temperance   178

Lesson 11-7: A Religious Revival in America   178

Lesson 11-8: Utopian Communities   179

Chapter 12: Manifest Destiny 185

Lesson 12-1: Settling the West   186

Lesson 12-2: Texas and the Alamo   187

Lesson 12-3: The Mexican-American War   188

Lesson 12-4: Internal Expansion   191

Lesson 12-5: Slavery in the South   194

Lesson 12-6: The Politics of Expansion   196

Chapter 13: The Road to Civil War 201

Lesson 13-1: The Compromise of 1850   202

Lesson 13-2: The Fugitive Slave Act   204

Lesson 13-3: Harriet Beecher Stowe   205

Lesson 13-4: The Ostend Manifesto   205

Lesson 13-5: Bleeding Kansas   205

Lesson 13-6: The Birth of the Republican Party   208

Lesson 13-7: The Dred Scott Decision   209

Lesson 13-8: The Lincoln-Douglas Debates   211

Lesson 13-9: John Brown's Raid   212

Lesson 13-10: The Election of 1860   212

Lesson 13-11: Secession   213

Chapter 14: A Nation Divided 219

Lesson 14-1: The Blue and the Gray   220

Lesson 14-2: Years of Conflict   223

Lesson 14-3: Union Victory   225

Lesson 14-4: The Impact of the War on American Society   227

Lesson 14-5: North and South   231

Answer Key 237

Glossary 275

Resources 309

Index 311

About the Author 319

Introduction

Welcome to *Homework Helpers: U.S. History!*

This two-book series was written with you in mind. It is my hope to make the study of history a bit easier. Each of the books in this series has been designed with 14 chapters that provide a review of the history of the United States. The first book covers the period from 1492 to the end of the Civil War in 1865, and the second covers the period from Reconstruction in 1865 to the present. It is meant to help you master the material from a U.S. history course and to help prepare you for review exams such as the SAT II U.S. History exam and the Advanced Placement U.S. History exam. The books are also flexible to fit a variety of needs for students. Some high schools offer the entire scope of U.S. history as their course, whereas other schools offer the second half of U.S. history from 1865 to the present. Students who need to study to prepare for state or national history exams will benefit from the scope of information in both books.

The vast amount of material you are presented with in a U.S. history course may at times seems a bit overwhelming, and many students can easily become intimidated. It can be a daunting task to think about people, places, and things from the times of Columbus and the founding of the colonies all the way to the terrorist attacks of September 11, 2001. That's a lot of history! If you learn to use a few tools along the way, you can begin to manage the vast amount of historical information. Don't get hung up thinking you have to memorize lists of dates and people. Although some dates and people are very important, it is a good idea to focus on themes and trends and make connections that way.

In this book, I hope to make terms and concepts easier to understand through the use of charts, maps, and easy-to-understand text. Although memorization does play a role in a course such as U.S. history, comprehension of the material leads to greater recall ability and more enjoyment of the subject matter.

Each chapter includes a review exam with test material in a multiple choice, matching, and short response format. Take time to complete each review exam. The correct answers and explanations are included for each exam! After you complete a review exam, go back and check your answers. If necessary, go back and review the material again and repeat the test. Practice does make perfect!

Each chapter begins with a brief time line of six major events that occurred during the time period discussed in that particular chapter. This is meant to help you keep the events in a chronological perspective.

Next, each chapter begins with a chart entitled "Trends and Themes of the Era." This chart is meant to provide a broad overview of the big ideas for the time frame covered in that particular chapter. These are good ideas to help anchor your review of the material.

The introductory paragraph in each chapter begins with three key words that will help act as a road map for that particular chapter. As you read the chapter, look for these concepts to be developed. Also, the introduction serves as a quick overview of the entire chapter by giving you a broad look at the landscape of that particular chapter. As you read each mini-lesson within the chapter, the details will be filled in.

Furthermore, most chapters contain maps! The entire two-book series contains more than 40 maps. Several different thematic maps are included to help guide you in the review of material. It is an excellent way to visualize important details on the maps: names of places, development of a particular theme for a map (such as land usage, trailblazing, property acquisitions, and so on). Take time when you are presented with a map to **stop** and **study** the map. Ask yourself very basic, yet important questions: "What information does this map provide?" or "How does this map relate to the important information in the chapter?"

Some chapters contain other forms of graphics, such as charts or political cartoons. Be sure to closely read all of the information in the charts. These are designed to provide you with a quick snapshot of vital information. Be sure to examine those graphics for unique information in a visual format.

Many state and national exams generally won't ask you specific questions about numerous facts during a particular war. Sometimes the names of leaders or the succession of major battles may be asked, but that's generally not the rule. Wars are often presented as being sandwiched between two bookends—the events leading up to and the events following the war. A short summary of the major war events is included in this book because it provides an important context for understanding the events preceding and following a war.

As you read this book, keep in mind several of the broad themes that begin occurring and look for various trends over time—economic trends, political trends, important legislative acts, tariffs, economic depressions, labor trends, foreign policy issues, domestic policy issues, court cases, immigration, and women and minorities in history. After reading a few chapters, you want to be able to make comparisons over periods of time from one decade to another, or by looking at trends over a 40- to 50-year period.

In order to guide your study of history you need to read the material in this book carefully! History is a story—so take time to enjoy it! Don't read all of the material in one setting! Take time to digest the material in each mini-lesson in the chapters. Pace yourself. You are a marathon runner running the 26.2 miles at the Boston Marathon, not just a track star running the 100-yard dash! Good studying takes a bit of preparation and endurance. Remember that good comprehension of a subject matter comes after sufficient review. Work on the material from this review book for a short period of time each night. It is my hope that this book helps bring comprehension, confidence, and enthusiasm to your study of history.

The Age of Exploration

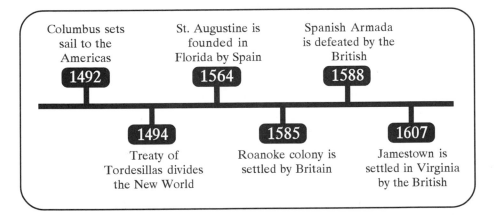

Columbus sets sail to the Americas
1492

St. Augustine is founded in Florida by Spain
1564

Spanish Armada is defeated by the British
1588

1494
Treaty of Tordesillas divides the New World

1585
Roanoke colony is settled by Britain

1607
Jamestown is settled in Virginia by the British

Trends and Themes of the Era

> Portugal and Spain take the lead in world exploration, trade, and colonization in the sixteenth century.

> The Old and New Worlds experience a large-scale exchange of people, crops, animals, and diseases.

> The British and French begin establishing a foothold in the New World by the end of the sixteenth century.

> Religion, commerce, and desire for land and power motivate Europeans to get involved on the world stage.

Gold, glory, and God! These goals changed the world by igniting more than 200 years of exploration and discovery. The opportunities for religious freedom, land, and the search for wealth in the New World motivated explorers and settlers. As explorers looked for the fabled Northwest Passage to the Orient, gold and other riches from the New World found their way back to Europe. This race for exploration set the nation-states of Europe on a course of conquest and domination. The resulting events intertwined the continents of Europe, Africa, and the Americas, and forever changed the destinies of each region.

Lesson 1-1: Europe Experiences Change

The feudalism of the Middle Ages was ending as the nation-states of England, Spain, Portugal, and France began exerting control on the European continent. The desire for trade with Asia and the exploration of the oceans would lead Europeans to the continents of Africa, Asia, South America, and North America.

By the mid-1400s, Europe's population was beginning to rebound after a century of decline from the ravaging effects of the Bubonic Plague, which was known as the **Black Death,** which killed nearly 30 percent of the population of Europe. Once areas began to recover, new population growth brought about a demand for land, food, and jobs. The practice of leaving the inheritance of all lands and titles to the eldest son left few options for younger children. Inflation, rising land values, lack of jobs, and food shortages resulted in conflicts.

Meanwhile, the Renaissance launched a remarkable rebirth of knowledge and ideas and a revival in the arts and education with the key figures and works of Michelangelo, Machiavelli, and Leonardo da Vinci. Furthermore, Johann Gutenberg's printing press in the 1450s gave people access to the written word. Not only did people begin to read the Bible and classical works of literature and philosophy, but they read about Marco Polo's adventures in China in the late thirteenth century and were captivated with the possibilities of Asian spices, silks, gold, and other riches.

Lesson 1-2: Religious Challenges in Europe

After centuries of domination by the Catholic Church, Martin Luther and John Calvin led Europe in the **Protestant Reformation.** Luther's message in 1517 that faith alone, not good works, would save Christians sparked upheaval in Roman Catholic communities throughout Europe.

In England, the Anglican Church was born when (among other issues) the Roman Catholic Church refused to grant an annulment to King Henry VIII's marriage to Catherine of Aragon in 1136. The king proclaimed himself head of the new reformed church. In Spain, the Jesuit order mounted a counter-reformation by sending missionaries and teachers to spread the Catholic faith to other parts of the world. In addition, the Catholic Church resorted to an inquisition to stop the spread of Protestant beliefs. When different groups encountered religious persecution in Europe, many saw the New World as a means of escape and a way to begin a new life.

Lesson 1-3: Beyond the Boundaries of Europe

European rivalries didn't let up during the quest for exploration. Portugal set out to establish trade routes with Africa with the goal of reaching the lucrative Asian market. However, a disturbing pattern began to develop as Portuguese killed the native people on islands off the coast of Africa, and then introduced labor-intensive crops such as sugar cane. The need for imported laborers led to the slave trade, with Africans being seized and then transported as forced slave labor. This slave trade would eventually result in more than 12 million Africans being forcibly moved from their homelands to colonies in North and South America. Over the next 300 years, this would become the largest forced migration in world history.

In Spain, Queen Isabella and King Ferdinand focused on finding a westward route to the Orient. In 1492 the Spanish financed **Christopher Columbus** with three ships, marking Spain's entrance on the world stage of exploration. Although he failed to find the shortcut to Asia (the fabled **Northwest Passage**—a shortcut from Europe to the Orient) during his four voyages to the Americas, Columbus did discover a new part of the world.

The competition between Spain and Portugal forced the Pope to divide the world for exploration. The **Treaty of Tordesillas** in 1494 split the world in half; the pope drew a line down the map and gave the western half to the Spanish, and the eastern half to the Portugese. Unfortunately, the line drawn by the pope gave Portugal only a small claim in the New World by granting it Brazil and everything east of the line, and everything west of Brazil was assigned to Spain. Other nations in Europe were left with two options: piracy, or rejecting the decree outright as undiscovered lands were settled.

The **Columbian Exchange** brought together the Old and New Worlds. Crops, animals, and diseases were exchanged and had a dramatic impact on the world stage. Crops and animals including corn, pumpkin, squash, chocolate, vanilla, turkey, sunflower, peanuts, and beans were introduced to Europeans, and bananas, oranges, lemons, sugar cane, coffee beans, grains, horses, and honey bees were brought over from the Old World. The Europeans introduced smallpox and measles, along with other diseases, and the Europeans brought back syphilis from the New World. Because of a lack of resistance to these new diseases, millions of people on both sides of the ocean died. Within a century of contact with Europeans, 90 percent of the Native American Indians had been wiped out.

Columbian Exchange

From the New World to the Old World

- Precious metals—gold and silver
- Plants—corn, sweet potatoes, potatoes, peppers, cocoa, vanilla beans, squash, pumpkins, and peanuts
- Disease—syphilis

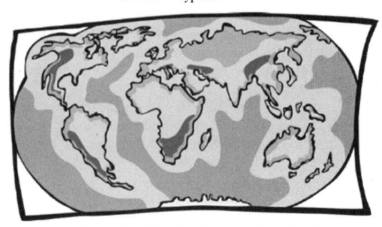

From the Old World to the New World

- Slaves
- Domesticated animals—cows, horses, pigs, chickens
- Diseases—small pox, measles, influenza, typhus
- Plants—wheat, barley, rice, coffee, sugar cane

Balboa, de Leon, Magellan, Cortes, de Vaca, Coronado, and de Soto were soldiers at the forefront of discoveries and conquests for the Spanish crown. As colonies were established, **mercantilism** came to dominate the Spanish economy. Spain relied on goods and wealth from the New World to support economic ventures at home, thus keeping new colonies subservient to the mother country. Spain, as well as other countries, believed in the old adage that land equals power, and that the more land one had the more power it also had. The great wealth that poured into Spain from the colonies in the New World provoked great interest on the part of the other European powers.

Spain's dominance faced several challenges. First, a former Spanish soldier-turned-priest, **Bartholome de Las Casas**, condemned the Spaniards' treatment of the American Indians. The Black Legend soon developed and was intended to make Roman Catholic Spain look evil in the eyes of the Protestant world. However, many Spanish priests established missions from current-day Florida to Texas, throughout the Southwest, and all the way to the coast of California.

Spain faced another challenge to its dominion of the New World. The French **Huguenots,** Protestant followers of John Calvin, tried to challenge Spain's authority in Florida by establishing a colony at Port Royal Sound in South Carolina in 1562. Two years later, French and Spanish troops clashed at the French colony of Fort Caroline on St. John's River (near present-day Jacksonville, Florida). The Spanish drove out the French and established a new colony at nearby **St. Augustine** in 1564. St. Augustine was the first permanent European settlement in what would become the United States. Spain's attempts at colonizing further north failed. Finally, Spain's role as the dominant world power ended when the British defeated the **Spanish Armada** in 1588. This paved the way for Britain to launch its own enterprises in the New World.

Great Britain turned its attention to the New World. As the British navy grew, it also looked for new trade outlets. Sir Francis Drake began plundering Spanish ships on the high seas and attacking Spanish outposts. His final victory came in 1588 when he helped capture and sink numerous ships in the defeat of the Spanish Armada.

Now the doors were opened for England to begin establishing a foot-hold in the New World. In 1585, Sir Walter Raleigh helped plant a colony on **Roanoke Island** just south of the Chesapeake Bay region. A year later, Drake took the disheartened settlers back to England. It was later abandoned, and a second effort two years later also proved a failure. When

John White returned to the island in 1590, he found the site of the "lost colony" deserted. It would be 20 years before the British would try again. The new attempt would be at Jamestown in 1607. This new colony would succeed, and North America would enter a new era.

The political climate in Great Britain changed after the death of Queen Elizabeth in 1603. During the reigns of King James I, and his son, King Charles I, economic and religious forces prompted many to seek their fortunes overseas. By the early 1600s, Britain began several attempts at colonization in the New World, securing England's place in its conquest for power and dominance.

Review Exam

Multiple Choice

1. By the 1400s, nations in Europe wanted to find a quicker way to trade with this region:
   a) Africa
   b) South America
   c) The Orient
   d) The Middle East

2. The race for exploration during the 1400s and 1500s eventually intertwined all of the following continental regions except:
   a) Africa
   b) The Americas
   c) Europe
   d) Australia

3. The adventures of this explorer to China sparked interests in spices, silks, and gold in the mid-1400s:
   a) Johan Gutenberg
   b) Marco Polo
   c) Martin Luther
   d) King Henry VIII

4. This European country began the slave trade with Africa in the 1400s:
   a) Portugal
   b) Spain
   c) England
   d) France

5. This explorer sailed from Spain in 1492 in search of the famed Northwest Passage to the Orient:
   a) Balboa
   b) Columbus
   c) de Leon
   d) Magellan

6. Within a century of contact with the Native Americans by the Spanish, what percentage of the native population was wiped out by either killings or diseases:
   a) 50 percent
   b) 75 percent
   c) 90 percent
   d) 65 percent

7. Bartholome de Las Casas, a priest in the New World, condemned this country's brutal treatment of the Native Americans:
   a) Spain
   b) England
   c) France
   d) Portugal

Matching

a. New World
b. Portugal
c. Northwest Passage
d. Renaissance

e. Old World
f. Black Death
g. Roanoke
h. France

i. Spain
j. St. Augustine
k. England
l. Mercantilism

_____ 8. the country that took the lead in world exploration in the 1500s

_____ 9. the country that took the initial lead in world exploration in the 1400s

_____ 10. the country that rose to dominance in the world after the defeat of the Spanish Armada in 1588

_____ 11. the country that was driven out by the Spanish in their attempt to set up a colony in Florida

_____ 12. the famed shortcut to the Orient

_____ 13. the plague that killed nearly 30 percent of Europe's population in the 1300s

_____14. a period of rebirth in Europe in the 1400s

_____15. the region made up of Europe and Africa

_____16. the region made up of North and South America

_____17. an economic system whereby the new colonies supplied goods and wealth

_____18. the first English attempt at establishing a colony in the New World

_____19. the first permanent Spanish settlement in present-day Florida

Short Response

20. What role did religion play in colonizing the New World in the sixteenth century?

21. What impact did colonization have on the Old and New Worlds in the 1500s?

22. How did the concepts of *"Gold, glory, and God"* change the world exploration of the 1500s?

Answers begin on page 237.

The Colonial Period

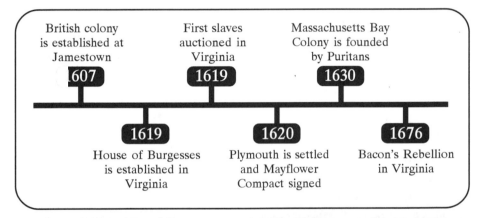

| British colony is established at Jamestown | First slaves auctioned in Virginia | Massachusetts Bay Colony is founded by Puritans |
| 1607 | 1619 | 1630 |

| 1619 | 1620 | 1676 |
| House of Burgesses is established in Virginia | Plymouth is settled and Mayflower Compact signed | Bacon's Rebellion in Virginia |

Trends and Themes of the Era

▶ After England defeated the Spanish Armada in 1588, the balance of power shifted in both Europe and the New World. Britain took the lead in world exploration, trade, and colonization.

▶ Colonial settlements began to build up along the eastern coast of North America, continuing through the seventeenth and eighteenth centuries.

▶ Puritan, Quaker, and Roman Catholic beliefs demonstrated religion's role in the founding of the colonies.

▶ Bacon's Rebellion illustrated the underlying political struggle between the elite planter class and the new landowners.

▶ By 1700 the colonies were distinguished by geographical, economic, and social adversity.

Land, opportunity, and freedom! At the beginning of the seventeenth century, religious, political, and economic forces in England encouraged migration to the New World. Many British immigrants sought a safe haven for religious practices; others wanted to seek their fortunes. By the end of the 1600s, Britain had gained a mighty stronghold in the New World by establishing several colonies along the Atlantic coast. But the successes in the colonies were not without challenges—geography, tolerance, and political upheaval divided and shaped the colonies. They began taking on their own identities separate from England, but also from each other. These differences helped establish a unique American character.

Lesson 2-1: The Colony of Jamestown

In 1607, a group of ships from the Virginia Company set out to claim for the British crown the "great and ample country of Virginia" from modern-day Maine to North Carolina. The employees of the Virginia Company of London were successful in their colonization attempt in a location near the Chesapeake Bay.

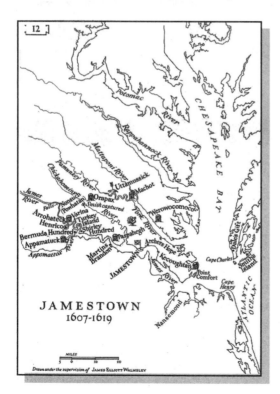

JAMESTOWN
1607-1619

The Virginia Company was financed as a **joint stock company**. Stock was sold to investors, who provided capital for the venture. In return for their investment, the stockholders gained wealth if the colony prospered. The leaders in the colonization ventures were often landless, second-born English sons, eagerly searching for wealth (in the form of gold) in the New World.

The geography of the **tidewater** region from the coastline to the furthest upstream river points created challenges for settlers. The poorly planned expedition of 105 men had but one goal in mind: "Dig, refine, and load gold." Disease, hunger, dwindling supplies, hard manual labor, fire, and exposure to the elements soon challenged their dreams. By the end of the first winter, more than half of the settlers had died. **Jamestown** became known as a "misery, a ruine, a death, a hell." When reinforcements arrived in 1608, only 38 colonists remained.

John Smith emerged as a prominent leader of the Jamestown community and organized work gangs to ensure that the colony had food and shelter. He made rules to control sanitation and hygiene. "He who shall not work shall not eat!" During the winter of 1608–1609, only 12 of 200 men died. Smith also maintained friendly ties with the nearby Powhatan Confederacy. When Smith was wounded in 1609 and returned to England, the colony began to decline. The deaths of many settlers, and deteriorating relations with the Native Americans, took its toll on the colony of Jamestown.

Building a Colony of Smoke

John Rolfe, an Englishman who married the Powhatan Indian leader's daughter, Pocahontas, introduced West Indian tobacco to the colony. Instead of gold or precious metals, tobacco proved to be the perfect crop for the colony. The addictive pleasures of smoking created new markets for trade. From 1616 to 1619, Jamestown's tobacco exports grew nearly twentyfold, and tobacco production increased dramatically, at the expense of all other pursuits. The first shipments of tobacco reached England in 1617. By the end of the seventeenth century, more than 30 million pounds of tobacco was being exported to England annually. By the eve of the American Revolution, more than 55 million pounds of tobacco was headed to Britain each year.

The Virginia Company instituted the **headright system** by dispatching money and supplies and awarding land grants of 50 acres to anyone able to pay for his own passage to Virginia, and an additional fifty acres was distributed for each person or laborer brought to the colony. The profits generated by the growth of tobacco saved Jamestown.

A unique one-crop economy, the supply and demand of the economic cycle, the need for increased land, and the demand for more labor brought challenges to Virginia over the next century. In an effort to fill jobs, **indentured servants** were lured to work in the colony. In exchange for payment for their trip to the colony and for their labor for five to seven years, the servants, often the lowest class of British society, received their freedom. When they gained their freedom and sought land, they often clashed with established landowners along the tidewater. They were forced to live in the unsettled frontier area in the western region of the colony.

The first Africans were brought to Jamestown in 1619 aboard a Dutch merchant ship and sold at auction as workers, along with one hundred women who were auctioned off as wives and workers. Originally, these Africans were sold as indentured servants. As time passed, however, colonists attempted to purchase African laborers for life, and by 1660 slavery was officially sanctioned by Virginia law.

Ruling the New Colony

In 1619, the colonists formed a general assembly, the **House of Burgesses**. This became the first representative government in the New World, though its power was limited because the Virginia Company could still overrule its actions. Landowners elected representatives to make laws for Virginia.

The year 1622 was tragic for Jamestown. High death rates from disease, the outbreak of a war with the Powhatan tribe, a slump in tobacco prices, and fraudulent practices by local officials all helped transform the rigors of colonial life into extremely hard times. Under this strain, the joint-stock company collapsed and King James I revoked its charter, making Virginia a **royal colony** in 1624. Relations with the Native Americans in Virginia proved to be troublesome as well. As the white population increased, the need for more land to cultivate tobacco grew, and hostilities mounted. On Good Friday in 1622, Chief Openchancanough led a massive assault, killing more than 75 percent of the white population. The colony's new leadership pursued a more aggressive policy, viewing the Native Americans as obstacles to the colony's success.

Seeds of Revolt

Overproduction and price fluctuations led to a bust in the tobacco market. In addition, social unrest began to swell under the leadership of **William Berkeley**. Taxes were being raised, and those who didn't own land saw their voting rights revoked. Tensions mounted between the elite planter class and those who lived along the frontier. Furthermore, disputes over access to land and confrontations with the American Indians reached a boiling point. **Nathaniel Bacon**, a wealthy newcomer, soon clashed with Berkeley and other elite landowners about their economic and political control over the colony.

Bacon challenged Berkeley's leadership, and violence erupted along the frontier with the Native Americans. Colonists then asked the House of Burgesses to raise taxes to support the militia in the frontier. Governor Berkeley refused to finance a war for the colony's poor frontier settlers. Several frontiersmen, indentured servants, and slaves sided with Bacon. In what became known as **Bacon's Rebellion**, Nathaniel Bacon and his men led an uprising in Virginia against the colonial government in 1676. High taxes, low prices for tobacco, and resentment against special privileges given those close to the governor provided the motive for the uprising. Berkeley claimed that Bacon and his fellow conspirators were "rebels and traitors." The ongoing conflict resulted in Bacon's forces capturing Jamestown and Berkeley's estate at Green Spring Plantation by the end of September. Jamestown was burned to the ground. A month later, after Bacon's sudden death from dysentery, the rebellion collapsed. Several men received amnesty by siding with Berkeley. Hundreds of Native Americans had been killed, and the revolt was crushed. Other consequences of the rebellion included the execution of 23 leaders of the rebellion and the removal of Berkeley's power by the king.

The revolt exposed a problem with the planters in the frontier being taxed and governed without their consent. The Native American campaign along the frontier fostered bitterness and resulted in the enslavement of many Indians. Along the tidewater region, fear of worker rebellions resulted in a division of the labor force, creating a permanent class of African slave laborers, so that by 1700, 28 percent of the population of Virginia consisted of slaves.

Lesson 2-2: Puritan New England

In 1620, 102 settlers sailed across the Atlantic on the *Mayflower*. These colonists agreed to send lumber, fish, and fur back to England for seven years before they could assume ownership of the land. Most of these settlers were English **separatists**, families who wanted to separate from the Anglican Church (the Church of England). Many of the separatists were living in exile in Holland and longed to live in a place where they were free to worship and raise their families in peace, according to the religion of their choice.

In November of 1620, the *Mayflower* landed at Plymouth Bay, outside the boundaries of British Virginia. Because they had no legal right to settle there, the leaders of the pilgrims insisted that all males sign the **Mayflower**

Compact, which established the colony of Plymouth Plantation as a "civil body politic" under the sovereignty of King James I of England. The Mayflower Compact is often described as the first example of true self government in the New World—a government based on the consent of the governed.

The pilgrims were unprepared for the very harsh New England winter, and about half of the settlers died by springtime. Those who survived owed their lives to the aid of English-speaking Native Americans, who taught the pilgrims how to grow corn. In addition to receiving help from the Native Americans, the pilgrims exhibited a powerful work ethic, unlike the greed that dominated much of Jamestown's history. The colony of Plymouth quickly grew and prospered through faith and hard work. Within a few years, the colony expanded into Cape Cod and the southeastern part of modern-day Massachusetts. Its lasting legacy is the American vision of sturdy, self-reliant, serious people who govern themselves freely.

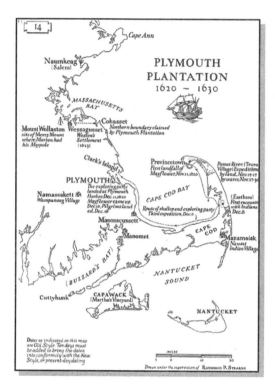

"A City on a Hill"

Religious and political oppression in England worsened during the first half of the seventeenth century. In 1629, the mainly middle-class **Puritans** received a royal charter for a joint-stock enterprise from the English government. The Puritans would leave England and settle north of the Plymouth Plantation, on the condition that they would have political control of their colony. The colonists' venture was well planned and funded, and they were able to shift the emphasis of their colony from trade to religion, setting up a rule by the word of God.

This settlement spurred the **Great Migration,** in which more than 20,000 people settled in the Massachusetts region by the mid-1640s. In 1630, under the leadership of Governor **John Winthrop**, a fleet of 17 ships began the migration by transporting a thousand people across the Atlantic to set up a colony in Massachusetts at the site of modern-day Boston and in 10 other towns across the area.

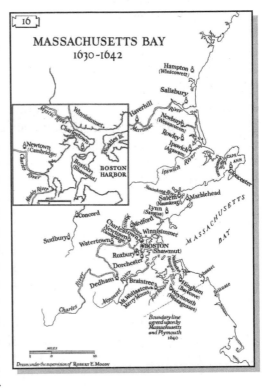

Winthrop's sermon onboard the ship *Arabella* envisioned **Massachusetts Bay** as a biblical "city upon a hill," a beacon of religious righteousness that would shine throughout the world. The collective group of professionals, merchants, and craftsmen saw themselves as God's chosen people. They were to "do more service to the Lord" and "love one another with a pure heart" as "the eyes of the world" looked up to them. Although they sold their property in Britain (making their venture permanent), many of the colonists were unprepared for the first winter. Almost 30 percent of the settlers died, but by mid-1631, the colonists had finally adapted, and the Massachusetts Bay Colony began to grow and thrive.

Religion and Massachusetts Bay

The Massachusetts Bay Colony operated under a system called **congregationalism.** Each independent church congregation served as the center of a community's political and social life, and those with good standing in the church could participate in government. Standards for church membership were very strict: People who could prove they were **predestined** (chosen by God) by describing their conversion experience were admitted.

Originally, only landholding Puritan men of the colony were allowed membership in the General Court, established by the original charter in 1629. Five years later, all free men, regardless of wealth or holdings, were allowed entrance. As the number of settlers increased and the General Court grew too large, the settlers instituted a representative government. Representatives from each district were elected to the legislative house of the General Court.

Problems in Paradise

Problems arose in the region, however, when some colonists broke with the Puritan leadership, and the desire for peace and purity gave way to intolerance for different points of view. One such dissenter was **Roger Williams,** who argued that total separation of church and state was the only way to maintain the purity of the church. Williams feared that without separation, the state would corrupt the church: "Forced religion stinks in the nostrils of God." He also proposed that the Native Americans be compensated for their land. Unable to be silenced, Williams was banished from Massachusetts in 1635. He eventually established the colony of Rhode Island in 1647, where the government renounced the Church of England and allowed religious freedom and the complete separation of church and state.

Another dissenter was **Anne Hutchinson**, whose religious teachings were taken by some as attacks on Puritan religious codes. She hosted religious discussions in her home, but the weekly meetings troubled the local authorities. Hutchinson's belief in the "Holy Spirit illuminating the heart of every true believer" put her at odds with the religious leaders. In 1637, Hutchinson and her followers were banished, and most of them settled in Rhode Island. After her husband's death in 1642, Hutchinson took most of her children to the Dutch colony in New York. A few months later, 15 Dutchmen were killed in a Native American raid, and in August 1643, the Mohicans raided the Hutchinson house and slaughtered Anne and five of her youngest children. Only her youngest daughter, Susanna, survived and was taken captive.

Mary Dyer, a one-time disciple of Anne Hutchinson, suffered for her religious beliefs after becoming a Quaker. Mary Dyer and her husband, William Dyer, were excommunicated from the Boston Puritan Church and banished from the colony, shortly after Anne Hutchinson was banished. After settling in Newport, Rhode Island, and living there for a time, Mary and her husband made a trip to England in 1652. While there, Mary became a follower of the Society of Friends (Quakers). When Mary Dyer returned to Boston, she was twice imprisoned due to her defiance of a new law passed in 1658 banishing Quakers under "pain of death." Eventually, she was expelled, but defied the court and returned to the city several times. Defiant to the end and refusing to repent, on June 1, 1660, she was led once more to the scaffold and this time executed by hanging. She hoped that her sacrifice would result in a change toward greater tolerance of religious faith. At the gallows, one of the onlookers was quoted as saying, "There she waves like a flag." Dissension, in any form, was not to be tolerated in or around Boston.

As in other regions of the colonies, dealings with the American Indians proved to be challenging in New England. When Winthrop settled the area in 1629, Native Americans weren't permitted to enter Puritan towns. Deaths from diseases had wiped out many of the local tribes. Some Puritans, such as John Elliot (a missionary to the Indians) set out to share their religious message and establish "praying towns" where converted Indians could live in as Christians. Relations with the Native Americans proved uneasy when focused on issues of land. As colonies continued to spring up in the Massachusetts area, more and more land was taken away from Indians and dispersed to new settlers, and sporadic tensions broke out between the colonists and the Native Americans. In 1637, when the Pequot Indians attempted to resist colonial expansion, John Winthrop recruited several hundred warriors from a neighboring Indian tribe and attacked and killed nearly 400 women, children, and old men at Mystic Village along the Connecticut River. The fighting ended a few months later with the deaths of the remaining Pequot warriors and the loss of their remaining land to the colonists. Struggles over dominance as well as land and expansion would continue for the next several decades.

In all of the New England colonies (except Rhode Island) the Puritan faith was the established church. But changing social and religious conditions challenged the status of the church, and dwindling membership left unconverted children outside the church. To be a full member of the established Puritan church one had to testify to a "religious conversion" experience. The next generation didn't share their parents' zeal for the faith, and they threatened the Puritan experiment by not always following in their parents' footsteps. To resolve this dilemma, adult church members (who had been baptized themselves as full members of the church) were allowed to have their unconverted children baptized, thus allowing them to become "halfway" members. This **halfway covenant** allowed for more lenient membership rules. While people were awaiting conversion, they could also participate in church affairs, with the exception of partaking in communion. At this time, women also began to outnumber men as full church members. Older members resisted the halfway covenant and other changes, however, feeling that it weakened the authority of the church.

The final challenge to the Puritan experiment came in 1692 with the **Salem Witchcraft Trials**. Betty Paris and her cousin, Abigail Williams, were seized with fits and began making wild gestures and speeches while playing magic with a black slave named Tituba. Soon, others were behaving strangely. The elders of the village extracted confessions that Tituba and two others in town were tormenting the villagers. Things got out of hand when a group of poor Puritan farmers sought to avenge themselves against other wealthier church members, charging their families and friends with witchcraft. By the end of the conflict, 175 men and women had been arrested, 19 people and one dog had been hanged, and one person had been pressed to death with stones. Ultimately, the hysteria and the mass executions illustrated the weaknesses within the Puritan faith and laid the groundwork for a religious revival.

Lesson 2-3: The Middle and Southern Colonies

The middle colonies included New York and New Jersey, and later Pennsylvania. Both New York and New Jersey followed the same standard political format: A royal governor and a general assembly governed each. Economically, the two colonies relied on grain production, shipping, and fur trading with the Native Americans.

New York was settled by Henry Hudson and the Dutch in 1609. Trading posts were established in New Netherland at Fort Orange (Albany) in 1624 and in New Amsterdam (New York City) in 1626. Although small in population, the New York colony was one of the most ethnically diverse settlements in the New World.

In 1634, Maryland was founded as a proprietary colony by the Calvert family. They established it as a refuge for English Catholics, and it was the only English colony in North America with a sizeable Catholic minority. Maryland quickly followed in the footsteps of neighboring Virginia by cultivating tobacco.

English Colonial Settlements, 1600s

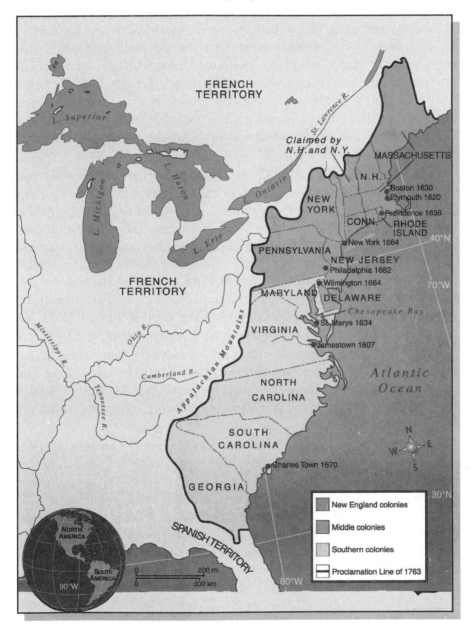

FRENCH TERRITORY

L. Superior

St. Lawrence R.

Claimed by N.H. and N.Y.

MASSACHUSETTS

L. Michigan

L. Huron

L. Ontario

N.H.

Boston 1630
Plymouth 1620

NEW YORK

Providence 1636

L. Erie

CONN.

RHODE ISLAND

40°N

New York 1664

PENNSYLVANIA

NEW JERSEY

FRENCH TERRITORY

Philadelphia 1682

70°W

Wilmington 1664

MARYLAND

DELAWARE

Chesapeake Bay

Mississippi R.

Ohio R.

Appalachian Mountains

VIRGINIA

St. Marys 1634

Jamestown 1607

Cumberland R.

NORTH CAROLINA

Atlantic Ocean

Tennessee R.

SOUTH CAROLINA

N

W E

S

Charles Town 1670

GEORGIA

30°N

NORTH AMERICA

SPANISH TERRITORY

New England colonies

Middle colonies

SOUTH AMERICA

90°W

| 0 | 200 mi |
| 0 | 300 km |

Southern colonies

Proclamation Line of 1763

80°W

The Carolina region was initially chartered as a proprietary colony. In order to attract settlers to the region, land was made available under the **headright system**. The new landowners were allowed to participate in the local government, but a distinction was made between the aristocracy and the poor. Colonists grew a variety of cash crops, including indigo, sugar, tobacco, and rice, along with raising cattle. Rice became the crop on which the region's stable economy was built, with the use of slave labor. In the earliest years of the colony, Native Americans were also captured and sold in New England and the West Indies. Later, in 1729, the colony split into North and South Carolina and became separate royal colonies.

In 1681, Charles II granted the last unclaimed tract of American land to **William Penn**, who launched a "holy experiment in living" by founding a colony based on religious tolerance. The **Quakers** had long been discriminated against, both in the Americas and England, for their religious beliefs, including the idea that God's inner light burned inside everyone, and for their pacifism. Seeking religious freedom, many Quakers flocked to Pennsylvania, along with Mennonites, Amish, Moravians, and Baptists. Pennsylvania soon became economically prosperous and religiously and racially diverse. By the 1750s, Pennsylvania's capital, Philadelphia, had become the largest city in the colonies, with a population of 20,000.

Pennsylvania also enjoyed better relations with the American Indians. Penn regarded the Native Americans as the rightful owners of the land and purchased it from them. Because of Penn's pacifist way of dealing with the Indians, many of the displaced tribes began migrating to the safe haven of Pennsylvania.

The last of the 13 colonies to be established was Georgia. In 1732, James Oglethorpe planned to settle the region with England's poorest people, and those from debtor prisons. Land ownership with land grants was kept small. Initially, the settlers weren't allowed to participate in the representative assembly, and slavery was banned. As settlers poured into the region, especially from South Carolina, they began to challenge the original rules for the colony. Within a few years, land ownership and slavery were increasing, and Georgia was taking on the characteristics of other southern colonies. Oglethorpe turned the colony back to the king in 1752.

Review Exam

Multiple Choice

1. By the 1600s, this European nation began to settle in North America and establish colonies along the Atlantic coastline:
   a) Spain
   b) France
   c) Great Britain
   d) Germany

2. Production of this crop (known as brown gold) literally transformed the colony of Jamestown and made it a viable colony:
   a) cotton
   b) tobacco
   c) rice
   d) indigo

3. More than half of the settlers in this colony died during their first winter in the New World due to their poor work habits:
   a) Jamestown
   b) Providence
   c) Plymouth
   d) Roanoke

4. Settlers in Jamestown were initially concerned about:
   a) retaliation from the Indians
   b) finding and refining gold
   c) growing enough crops for survival
   d) the boats for the return voyage to England

5. In 1619, these people were brought to Jamestown for the first time to provide a new source of labor for the colony:
   a) indentured servants
   b) prisoners
   c) women
   d) slaves

6. He led a rebellion against the elite wealthy landowners in Virginia in 1676:
   a) Nathaniel Bacon
   b) John Smith
   c) William Berkeley
   d) Chief Powhatan

7. English separatists on the *Mayflower* settled in this region of the New World in 1620:
   a) Boston
   b) Providence
   c) Plymouth
   d) Salem

8. In addition to their strong work ethic, this group of settlers received help from the American Indians, which allowed them to prosper in the New World:

   a) pilgrims   c) slaves

   b) indentured servants   d) Jamestown

9. While on board the *Arabella* in 1630, John Winthrop delivered a sermon in which he declared that the new colony they were settling would be similar to:

   a) "a new colony like no other"

   b) "a city on a hill"

   c) "a colony free of slaves"

   d) "a colony free of indentured servants"

10. Roger Williams was banished from the Massachusetts Bay Colony for proposing this policy:

    a) open church membership

    b) return to England within the next five years

    c) compensating Indians for their land

    d) not favoring the separation of church and state

11. Anne Hutchinson was banished from Massachusetts Bay Colony in 1637 for:

    a) stepping out of her traditional role as a submissive woman

    b) hosting religious discussions in her home

    c) the belief in the Holy Spirit enlightening the heart of every believer

    d) all of the answers on the list

12. In all of the New England colonies (except for Rhode Island) this faith was the "established church" that combined religious and political beliefs:

    a) Puritan   c) Old Light

    b) Quaker   d) Separatist

13. The Salem Witchcraft Trials in 1692 resulted in all of the following *EXCEPT*:

    a) the hanging of 19 people and one person being pressed to death

    b) the accusations and arrest of more than 175 people suspected of witchcraft

c) demonstrating the lack of religious commitment from the founding of the colony in 1630

d) strengthening of the power and authority of the church

14. All of the following demonstrated problems of the Puritans straying from John Winthrop's original goal for the colony in Massachusetts Bay region *EXCEPT*:

a) the halfway covenant

b) the hanging of Mary Dyer for her religious beliefs

c) the hysteria of witchcraft in Salem

d) having the Puritan church be the only accepted church in the colonial region

15. Pennsylvania was founded as a "safe haven" against persecution for which of the following groups:

a) Quakers

b) Puritans

c) Catholics

d) Separatists

Matching

a. indentured servants

b. House of Burgesses

c. John Winthrop

d. royal colony

e. Mary Dyer

f. Henry Hudson

g. joint stock company

h. Mayflower Compact

i. predestination

j. John Smith

k. William Berkeley

l. Rhode Island

m. halfway covenant

n. headright system

o. James Oglethorpe

p. William Penn

q. Great Migration

_____16. a group of investors who bought stock to provide capital for colonial ventures; in return, they hoped to make great wealth on their investments

_____17. the person who made the rule for the Jamestown colony that "he who shall not work shall not eat"

_____18. remained under the direct rule by the king

_____19. the document that is the first example of true self-government in the colonies

____20. served for five to seven years to provide labor in exchange for their payment for the trip to the New World

____21. the leader of the Virginia colony who clashed with others over land ownership and political control of the colony

____22. the founder of the colony at Massachusetts Bay by proclaiming it to be "a city on a hill"

____23. the first colonial assembly that provided the first representative government in Virginia

____24. the religious belief that adhered to the teaching that people were chosen by God for salvation

____25. a disciple of Anne Hutchinson who was hanged for refusing to repent her differing religious beliefs

____26. the colony founded by Roger Williams in 1647 that allowed for religious freedom and separation of church and state

____27. sought to allow unconverted Puritan children to be baptized and brought into partial church membership

____28. awarded a land grant of 50 acres for each indentured servant whose passage was paid for by a landowner in Virginia

____29. a Quaker who helped launch a "holy experiment of living" by founding a colony in Pennsylvania

____30. the person who planned to establish a colony in Georgia in 1732 by using England's poor people and prisoners

____31. the time from 1620 to 1640 when more than 20,000 people settled in the Massachusetts region of New England

____32. the person who founded the colony of New York in 1609 and helped establish trading posts for commerce

Short Response

33. What role did religion play in colonizing the New World in the sixteenth century?

34. Although mainly British, the colonies began to differ by region. What items began to account for this difference in the colonial regions?

35. How did the concepts of *land, opportunity, and freedom* encourage settlement in North America in the 1600s?

Answers begin on page 238.

Colonial Society Comes of Age

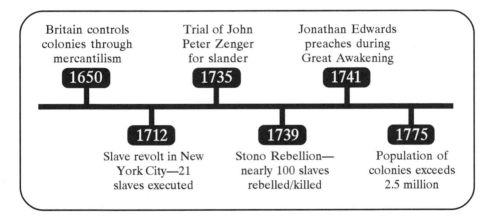

Britain controls colonies through mercantilism	Trial of John Peter Zenger for slander	Jonathan Edwards preaches during Great Awakening
1650	**1735**	**1741**

1712	**1739**	**1775**
Slave revolt in New York City—21 slaves executed	Stono Rebellion— nearly 100 slaves rebelled/killed	Population of colonies exceeds 2.5 million

Trends and Themes of the Era

▶ Britain led in world trade while taking advantage of the resources and the labor pool in the colonies.

▶ Geography, population, economics, and religion played a role in the identities of colonists in the three main regions.

▶ The Enlightenment's use of reason and the scientific method to obtain knowledge conflicted with traditional beliefs.

▶ The Great Awakening challenged and renewed religious beliefs in America.

▶ Slave labor increased in the colonies.

Economics, growth, and revival! During the first half of the eighteenth century, the colonies experienced tremendous growth. The lure of freedom, new challenges, and a fresh lease on life appealed to many people. As the population and materialism increased, the colonies began to mature. Although predominantly British, the colonies were becoming more diverse. Each geographic region began to develop unique characteristics that shaped the identity of the colonists in that area. Mercantilism, triangular trade, indentured servants, and slave labor created a unique economic system in colonial America. The colonists began to feel a unique sense of identity.

Lesson 3-1: The Colonial Economy of Mercantilism

Beginning around 1650, the British government pursued a policy of **mercantilism** in order to compete with France and the Netherlands. The mercantile theory of trade said that a nation could build economic strength only by exporting more than it imported. This policy also kept the colonies in a subservient role, providing raw materials and trade outlets for Britain.

To achieve this favorable balance of trade, the English passed a series of regulatory laws that benefited the British economy exclusively. The laws created a trade system in which the colonies provided raw materials to Britain, and Britain used the raw materials to produce manufactured goods to sell in European markets and back in the colonies. As only the suppliers of raw materials, the colonies couldn't compete with Britain in manufacturing, which kept them at Britain's mercy for supplies. English ships and merchants were always favored in this trade strategy, preventing other countries from sharing the British Empire's wealth.

Between 1651 and 1673, the English Parliament passed four types of legislation that became known as the **Navigation Acts.** The acts were intended to ensure the proper mercantilist trade balance between the colonies and England. The acts declared that:

> ▶ Only English ships could transport cargo between imperial ports. The crews on the ships were required to be at least 50 percent British. This greatly increased the number of British ships sailing the seas and created the shipping industry in the northern colonies.

▶ Certain goods known as enumerated products, including tobacco, rice, indigo, cotton, and furs, couldn't be shipped to foreign nations except first going through England or Scotland for taxation purposes. All European goods had to pass through British ports before being shipped to the colonies. This allowed Britain to tax these goods as well.

▶ The English Parliament would pay "bounties" to Americans who produced certain raw goods, while raising protectionist **tariffs** (tax on imports) on the same goods produced in other nations.

▶ Restrictions on large-scale manufacturing of certain goods in the colonies (wool, felt hats, and iron) protected businesses in England.

The colonists initially complained about these trade restrictions. Many colonists, in New England in particular, resorted to smuggling to get around the restrictions of the Navigation Acts. Customs officials in the colonies could easily be bribed to look the other way.

Despite the trade limitations, the colonists saw their economy grow nearly twice as fast as that of England. This was partly because of the policy of **salutary neglect** toward the colonies. In general, Britain didn't enforce the trade laws that most hurt the colonial economy.

Internal problems in England affected its control and focus in governing the colonies. The most drastic change in England was the monarchy agreeing to a Bill of Rights for British subjects. British officials knew that if they appeased the colonists, they would have the colonists' support if they later clashed with the French over control of the continent. The British didn't want to alienate their much-needed allies through aggressive trade restrictions.

Triangular Trade

By the mid-seventeenth century, the Atlantic was a busy thoroughfare of international trade. It was part of an expanding world market economy that saw growth in trade, population, and wealth. British mercantilism manifested itself in the form of the **triangular trade** that linked the American colonies, the West Indies, Africa, and Great Britain. New England rum was shipped to Africa and traded for slaves, who were brought to the West Indies and traded for sugar and molasses, which went back to New England. Other raw goods were shipped from the colonies to England, where they were swapped for a cargo of manufactured goods.

Colonial Overseas Trade, 1740

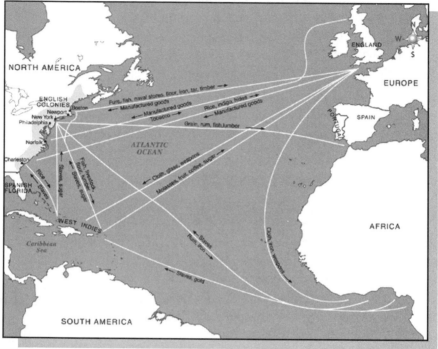

Mercantilism and the triangular trade proved quite profitable for New England tradesmen and shipbuilders. In the southern colonies, however, where the Navigation Acts had greatly lowered tobacco prices, colonial economies suffered until farmers diversified into other crops. West Indian sugar and colonial tobacco were the two leading exports from the colonies, but rice, indigo, and wheat also became important exports. The triangular trade boosted the merchant population, creating a class of prosperous elites who dominated both trade and politics throughout the colonies.

Lesson 3-2: Life in Colonial America

By 1700, more than 250,000 people of European origin or descent lived in the colonies along the Atlantic coast. At the outset, 80 percent of the population was of British descent. Within the next five decades, the population increased to more than 2.5 million and became extremely diverse. Benjamin Franklin would attribute this growth to "the great increase of offspring." By 1775, only 52 percent were British, whereas 20 percent were African. Other countries that had colonists settle in the

New World included Scotland, Ireland, Wales, France, Sweden, and Germany. Some of the colonial population also included convicts from Britain. These settlers covered much of the eastern seaboard, but they generally lived within 50 miles of the coastline. Each region of colonization was geographically, economically, and socially distinct, and each area developed differently, based on immigrant culture.

The New England Colonies

The New England colonies stretched over the area of modern-day Massachusetts, New Hampshire, Maine, Connecticut, and Rhode Island. Large families, early marriage, economic opportunities, and healthy climates helped this region to grow quickly. Because of the rocky soil and long, harsh winters, New England's economy centered on small farming, fishing, and at-home manufacturing, as well as sea trade and shipbuilding. Colonial cities in this region became centers of commerce. Boston became a hub for international commerce. The region quickly expanded as immigrants streamed in and colonists produced large families.

The New England Colonies

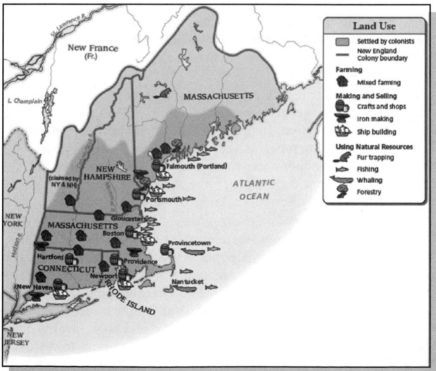

The New England Colonies

Geography	thin, rocky soil, cold coastal waters, natural harbors
Climate	harsh winters, shorter growing season
Economy	small farming, fishing, at-home manufacturing, lumber, rum, shipbuilding, trade
Major cities	Boston became the major economic and political center
Colonies	Massachusetts, New Hampshire, Connecticut, Rhode Island

Life was stable for New Englanders. They generally lived 15 to 25 years longer than Englishmen or colonists from other regions, in part because of better diets. Because of the colonists' emphasis on family, the population was more stable.

Close communal ties united New England's Puritan society. The Puritans sought to create their own version of the "right and perfect way." Because Puritans believed that all followers of God should be able to read the Bible, they emphasized education, and New England became the most literate area in the colonies. **Harvard University,** the first institution of higher learning in the colonies, was founded in 1638 to train ministers.

The church controlled most New England community affairs. Religion dominated nearly every aspect of life, from politics to legal proceedings and social interaction. In order to vote or hold office, a person had to be considered a member of the church. Religious dissenters were often subjected to public spectacle; sometimes they were even banished. Although the church was a unifying force for colonies in New England, it began to demonstrate internal weakness by the late 1600s.

The New England colonies quickly established a tradition of self-government. Male landowners were granted the right to vote and were encouraged to participate in the political process. **Town meetings** often covered a wide range of local government concerns. These meetings not only served as the basis of local control, but became important decision-making institutions as resistance to the British crown increased before the Revolutionary War. In addition to the town meetings, taverns quickly became places not only for food and drink, but also places to discuss the news of the day.

England saw these attempts to unite the colonists as potentially dangerous to its own interests. In 1735, **John Peter Zenger**, a New York printer, went to trial for libel for his printed attacks on the royal governor. His acquittal helped expand freedom of the press and encouraged the growth of more newspapers to express diverse colonial opinions over the next few years. By the eve of the Revolutionary War, Boston would be the hotbed of resistance against the crown. At the outbreak of the Revolutionary War, 39 newspapers were being published in the colonies.

The Middle Colonies

The middle colonies included the areas of New York and New Jersey, and later Pennsylvania. This region offered rich land and abundant water power. Both New York and New Jersey followed the same political format: A royal governor and a general assembly governed. Economically, the region relied on grain production, shipping, and fur trading with the local Native Americans.

The Middle Colonies

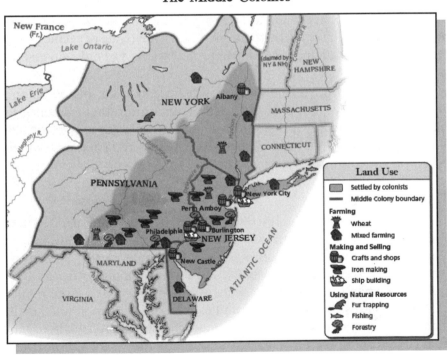

The Middle Colonies	
Geography	fertile soil, cold coastal waters, natural harbors
Climate	moderate winter, longer growing season
Economy	trade, furs, livestock, wheat, shipping, rum, shipbuilding, foodstuffs
Major cities	New York (25,000 population) and Philadelphia (30,000 population) became the major cities for economics and politics
Colonies	New York, Delaware, New Jersey, Pennsylvania

In Pennsylvania, **William Penn** launched his "holy experiment," a colony based on religious tolerance. The original plan (never fully realized) was to create a society that banished violence, religious intolerance, and capricious rule. The industrious Quaker work ethic helped Pennsylvania become economically prosperous, and the Quaker belief in pacifism encouraged peaceful relations with a wide range of ethnic groups. By the 1750s, Philadelphia had become the largest and most diverse city in the colonies.

This region also became known as the breadbasket of the colonies because of the large amount of wheat and other crops that farmers grew. Increasingly, the colonial regions began to specialize economically, with New England turning to commerce as the middle and southern colonies relied on agriculture.

The Southern Colonies

With its center in Jamestown, Virginia dominated the southern colonies, which included the Chesapeake colonies, Maryland, and the Carolinas. The region was more religiously and ethnically diverse than the middle or New England colonies, harboring immigrants from all over Europe, Roman Catholics (especially in Maryland), and a large number of African slaves. In the South, families were less common and smaller than in other regions, because adult men far outnumbered women. More than 50 percent of the population south of New England was non-British. This helped to create a unique and diverse population of a variety of ethnic groups from Pennsylvania to South Carolina.

The Southern Colonies

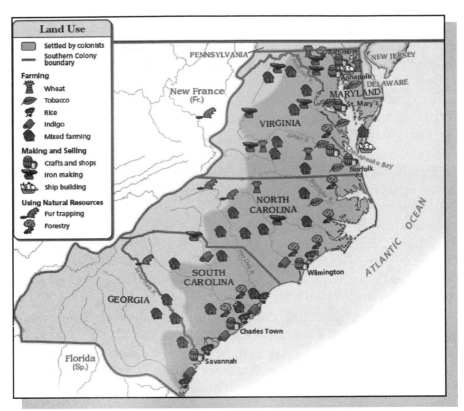

The Southern Colonies	
Geography	rich, fertile soil, lack of natural harbors
Climate	mild winters, long growing season, abundant rainfall
Economy	tobacco, rice, indigo, cattle, grain, indentured servants and slave labor
Major cities	Jamestown and Charleston became the major cities for economics, but were small in population compared to other major cities in the colonies
Colonies	Virginia, Maryland, North Carolina, South Carolina, Georgia

Plantations, which produced tobacco, rice, and indigo, influenced all aspects of life in the South. Agriculture dominated the economy, and oftentimes a single crop, such as tobacco or rice, would dominate an area. As more land was set aside for agriculture and soil was depleted, farmers competed for fresh land along the frontier, and new colonies became vital for the region's economic growth. Land ownership was a status symbol, and wealthy landowners dominated political and social life. The importance of plantations, in turn, limited the development of cities and a merchant class.

As plantations increased in size, labor was in great demand. Land-owners met this need by using **indentured servants** and slave labor. In-dentured servants were adult men and women, usually white, who bound themselves to labor on plantations for a fixed number of years until they had earned their freedom, and, with it, a small plot of land. The New England colonies also relied on indentured servants as a labor supply. Once they were free, however, indentured servants still had to struggle to survive, and great tensions arose between the freed servants and the in-creasingly powerful plantation owners.

Because of the limitations of indentured servitude, slavery became a more profitable and stable labor source in the South. After laws in the South officially sanctioned slavery by the 1660s, the slave population grew so much that, by the mid-1700s, many areas of the southern colonies had populations that were nearly 40 percent slaves.

Lesson 3-3: Colonial Culture in the Age of Reason

In eighteenth-century Europe, the intellectual movement known as the **Enlightenment,** or the Age of Reason, embodied the principles of rationalism and logic, and the Scientific Revolution worked to demystify the natural world. The Enlightenment movement questioned how the world was viewed and sought to apply reason and the scientific method to ob-tain knowledge. It didn't always follow religious or traditional values, but instead advocated natural laws that governed the world and the universe. The movement studied connections between society, politics, and eco-nomics. In addition, the movement questioned the idea of a vengeful God and exalted man's capacity for knowledge and social improvement. News-papers helped spread these ideas throughout Europe and the colonies.

As the Enlightenment traveled across the Atlantic to America, upper-class Americans—including many of the colonists who would eventually lead the Revolution—were heavily influenced by these new philosophies, such as faith in the power of human reason and skepticism toward beliefs that couldn't be proven by science or clear logic. Outstanding European Enlightenment figures in the 1600s included Nicolaus Copernicus, Galileo Galilei, Isaac Newton, René Descartes, and John Locke.

Thomas Jefferson and **Benjamin Franklin** were the American counterparts in this movement in the early to mid-1700s. Benjamin Franklin devoted his life to the intellectual pursuit of social, political, and economic improvements. He conducted experiments with electricity and developed several inventions, including spectacles, a wood stove for heating, and the lightening rod. Franklin also founded a library in Philadelphia, and in 1769 he created a scientific organization known as the American Philosophical Society. His published work in *Poor Richard's Almanac* in 1732 contained a collection of proverbs and information about colonial life. Franklin, along with his close friends John Adams and Thomas Jefferson, later played a pivotal role in the independence movement that would sweep across the colonies.

Thomas Jefferson's writings reflected **John Locke's** earlier works in England about the contract theory of government and the need for a government to protect a person's "life, health, liberty, and possessions." Jefferson assumed responsibility for drafting the **Declaration of Independence** in 1776. He worked closely with Benjamin Franklin, John Adams, Roger Sherman, and Robert Livingston. Jefferson crafted his writing by basing it on John Locke's work that stated that the power of any government rested in the people themselves and that the power of any ruler was conditional. Jefferson would later play a key role in the foundation of the United States by serving as a diplomat, secretary of state, vice president, and eventually president.

Lesson 3-4: The First Great Awakening

In response to the waning of religion and the spread of skepticism bolstered by the Enlightenment, the 1730s and 1740s ushered in a broad movement of religious commitment called the **First Great Awakening**. Many people had moved away from their parents' faith, enticed by materialism and other worldly pleasures. Others challenged the dominance of the Congregational Church in New England and the Anglican Church in the southern colonies.

During this time, revival ministers John and Charles Wesley, George Whitefield, Jonathan Edwards, and others stressed the emptiness of material comfort, the corruption of human nature, and the need for immediate repentance to avoid incurring divine wrath. George Whitefield held several large revival meetings throughout different regions of the colonies. Audiences at these revival meetings came from all parts of society and had a wide range of religious backgrounds. Jonathan Edwards's impassioned sermon, "Sinners in the Hands of an Angry God," proclaimed that man must save himself by immediately repenting his sins. He claimed that salvation and virtue were matters of the heart and not the head. After a revival speaker had come to town, often the community talk turned to religion, and community members offered evidence of their changed lives.

The message of repentance, the sovereignty of God, the depravity of man, salvation by grace alone, and the fear of hell and damnation appealed to a broad range of people, including young men, the poor, slaves, and Native Americans. The Great Awakening is often credited with democratizing religion, because revivalist ministers such as Whitefield stressed that anyone who repents can be saved by God, not just those who are prominent members of established churches.

Because of its message, the Great Awakening divided American Protestants, pitting the revivalists (called New Lights) against the more established ministers (called Old Lights). Out of this division, Baptists, Methodists, Presbyterians, and other religious congregations gained strongholds. The schism also resulted in the formation of many new universities to teach ministers in the early 1700s, including Yale, Princeton, Columbia, Brown, and Dartmouth.

Lesson 3-5: The Slave Trade

The Portuguese slave trade in the mid-1400s launched the nearly 400 years of the **Middle Passage** for Africans. An estimated 10 to 12 million Africans had been transported from Africa to the New World by 1810 (76 percent of them arrived from 1701 to 1810). This was the largest forced migration in history. By the time the slave trade ended, more than 520,000 slaves had been transported to America. By the 1730s, British ships controlled the biggest share of the Atlantic slave trade, and this would continue for the next 70 years. In fact, more Africans than Europeans came to the New World during the colonial period. What began as an attempt to end the labor shortage on New World sugar plantations expanded to include labor in other areas of agriculture, domestic needs, and artisans. Slavery became extremely important to the South's economy, and soon was central to the region's way of life. Slavery eventually replaced the need for indentured servants. Because of the time limit for the use of indentured servants, the labor supply of indentured servants had to be continually renewed. The use of slave labor solved those problems by providing a pool of labor based on a lifetime of servitude.

Within a generation of the first slaves brought to Virginia in 1619, slavery became hereditary. Slavery soon continued as an inherited racial status, meaning that the children of slaves were born into a lifetime of slavery. The words *negro* and *slave* quickly became interchangeable. Cheap land and the high cost of labor added urgency to the slavery issue. Slaves became the chattel or property of their masters, making slave ownership a profitable long-term investment. **Slave codes** were soon established, governing slavery and reducing the enslaved people to property, deprived of basic civil rights. These laws developed out of fear that the increasing black population needed to be kept under control.

New York became involved with the slave trade with the importation of 11 black slaves in 1625 by the Dutch West India Company. These slaves worked as farmers, fur traders, and builders. During most of the 1700s, the large slave population in colonial New York City ranked second only to the slave population in Charleston, South Carolina. New York City's economy also prospered, as it served as a center of the slave trade.

Because of its involvement in the Caribbean trade, New York City had a sizeable slave population that lived and worked alongside the indentured servant population. In April 1712, a group of more than 20 slaves armed with weapons burned a building in the middle of town. As the flames continued, colonists tried to put out the blaze. They were attacked by the rebels and nine whites were shot or stabbed. Afterwards, 21 slave rebels were executed. Because of this rebellion, tougher slave codes were enacted, including limiting the size of gatherings of gatherings to no more than three, limiting the possession of weapons, punishing crimes of rape or theft by death, restricting the freeing of slaves, and giving slave owners more leeway in punishing slaves. These new laws sought to govern nearly every aspect of their lives from morning to night. Despite new legislation, the laws failed to prevent another uprising in New City in 1741 when an

Slavery in the Colonies

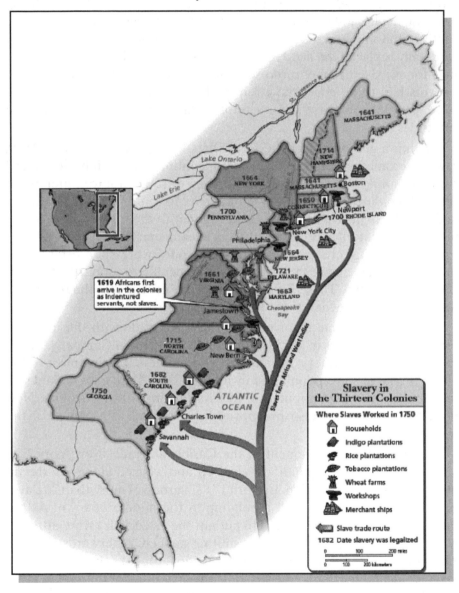

1619 Africans first arrive in the colonies as Indentured servants, not slaves.

Slavery in the Thirteen Colonies

Where Slaves Worked in 1750

- Households
- Indigo plantations
- Rice plantations
- Tobacco plantations
- Wheat farms
- Workshops
- Merchant ships

Slave trade route

1682 Date slavery was legalized

outbreak of several fires were blamed on yet another slave rebellion. Following this latest scare, more than 24 blacks were killed and several slaves were deported from the region.

In September 1739 outside of Charleston, South Carolina, the **Stono Rebellion** occurred when 20 slaves broke into a store for weapons and ammunition. As they marched toward freedom in St. Augustine, Florida, they gathered recruits, attacked and burned houses, and killed 20 white men, women, and children. At each plantation, they recruited other slaves, and as they moved south, their numbers grew. That afternoon, several planters caught up with the large band of rebel slaves. More than 20 whites and 40 slaves were killed before the suppression of the rebellion. They were captured and put to death. This rebellion sparked a fear of uprisings in the minority white population in the southern colonies and led to stricter slave codes, including a ban of assembling in groups, earning their own money, or learning to read. This rebellion became the largest slave uprising in the colonies prior to the American Revolutionary War.

Although some people saw slavery as morally degrading and danger-ous to maintain, others found it too profitable to give up. As the number of enslaved blacks continued to increase in the colonies, the presence of free blacks began to be seen as a threat, and free blacks faced discrimina-tion in many parts of the colonies. From the time the first slave entered the colonies in 1619 until the ending of slavery with the 13th Amendment in 1865, and the push for civil rights, the economic, political, and social fabric America became intertwined with slavery.

Review Exam

Multiple Choice

1. Great Britain attempted to control the colonies in North America with the policy of mercantilism by:
   a) increasing exports to the colonies
   b) providing raw materials to Britain
   c) limiting manufacturing in the colonies
   d) all of the answers on the list

2. All of the following are true about the Navigation Acts imposed on the colonies by Great Britain *EXCEPT*:
   a) any ships could be used to transport goods to the colonies
   b) Britain imposed taxes on all goods being shipped to the colonies

c) placing restriction son colonial manufacturing

d) Britain imposed taxes on all products being shipped from the colonies to other countries (after stopping at a British port)

3. Despite the regulations placed on the colonies, they enjoyed nearly a century of economic growth because of:

a) the policy of salutary neglect

b) Britain's lingering European problems caused her to ignore the colonies

c) the desire of Britain to eventually allow the colonies to become independent

d) *a* and *b* only

4. Which crop was *NOT* a major export from the colonies to Britain by the mid-eighteenth century:

a) rice

b) indigo

c) cotton

d) tobacco

5. The economy of the colonies continued to flourish from the mid-seventeenth century to the mid-eighteenth century because of:

a) salutary neglect

b) indentured servants and slave labor

c) population growth in the colonies

d) all of the answers on the list

6. By the 1750s, the population in the colonies reflected:

a) a decrease in the slave population

b) an increase to 2.5 million people in the colonies

c) a population that was more than 75 percent British

d) a decrease in the population due to disease

7. The middle passage was significant in that it:

a) was the route used to transport 12 million Africans to the New World by 1810

b) was the route used to transport more than a million slaves to America by the late eighteenth century

    c) became a major route of slaves returning to Africa

    d) was the major trade route used to transport slaves to Europe

8. Slave labor began to be used in the colonies to:
    a) replace child labor
    b) fill a labor shortage in the New England colonies
    c) replace indentured servants
    d) fill a short-term need for labor in the southern colonies

9. The Great Awakening was a time period in which:
    a) large numbers of Puritans in New England converted to the Quaker faith
    b) churches remained unchanged
    c) the colonies experienced a series of religious revivals resulting in the conversion of many colonists
    d) scientific ideals were widely accepted over religious teachings

10. The middle colonies became known for their:
    a) diverse population
    b) religious tolerance
    c) large slave population
    d) lack of diversity

11. The slave rebellions in New York City in 1712 and 1741 and the Stono Rebellion in South Carolina in 1739 were significant because:
    a) they increased fears of more slave rebellions
    b) after the rebellions, strict slave codes were enacted
    c) slavery was not just limited to the southern colonies
    d) all of the answers on the list

12. Because of the strong agricultural base in the southern colonies, both political and economic power became dominated by:
    a) the merchant class
    b) a small number of plantation owners
    c) a large number of plantation owners
    d) indentured servants

Matching

a. Puritans	j. Enlightenment
b. John Peter Zenger	k. Thomas Jefferson
c. indentured servants	l. African slaves
d. southern colonies	m. Great Awakening
e. triangular trade	n. Benjamin Franklin
f. William Penn	o. Jonathan Edwards
g. Mercantilism	p. slave codes
h. George Whitefield	q. middle colonies
i. New England colonies	r. John Locke

____13. the trade system involving rum, sugar, and slaves that linked Britain, the colonies, and the West Indies and Africa together

____14. the person who developed a philosophical belief in the contract theory of government, that stated that the sole purpose of a government was to protect the basic rights (life, health, liberty, and possessions) of its citizens

____15. the group that comprised nearly 20 percent of the colonial population by the 1750s

____16. the group that sought to create a unique religious settlement in the New World and to live "the right and perfect way"

____17. the Age of Reason that relied on the principles of scientific logic to explain how the world was viewed

____18. the region that was dominated by thin rocky soil and short growing seasons, but had several natural harbors that would aid in commerce and trade

____19. adult men and women who provided a short-term labor source (generally five to seven years) in the colonies in return for their passage to the colonies

____20. the person who launched his "holy experiment" with a colony based on religious tolerance and helped plan the city of "brotherly love" (Philadelphia)

____21. the region that offered rich farmland and abundant water power

____22. a religious revival in the colonies in the 1730s and 1740s

____23. laws established to regulate the institution of slavery by making slaves property of their masters and depriving them of basic civil rights

____24. a famous revival speaker with his sermon, "Sinners in the Hands of an Angry God"

____25. the person who borrowed extensively from Locke's contract theory of government when writing the Declaration of Independence

____26. the economic policy of using raw materials from colonies and keeping the colonies subservient to the mother country in an attempt to aid the growth of the mother country

____27. a prominent revival preacher during the Great Awakening whose message of salvation impacted many lives and brought about several new religious groups (similar to the Methodists, Baptists, and Presbyterians)

____28. an American counterpart in the Enlightenment who not only authored *Poor Richard's Almanac* but devoted his life to social, political, and economic improvements

____29. the region that had an abundance of rich, fertile soil and long growing seasons

____30. the person who was placed on trial for libel for printing attacks against the British royal governor (he was acquitted)

Short Response

31. What factors contributed to the switch from indentured servants to slave labor?

32. Create a t-chart to compare and contrast the three major colonial regions—northern, middle, and southern—in relation to economics, geography, and climate.

33. How did *economics, growth,* and *revival* impact the lives of colonists from the mid-seventeenth century to the mid-eighteenth century?

Answers begin on page 241.

The Road to Revolution

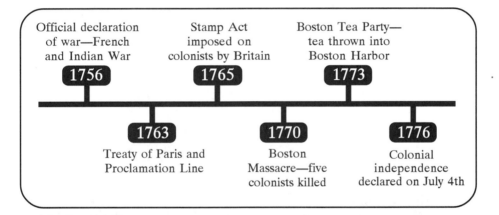

Official declaration of war—French and Indian War **1756**	Stamp Act imposed on colonists by Britain **1765**	Boston Tea Party— tea thrown into Boston Harbor **1773**

1763 Treaty of Paris and Proclamation Line	**1770** Boston Massacre—five colonists killed	**1776** Colonial independence declared on July 4th

Trends and Themes of the Era

▶ When Britain increased its taxation of the colonies after the French and Indian War, tensions mounted as colonists felt they were being taxed without representation.

▶ Colonial resistance to British taxation and other legislation led the British to implement stricter taxes and clamp down on rebellion. The colonists' opposition grew fiercer and more violent.

▶ During this period, colonial resistance efforts became increasingly unified.

▶ Colonists felt the British were denying them their natural rights. As revolution became more likely, many colonists hoped to implement a government independent of the British crown, one that would secure their rights as Americans.

Regulations, taxes, and protests! For more than 100 years, the colonists enjoyed a relatively peaceful "tradition of neglect." As loyal British subjects, they enjoyed being ruled by the British crown, while at the same time having a certain degree of freedom in the colonies. The colonists began to respond to rapid changes in how the colonies were governed by the British crown after the French and Indian War. By 1776, the colonists were primed for rebellion. Benjamin Franklin wrote, "American independence couldn't happen without the most grievous tyranny and oppression." Patrick Henry boldly proclaimed, "I am an American!" The conflict with the British would force the colonists to make a fateful decision. Were they simply Britons who happened to live in America, or were they Americans separate from the British crown? When 56 men in a Philadelphia meeting house "pledged their lives and fortunes and sacred honor to one another" on July 4, 1776, there would be no turning back.

Lesson 4-1: Crisis in the Colonies

By the late 1600s, the French and English emerged as the two dominant forces in North America. They vied for position in both Europe and the New World, resulting in occasional wars on both continents. This series of wars, which ranged through the first half of the eighteenth century, culminated in the **French and Indian War** of 1754–1763.

The Path to Conflict

In the early 1750s, Virginia, Pennsylvania, France, and the Iroquois tribe all claimed ownership of the Ohio Valley. The French began constructing forts to stave off English colonial advances and to maintain their fur trade with local Native Americans. In 1754, a young George Washington (on the orders of the Virginia governor) led about 400 Virginia militiamen against the French. French troops repulsed the Virginia force and captured Washington and the garrison at **Fort Necessity**. With 30 percent of his men lost in the conflict, Washington surrendered on July 4, 1754.

Around the same time, an intercolonial meeting in New York, known as the **Albany Congress,** met to discuss matters with the Iroquois Indians. Representatives of seven colonies gathered with 150 Iroquois chiefs. At the meeting, Benjamin Franklin submitted the **Albany Plan of Union**, which called for the colonies to unify in the face of French and Native American threats. They would have the power to coordinate a colonial defense, levy taxes, and regulate Native American affairs. Remarkable for its attempt to establish a unified colonial government, the Albany Plan won the support of the delegates but was rejected by the separate colonies, because they weren't yet ready for union. The Iroquois left the meeting with no commitment to fight against the French, and British officials in Parliament didn't push for the union because they were fearful of the powerful colonial assembly it would create.

J O I N, or D I E.

Ben Franklin' Pennsylvania Gazette, May 9, 1754

Lesson 4-2: The French and Indian War

The French felt that if they lost the Ohio region, it would threaten their control of the Mississippi River. Soon after the Albany meeting, certain Native American groups allied themselves with the French for two years of fighting against the British. This led to the **Seven Years War** in Europe (1756–1763) and its counterpart, the **French and Indian War** in the colonies.

British army and colonial ranks had to conform to European professional standards, enforced by iron discipline and savage punishment. The men in the colonial ranks became irritated at the demands of fighting under British commanders. Each side blamed the other for struggles in defeating the French. During the conflict, the colonists learned much about British fighting tactics and how British military commanders responded. These lessons would be remembered years later as the colonists united for the Revolutionary War.

Although the colonial regiments were assigned to separate units under a British commander during the war, they would share in the victory at the war's end. When the war began, England held a great advantage in men and supplies; yet, in the first two years, the cunning guerrilla tactics of the French and their allies resulted in numerous humiliating losses for the English.

William Pitt's goal was to expel France from the New World colonies. Under his leadership, England managed to push France out of the Ohio Valley and into Canada. **General Braddock** led an expedition to expel the French from Fort Duquesne, but instead was ambushed and killed by the French. In 1755, the British were successful in forcibly deporting nearly 10,000 Arcadians (French-speaking settlers) to Louisiana (were they formed the Cajun community). By 1758, the British troops had almost completely defeated the French. The remainder of the war was a contest in which the larger, better-supplied army would triumph. In 1759, English forces captured Quebec, and in 1760 they captured Montreal, thus ending the war in North America. The Iroquois allied themselves with the British in 1760. In Europe, the war raged on until the British victory in 1763. Under the terms of the **Treaty of Paris** (1763), Britain gained all of the land in North America east of the Mississippi, and France lost all of its claims in North America except the city of **New Orleans**.

The French and Indian War 1754–1763

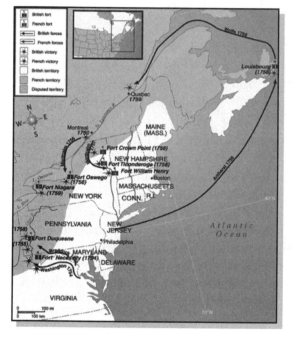

The excitement of victory, however, was short-lived. Because of the war's costs, England faced tough financial difficulties. The British government had accumulated a massive debt fighting the French and Indian War, and acquired a huge new piece of territory to govern. It now looked to the American colonies to help pay for their share of the war expenses. **King George III** and his prime minister, **George Grenville**, noted that the colonists had benefited most from the expensive war and yet had paid very little compared with citizens living in England. They reasoned that, because the colonies benefited most from the war, they should be taxed to pay for England's war debt. England was ending its century-long policy of salutary neglect. This dramatic change in policy sparked escalating tensions between England and its colonists that eventually led to the American Revolution.

Lesson 4-3: British Demands and Colonial Resistance

After the French and Indian War, Britain was the foremost colonial power in North America. While eliminating the French as a threat, the Treaty of Paris (1763) more than doubled the size of British territories in North America. Despite the fact that the British were now firmly in control of the colonies, signs of trouble lingered on the horizon. The British superiors began to make plans to rein in the mismanaged colonies.

To begin with, the British changed the purpose of the war to say that it was waged to "protect the colonists and expand their opportunities for settlement." Despite this goal, Britain lacked supplies and troops at various times in the conflict. The colonists not only had different views about armed conflict, but they resented being imposed upon to quarter British troops in local communities by providing them with shelter, wood, and candles during the war. Colonists who profited by the war saw those wartime profits dry up at the end of the war with a spike in prices and a sharp rise in unemployment. Following the war, Parliament passed a series of acts designed to secure revenue from the colonies. This new financial plan revoked the policy of salutary neglect, enforced the Navigation Acts, and instituted new taxation measures. These measures angered many colonists, who felt harassed by the tight British control. The new interpretation showed the British government's increasing doubts about colonial support of British policies.

The Writs of Assistance

One of the first sources of tension between the colonies and England surfaced during the French and Indian War. In order to avoid English taxes on molasses, rum, and sugar imported from non-British territories (which were set by the 1733 **Molasses Act**) colonial traders smuggled French goods from the French West Indies during the war. But England wanted stricter enforcement of the Molasses Act to raise revenue from the colonies.

In 1760, as its war debt accumulated, England authorized British revenue officers to use **writs of assistance**. The writs served as general search warrants, allowing customs officials to enter and investigate any ship or building suspected of holding smuggled goods. The writs of assistance meant officials could enter and ransack private homes and ships without proving probable cause for suspicion.

Although the writs of assistance proved to be a useful tool in fighting smuggling, they greatly angered colonists. In 1761, Boston merchants challenged the constitutionality of the writs before the Massachusetts Supreme Court, arguing that the writs stood "against the fundamental principles of law." Even though they lost the case, the merchants and other colonists continued to protest against the writs, believing the government had overstepped its bounds.

The Proclamation Line

In 1763, in efforts to keep peace with the Native Americans, the British government established the **Proclamation Line** to bar colonial settlement west of the Appalachian Mountains. Britain claimed the line was needed

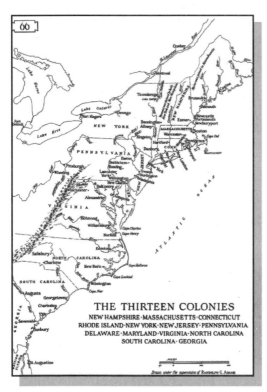

THE THIRTEEN COLONIES
NEW HAMPSHIRE·MASSACHUSETTS·CONNECTICUT
RHODE ISLAND·NEW YORK·NEW JERSEY·PENNSYLVANIA
DELAWARE·MARYLAND·VIRGINIA·NORTH CAROLINA
SOUTH CAROLINA· GEORGIA

to protect the colonists from attacks on the wild frontier. The terms of the Proclamation Line stated that colonists already settled in the region must leave, negating their claims to the West and limiting colonial expansion. Lands west of the mountains would be reserved for Indian nations, and the colonists would be confined to the region east of the Appalachian Mountains. Several land speculators, such as George Washington and Benjamin Franklin, saw their profits from western land investments threatened.

The Proclamation Line directive angered many colonists and signaled yet another change in British policy. Native Americans were also upset by the loss of French business and the prospect of British colonists moving farther west. In 1763, **Chief Pontiac** led an unsuccessful effort to resist the British in the Ohio Valley regions formerly claimed by France. The small garrisons of British troops found it difficult to enforce the policy, and tensions rose with land speculators and frontier settlers.

The Sugar Act

In 1764, Parliament passed the **Sugar Act** to counter smuggling of foreign sugar and to establish a British monopoly in the American sugar market. The act lowered the import tax on foreign sugar while raising the stakes for smugglers. Royal officials could seize colonial cargo with little prompting or legal cause. If caught, smugglers would face a trial in a vice-admiralty court, where a conviction was more likely. Unlike previous acts, which had regulated trade to boost the entire British economy, the Sugar Act was a profit-seeking measure geared toward getting revenue from the colonists for the English government. The colonists felt the British were levying an unfair tax and began to question whether some actions of the British government warranted resistance.

The Stamp Act

As another way to force the colonies to help pay off the war debt, Prime Minister Grenville pushed the Stamp Act through Parliament in March 1765. This was the first direct tax on the colonies to raise money by taxing vital goods and services. The act, passed over the authority of local colonial assemblies, required Americans to buy special watermarked paper for 15 classes of documents that included everything from wills and property deeds to newspapers, almanacs, diplomas, marriage licenses, and even playing cards. Violators faced juryless trials in vice-admiralty courts, where presumption of guilt was standard until the defendant was proven innocent.

Both the Sugar Act and the Stamp Act were passed to raise revenue from the colonists. They met with fierce resistance. In the colonies, legal pamphlets condemned the acts on the grounds of "taxation without representation." Colonists believed they shouldn't have to pay parliamentary taxes because they didn't elect any members of Parliament. Many believed that only the colonial legislatures had the right to impose direct taxes on the colonists.

Prime Minister Grenville and others in Parliament argued that Americans were obligated to pay taxes because they enjoyed the same status as British subjects in England. Grenville claimed that all British citizens were "virtually represented" in Parliament. This theory of **virtual representation** meant that Parliament members not only represented their specific geographical constituencies, but that they also considered the welfare of *all* British subjects.

Opposition to the Stamp Act

The Stamp Act generated the first round of significant, widespread colonial resistance to British rule. Elite colonists and poor colonists alike began to unite with their common resentment against royal officials. By May 1765, the Virginia House of Burgesses had passed the **Virginia Resolves**, which denied Parliament's right to tax the colonies under the Stamp Act. Word of these resolutions spread, and by the end of the year, eight other colonial legislatures had adopted similar positions. Grenville said that because the Americans were "children planted with great care, nourished by British indulgence, protected by British arms, would they now begrudge to contribute their mite to reduce the British people from the heavy burdens they suffered?" Americans claimed it was not "British care" but rather "British oppression."

Dissent spread throughout the colonies and became more organized as the colonists openly challenged Britain's right to exercise its authority over the colonies. Radical groups calling themselves the **Sons of Liberty** formed throughout the colonies to channel the widespread violence, often burning stamps and threatening British officials. Merchants in New York began a **boycott** of British goods, and merchants in other cities soon joined. Patrick Henry asserted that the Stamp Act was evidence of the tyranny of King George. Representatives of nine colonial assemblies met in New York City at the **Stamp Act Congress**, where they prepared a petition in which Parliament was asked to repeal the Stamp Act because it violated the principle of "no taxation without representation." The congress argued that Parliament couldn't tax anyone outside of Great Britain and couldn't deny anyone a fair trial. The Stamp Act Congress and the boycotts were major steps in uniting the colonies against the British. Mob violence and formal legislative protests were having an impact.

Under strong pressure from the colonies, and with the British economy slumping because of the American boycott of British goods, Parliament repealed the Stamp Act in March 1766. At the same time, Parliament passed the **Declaratory Act** to strengthen British rule in the colonies. The Declaratory Act stated the absolute right of Parliament to pass legislation and raise taxes "in all cases whatsoever." In the euphoria of celebrating the Stamp Act repeal, the colonists ignored Parliament's continued right to tax the colonies.

The Townshend Duties

Because of the shortfall in the British treasury, Charles Townshend, leader of the British government from 1766 to 1770, proposed new taxes—including taxing imports into the colonies to recover Parliament's lost revenue—and secured passage of the Revenue Act of 1767. Referred to as the Townshend Duties, the Revenue Act taxed glass, lead, paint, and paper, and instituted a three-penny tax on tea entering the colonies. The profits from these taxes would pay the salaries of the royal governors in the colonies. Townshend also enacted the 1766 Quartering Act, requiring colonists to provide room and board for troops stationed in the colonies. In practice, however, the Townshend Duties yielded little income because the colonists planned a well-organized boycott in resistance to the new taxes. Some colonists, such as Samuel Adams in Boston, began questioning the need for a standing army in a time of peace.

Opposition to the Townshend Duties

The Townshend Duties may not have raised much revenue, but they stirred up a great deal of political dissent in the colonies. New customs regulations attempted to ensure payment of the taxes and to curb smuggling and evasion of payments. Protest against the taxes first took the form of intellectual and legal dissent, and then erupted in violence.

In December 1767, colonist John Dickinson published "Letters From a Pennsylvania Farmer" in the *Pennsylvania Chronicle*. This series of letters argued against the legality of the Townshend Duties and soon appeared in nearly every colonial newspaper. Dickinson argued the fallacies of virtual representation of all British citizens in Parliament and wrote about the need for actual representation of elected men to speak for the rights of all Englishmen in Parliament. The colonial media quickly became tools to spread opposition to the royal crown, as people throughout the colonies read the articles. Political opposition to the Townshend Duties spread, and colonial assemblies passed resolves denouncing the act and petitioning Parliament for its repeal.

John Hancock became personally involved with Samuel Adams and other patriots in their opposition to various acts instituted by Parliament when in 1768, Hancock's own ship, *Liberty*, was seized for smuggling during the opposition to the Townshend Acts. He became one of the leading spokesmen in opposition to British measures.

Boycotts of British goods demonstrated the colonists' resolve and showed how dissent had crossed social barriers. Colonists even appealed to women to help boycott British goods. To avoid buying material spun in Britain, the **Daughters of Liberty** met in large spinning bees to spin wool into yarn and to weave it into a rough fabric known as homespun.

Although colonial boycotts were somewhat successful at keeping British imports out of the colonies, they prompted many British merchants and artisans to mount a significant movement to repeal the Townshend Duties. Sailors joined the resistance by rioting against corrupt customs officials. Many customs officials were exploiting the ambiguous and confusing wording of the Townshend Act by claiming that small items stored in a sailor's chest were undeclared cargo. The customs officers then seized entire ships based on that charge. Often, they pocketed the profits. Known as customs racketeering, this behavior amounted to little more than legalized piracy.

Lobsterbacks and Martyrs

In 1768, 4,000 British troops (who wore red coats, hence the nickname "lobsterbacks" or "redcoats") landed in Boston to stop further

violence, and the following year passed relatively peacefully. Britain continued to move troops from the interior to major port cities. With the presence of so many soldiers around the volatile environment of Boston, many people began to wonder if open violence was inevitable. **Samuel Adams** and some of his close friends encouraged the hostile feelings by publishing newspaper accounts of supposed confrontations and threats from British soldiers in and around Boston. In 1772, Adams also helped form the Boston Committee of Correspondence to continue the protest efforts against Britain.

Tensions flared with the **Boston Massacre** in March 1770 when an unruly mob, ready for a fight, bombarded British troops with rocks, snowballs, and insults. In the ensuing chaos, five colonists were killed. A later report claimed that former slave Crispus Attucks, along with four other men, had been "killed on the spot" by British redcoats. James Bowdoin's short narrative called "The Massacre in Boston" gave a vivid account of the five "martyrs" and 11 wounded, and along with a wood engraving by **Paul Revere,** depicted the horrors of the event. It was widely circulated throughout the colonies. The image of British cruelty and brutality helped to inflame anger toward the British.

Because of the colonists' vocal and violent opposition to the various taxes, Parliament finally relented and repealed most of the Townshend Duties in March 1770. Lord North, the new prime minister, eliminated most of the taxes but insisted on maintaining the profitable tax on tea. In response, Americans ended their opposition but maintained voluntary agreements to boycott British tea. Nonconsumption kept the tea tax revenues far too low to pay the royal governors, effectively nullifying what remained of the Townshend Duties.

Lesson 4-4: "If This Be Treason..."

From 1770 to 1772, the British ignored the colonies and tensions cooled substantially. But in the fall of 1772, Lord Frederick North began preparations to pay royal governors out of customs revenue rather than letting the colonial assemblies control payment, denying the assemblies their taxation privileges. In response to this threat, Samuel Adams urged Massachusetts communities to appoint a committee to coordinate colony-wide measures protecting colonial rights. Within the year, nearly 250 **Committees of Correspondence** had formed throughout the colonies. These committees not only linked political leaders of almost every colony in resistance to the British, but they became the method by which the colonies coordinated their efforts to preserve their rights.

In addition, the citizens of Boston commemorated "Massacre Day" each year with orations and remembrances, keeping memories of the incident alive. Acts of violence began spreading to other colonies. In Rhode Island, several angry colonists scuttled the confiscated ship *Liberty*. Another ship, the *Gaspee*, ran aground in Narragansett Bay and was set ablaze by an angry mob from Providence.

The Boston Tea Party

The **British East India Company** suffered from the American boycott of British tea. By the 1770s, 90 percent of American tea was contraband to escape British taxes. In an effort to save the company, in 1773 Parliament passed the Tea Act, which eliminated import tariffs on tea entering England. The act allowed the company to sell directly to consumers rather than through merchants, giving it a monopoly on the tea trade. These changes lowered the price of British tea below that of smuggled tea, which the British hoped would end the boycott. Parliament planned to use the profits from tea sales to pay the salaries of the colonial royal governors, a move that particularly angered colonists.

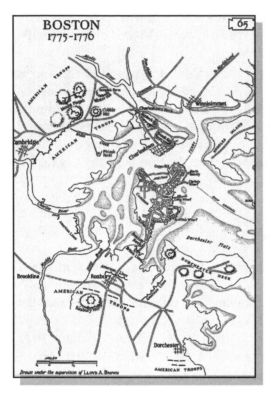

Though colonists protested the Tea Act by boycotting tea and burning tea cargos throughout the colonies, the response in Boston was well organized and aggressive. Samuel Adams was among those who helped plan and coordinate Boston's resistance to the Tea Act that culminated in the infamous Tea Party. In December 1773 (with several thousand onlookers) a group of colonists dressed as Native Americans dumped nearly 700,000 pounds of tea into Boston Harbor. Dubbed the **Boston Tea Party**, the event achieved an epic status. A similar incident took place in New York City a few months later, when protesters threw tea overboard, then paraded the empty tea chests through the town and burned them outside the city. These protests became powerful symbols of resistance and continued to unite the colonists in their opposition to the royal crown. Samuel Adams later worked for the creation of the Continental Congress, helping propel it into supporting Massachusetts in the crisis following the Tea Party incident.

The Intolerable Acts

Parliament responded swiftly and angrily to the actions in Boston with a string of legislation known as the **Intolerable Acts**, which included the four Coercive Acts of 1773 and the Quebec Act. The four Coercive Acts:

▸ Closed Boston Harbor to trade until the city paid for the lost tea.

▸ Removed certain democratic elements of the Massachusetts government, most notably by making formerly elected positions appointments by the crown.

▸ Restricted town meetings, requiring that their agendas be approved by the royal governor.

▸ Declared that any royal agent charged with murder in the colonies would face trial in Britain.

▸ Instituted a new **Quartering Act**, forcing civilians to provide room and board in town to support British soldiers.

The Quebec Act, unrelated to the Coercive Acts but just as offensive to the colonists, established Roman Catholicism as Quebec's official religion, gave Quebec's royal governors wide powers, and extended Quebec's borders south to the Ohio River and west to the Mississippi, inhibiting westward expansion.

Colonial opposition to the latest round of British legislation was widespread. Not only did the acts impose a heavy military presence in the colonies, but in the colonists' minds, they effectively authorized the military to murder colonists with immunity. Many saw the Intolerable Acts as a British plan to starve the New England colonists while reducing their ability to organize and protest. Sympathy for the economic and political turmoil in Boston spread throughout the colonies, and farmer-soldiers in Massachusetts formed a colonial militia known as the **minutemen.** As protests against British officials continued, the protest spread from the urban centers to the rural countryside.

The First Continental Congress

In September 1774, the Committees of Correspondence of every colony except Georgia sent delegates to the **First Continental Congress.** Although the delegates differed in their political views and regional interests, the event further unified the colonists. The congress endorsed Massachusetts' Suffolk Resolves, declaring that the colonies didn't have

Legislation Along the Road to War at a Glance

Legislation	Provision	Reaction
Sugar Act 1764	Duties on sugar, coffee, tea, and other imports	Protests
Currency Act 1764	Didn't allow colonies to print paper money, so colonists would have to pay for goods in gold or silver	Continued smuggling of goods
Stamp Act 1765	Ordered that all printed documents had to bear a stamp	Riots
Quartering Act 1765	Colonists ordered to provide British troops with housing and other items	Protest in local assemblies
Declaratory Act 1766	After repeal of Stamp Act, Parliament's sovereignty over the colonies declared in "all cases whatsoever"	Ignored by colonists
Townshend Duties 1767	New taxes on glass, lead, paper, paints, and tea	Boycotts, assembly protests, newspaper attacks
Tea Act 1773	Gave East India Company a monopoly and the right to sell tea directly to colonists	Protests
Intolerable Acts 1774	Closed Port of Boston, restricted town meetings	Boycott of British goods, First Continental Congress convened
Prohibitory Act 1775	Embargo placed on American ships and American ships seized	Further justification for the decision for independence

to obey the Coercive Acts because they infringed upon basic liberties. The delegates also voted for an organized boycott of all British goods. In preparation for possible British retaliation, the delegates called upon all colonies to raise and train local militias.

By the spring of 1775, colonists had established provincial congresses to enforce the decrees of the Continental Congress. The final business agenda was an agreement to meet again in May 1775 for a second congressional gathering. King George's response to the committee was that "the line of conduct seems now chalked out...the New England governments are in a state of rebellion, blows must decide whether they are to be subject to this country or independent."

The Shot Heard 'Round the World

In April 1775, colonial minutemen met near Boston and exchanged fire with British soldiers who were attempting to seize a supply stockpile in Concord and to arrest John Hancock and Samuel Adams. The first confrontation came in Lexington, a town in New Hampshire. Once in Concord, the British troops faced a much larger colonial force. Riders **Paul Revere** and William Dawes warned of the impending arrival of the redcoats. In the skirmish, the British lost 273 men and were driven back into Boston.

The **Battle of Lexington and Concord** persuaded many colonists to take up arms. General Thomas Gage, colonial governor of Massachusetts

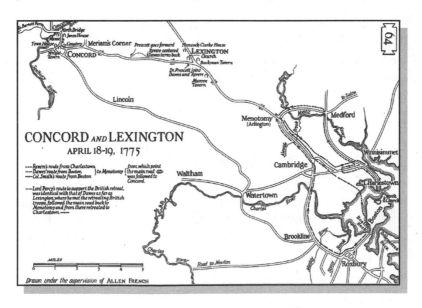

from 1774 to 1775 and head of the British army in America, later complained that the Americans displayed "a conduct and spirit against us they never showed against the French," and a colonist commented that the British were much mistaken in the people they had to deal with.

The next night, 20,000 New England troops began a month long siege of the British garrison in Boston. On June 17, 1775, the English attacked the colonial stronghold outside Boston on Breed's Hill in what became known as the **Battle of Bunker Hill**. The English redcoats successfully dislodged the colonials from the hillside stronghold but suffered a 40 percent casualty rate.

Attempted Reconciliation

As violence erupted all over New England, the Second Continental Congress convened in Philadelphia in May 1775. New England delegates urged independence from Britain, although other delegates, from the middle colonies, wanted a more moderate course of action. Most delegates still fervently opposed complete separation from England. In an effort to reconcile with the king, Dickinson penned the **Olive Branch Petition**, offering peace under the following conditions:

▸ A cease-fire in Boston.

▸ Repealing of the Coercive Acts.

▸ Negotiations between the colonists and Britain.

The Olive Branch Petition reached Britain the same day as news of the Battle of Bunker Hill. King George III rejected reconciliation and declared New England to be in a state of rebellion in August 1775. In the colonies, the Second Continental Congress issued a Declaration of Causes and Necessity of Taking up Arms. Years of resistance to Britain had given the colonists a new political identity, and they marched for independence.

Lesson 4-5: Independence Declared

In June 1775, the Second Continental Congress elected **George Washington** commander in chief of the newly established American Continental Army. Meanwhile, the British forces abandoned Boston and moved to New York City, which they planned to use as a staging point for conquering New England.

In January 1776, **Thomas Paine**'s pamphlet *Common Sense* was published and widely distributed. Paine called for economic and political independence, and he proposed that America become a new kind of nation founded on the principles of liberty. "We have it in our power to begin the world over again." In the first three months, more than 120,000 copies were sold. Paine's greatest contribution was persuading the common man to sever ties with Great Britain.

In June, the Second Continental Congress adopted a resolution of independence, officially creating the United States of America. Thomas Jefferson's draft of the **Declaration of Independence** was officially approved on July 4th. The Declaration of Independence was a formal justification for the colonists' actions and proclaimed a complete and irrevocable break from England. In borrowing from John Locke's government theories, Jefferson argued that the British government had broken its contract with the colonies and failed to protect the colonists' universal rights of "life, liberty, and happiness." The British people weren't condemned, but the king was openly attacked personally as a tyrant, whose repeated abuses of power were spelled out repeatedly in the document.

By declaring independence and forming a new entity, Americans dramatically raised the political and military stakes in their struggle with Great Britain. Although not totally united in this new spirit of independence, many colonists, apart from the loyalists, redefined themselves and their protest against Britain. Many merchants, farmers, slaveholders, laborers, artisans, and housewives had a new cause. "Life, liberty, and the pursuit of happiness" became the new rallying cry.

Review Exam

Multiple Choice

1. The French and Indian War's first skirmish involved the surrender of George Washington at:
   a) Quebec
   b) Fort Necessity
   c) Fort Duquesne
   d) Fort Ohio

2. Benjamin Franklin's early proposal to unify the colonies was known as the:
   a) League of Colonies
   b) Colonial Confederation
   c) Albany Plan of Union
   d) Colonial-Iroquois Union

3. The Albany Plan of Union was ultimately rejected for all the following reasons *EXCEPT*:
    a) a lack of unity
    b) a lack of identity
    c) the colonies were not ready to break with Great Britain
    d) for a lack of support from the French and Iroquois

4. During the French and Indian War, the British did all of the following *EXCEPT*:
    a) raise taxes in the colonies to help finance the war effort
    b) require strict discipline of the colonial troops
    c) require colonial troops to be commanded by British commanders
    d) raise taxes in Great Britain to help finance the war effort

5. At the end of the French and Indian War, all of the following occurred *EXCEPT*:
    a) New Orleans was under British control
    b) Britain emerged as the dominant power in North America
    c) France lost all its claims to North America
    d) the land west of the Appalachian Mountains to the Mississippi River became British territory

6. King George ignored this long-standing policy of and began to focus on the colonists:
    a) mercantilism
    b) salutary neglect
    c) virtual representation
    d) the Navigation Acts

7. Colonists at first resorted to this in order to avoid paying taxes under the Molasses Act:
    a) smuggling goods
    b) boycotting British goods
    c) paying taxes under protest
    d) working to have the act repealed

8. The Proclamation Line of 1763:
    a) allowed for limited movement west of the Appalachians
    b) barred colonial movement west of the Appalachian mountains
    c) allowed for a five-year limit of movement west of the Appalachian mountains
    d) allowed for land speculators to continue the sale of land

9. Great Britain began taxing the colonists in order to:
    a) raise revenue to pay for war expenses
    b) exert authority over the colonists
    c) limit profits from smugglers
    d) all of the answers on the list

10. The Stamp Act represented:
    a) a direct tax on the colonists
    b) an attempt by Britain to raise revenues by taxing a variety of goods and services
    c) a tax passed without the consent of local colonial assemblies
    d) all of the answers on the list

11. The rally cry of the colonists protesting increased taxation measures by Great Britain was:
    a) "Down with taxes!"
    b) "No taxation without representation!"
    c) "Read my lips, no new taxes!"
    d) "No new taxes, period!"

12. Colonial protests against the actions of Parliament included:
    a) the Daughters of Liberty spinning cotton to make their own homespun cloth
    b) dumping crates of tea overboard in Boston and New York harbor
    c) the Sons of Liberty burning stamps and tar, and feathering tax collectors
    d) all of the answers on the list

13. As taxation measures and other actions by the British government continued:
   a) colonists began to deeply resent these actions as infringements on their liberties as British subjects
   b) colonists elected colonial officials to Parliament
   c) colonists began to accept the added measures as necessary
   d) protests died down after Britain removed its troops from the colonies

14. The Boston Massacre resulted in not only the death of Crispus Attucks, a former slave, but also resulted in:
   a) the deaths of four other colonial men
   b) the horrors of the event being widely circulated throughout the colonies
   c) the event being depicted in a wood engraving and printed in newspapers long with news articles describing the event
   d) all of the choices on the list

15. "The line of conduct seems now chalked out...the New England governments are in a state of rebellion, blows must decide whether they are to be subject to this country or independent." This statement about the Continental Congress was made by:
   a) King George
   b) Patrick Henry
   c) George Washington
   d) Benjamin Franklin

16. The significance of Thomas Paine's publication, *Common Sense*, in January 1776 was that:
   a) it called for economic and political independence from Britain
   b) it sold more than 120,000 copies within the first three months of publication
   c) it persuaded colonists to sever ties with great Britain
   d) all of the answers on the list

17. The major foundation principle of the Declaration of Independence were Thomas Jefferson's words of:
   a) "Life, liberty, and property..."
   b) "One nation, under God..."
   c) "Life, liberty, and the pursuit of happiness..."
   d) "When in the course of human events..."

Matching

a. Writs of Assistance

b. John Hancock

c. Lobsterbacks

d. British East India Company

e. George Washington

f. John Dickinson

g. Committees of Correspondence

h. Patrick Henry

i. William Pitt

j. General Thomas Gage

k. French and Indian War

l. King George III

m. Coercive Acts

n. Samuel Adams

o. Arcadians

p. Minutemen

q. Chief Pontiac

r. Bunker Hill

s. Olive Branch Petition

_____18. more than 250 of these colonial groups were formed to coordinate their protest efforts to preserve their rights

_____19. he boldly proclaimed "I am an American" prior to American Independence in 1776

_____20. he encouraged the hostile feelings by publishing newspaper accounts of threats from British soldiers in and around Boston and helped form the Boston Committee of Correspondence

_____21. a British leader who looked to the colonies after 1763 to have them help share the tax burden for all British subjects

_____22. he led an unsuccessful effort to resist the British troops in the Ohio Valley in 1763

_____23. the war (also called the Seven Years War) in the colonies that was fought between Britain and France over control of North America; it resulted in the French losing and being forced out of North America

_____24. French-speaking settlers in Canada who were forcibly relocated to Louisiana (where they formed the Cajun community)

_____25. a nickname associated with the British Redcoats

_____26. the British commander whose goal was to expel France from North America

_____27. the farmer-soldier colonial militia formed to respond quickly in case of a battle

_____28. general search warrants that allowed British customs officials to enter and investigate any ship suspected of holding smuggled goods

_____29. he published "letters from a Pennsylvania Farmer" written in protest to the Townshend Duties and printed in several colonial newspapers

_____30. a British tea company that attempted to establish a monopoly on the tea trade in the colonies

_____31. a patriot who became personally involved by speaking out against British measures (and was the first to sign the Declaration of Independence)

_____32. the commander of the newly formed American Continental Army

_____33. the acts that were included in the Intolerable Acts and were meant to punish Boston for the Boston Tea Party by closing the port and forcing the colonists to pay for the tea

_____34. the head of the British army in America at the time of the battles of Lexington and Concord and also colonial governor of Massachusetts

_____35. the document from the Second Continental Congress that attempted a reconciliation with Britain in 1775

_____36. the battle that was fought in June 1775 and resulted in a British victory over colonial troops

Short Response

37. How did the outcome of the French and Indian War impact the colonists in their dealings with Great Britain?

38. What events had a major impact upon the colonists as they were beginning to develop a unique sense of **identity** during the time period 1754 to 1776?

39. What events had a major impact upon the colonists as they were beginning to develop a unique sense of **unity** during the time period 1754 to 1766?

40. What role did the media play in colonial affairs from 1763 to 1776?

41. In light of *regulations, taxes, and protests*, could the Revolutionary War have been avoided?

Answers begin on page 244.

The Revolutionary War

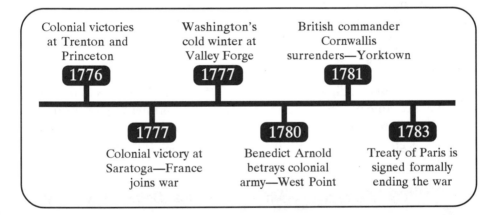

Colonial victories at Trenton and Princeton
1776

Washington's cold winter at Valley Forge
1777

British commander Cornwallis surrenders—Yorktown
1781

1777
Colonial victory at Saratoga—France joins war

1780
Benedict Arnold betrays colonial army—West Point

1783
Treaty of Paris is signed formally ending the war

Trends and Themes of the Era

- The Revolutionary War affected women, African Americans, Native Americans, patriots, and loyalists in varying degrees.

- As battles raged on from 1775 until 1781, the strengths and weaknesses of the combatants influenced the eventual outcome.

- The negotiations of the Treaty of Paris (1783) affirmed American independence and greatly enlarged the country's territorial claims in North America.

- The war challenged Americans' expectations about individual rights and social equality.

Freedom, democracy, and independence! From Lexington and Concord to Yorktown, the colonists waged a war that ended in the sovereignty of America apart from Great Britain. Political ties were dissolved with the resolution that "these United States are, and of right ought to be free and independent states absolved from all allegiance." Although the war wasn't popular with the entire population, the patriots dared to challenge the formidable power of Great Britain. Britain anticipated that a mere showing of force would intimidate the rebels, but the ideological pull of independence kept the American soldiers steadfast. By September 1781, Washington's troops had emerged victorious against the most powerful nation in the world. Years later, John Adams commented, "The Revolution was effected before the war commenced. The Revolution was in the hearts and minds of the people." Following the end of the war, the greatest challenge for the new country lay in securing its freedom.

Lesson 5-1: The Continental Army versus the Redcoats

In the events leading up to July 4, 1776, Great Britain was unwilling to make any concessions to colonial demands. Colonial militias prepared for the inevitable conflict. After the delegates at the Second Continental Congress signed the Declaration of Independence, the two sides readied for war.

Sizing up the Competition: Great Britain

Advantages	Disadvantages
Well-trained army	Increase in national debt during the war
Large navy	Underestimated colonial resistance
Large population of 11 million	
Ability to hire Hessians	Distance dividing England and America
Strong centralized government	
Support from loyalists in America	Unfamiliar with terrain
	Deserters in the army and navy
	Also fighting France and Spain

Sizing up the Competition: America

Advantages	Disadvantages
Familiar with terrain/guerilla warfare	Smaller population of 2.5 million
Widespread resistance against England	Only 40 percent of population supported
Inspiring cause of freedom	20-percent loyalist population
Washington's leadership	Lack of military training
Alliances with France, Spain, and the Netherlands	Virtually no navy
Victories in various battle strategies	Lack of centralized government

At the outset, Great Britain clearly had a distinct military and economic advantage over the newly formed states in America. Americans were inspired by their noble cause of fighting for freedom and "pledging to each other [their] Lives, Fortunes, and sacred Honor." By the war's end in 1781, George Washington's troops, with the aid of the French allies, managed to wear down the British and emerge triumphant with their new found cause for war intact. "That these United States are, and of right ought to be free and independent states; that they are absolved from all allegiance to the British crown, and that all political connection between them and the state of Great Britain, is and ought to be totally dissolved."

Division Among the Colonists

Similar to the British, the Americans suffered from several disadvantages. Not only was the American population smaller at 2.5 million, but it was divided over the war effort. The signing of the Declaration of Independence led to a sharp break in the colonies between the **Whig party**, who favored independence, and the **Tories**, who were British loyalists and sympathizers.

Only about 40 percent of Americans supported the war effort. Almost 20 percent of the population was enslaved, with 5,000 blacks serving in the Continental Army during the war.

Approximately 100,000 **loyalists**, or Tories, fled America during the war; another 20,000 served in the British army or local militias. Estimates of the number of loyalists run as high as 500,000, or 20 percent of the white population of the colonies. Tory influence was strongest in the middle colonies and in Georgia. The most prominent Whig strongholds were New England, Virginia, and South Carolina. Others, meanwhile, remained silent or neutral throughout the conflict.

Lesson 5-2: Fighting the War for Independence

One of Great Britain's biggest failures in fighting the war was in thinking that colonial resistance was limited to a few localized groups of radicals. They failed to see that colonial resistance was widespread throughout all 13 colonies. During the ensuing conflict, the colonial militia were able to capitalize on their cunning guerilla war tactics and knowledge of the local terrain. Both sides seemed reluctant to risk all their manpower and resources in battles. Each side would have to determine how far it was willing to go to secure victory in the conflict.

The War in the North

Early in the war, George Washington's forces around New York were driven back to Pennsylvania by the stronger British forces that used New York City as their base of operations. Much to the surprise of the British (and their hired German Hessian troops) Washington's Christmas victories in 1776 at **Trenton and Princeton,** New Jersey, helped revive the lagging spirits of the American troops. Washington's Christmas-night crossing of the Delaware River ended up surprising the British and the Hessian brigades and brought about a much-needed American victory. This would be followed a few days later with another crossing and victory at Princeton. In addition, Thomas Paine offered inspiration to the troops in his new article "The Crisis" in December of 1776 in which he stated, "These are the times that try men's souls. The summer soldier and the sunshine patriot will, in this crisis, shrink from the service of their country; but he that stands by it now, deserves the love and thanks of man and woman. Tyranny, like hell, is not easily conquered; yet we have this consolation with us, that the harder the conflict, the more glorious the triumph." Washington had this read aloud to his troops. The gamble for a victory and words of inspiration helped fuel the lagging spirits of the troops.

In October 1777, the Continentals won another decisive victory at the **Battle of Saratoga.** Led by Benedict Arnold, the Americans pushed back the British. During this battle in New York, American forces under **General Horatio Gates** surrounded the British troops, forcing **General Burgoyne** to surrender his entire army. The British defeat not only raised the American army's morale, but it also persuaded France to recognize American independence and to join the battle against Britain.

In early December 1777, 11,000 troops under Washington's command marched through the snow to spend a long, cold winter at **Valley Forge**, Pennsylvania, where they regrouped and trained. In June 1778, these newly trained troops met the British at the Battle of Monmouth Courthouse. It ended with the redcoats' retreat, bringing the Americans victory in the North. This was the last major engagement in the North, as the war shifted to other fronts signaling the failure of the British to isolate the North from the rest of the region. The British strategy of attempting to win the war by capturing major cities failed. Despite setbacks, the colonial population failed to become demoralized during the war.

Revolutionary War in the North and West, 1776–1780

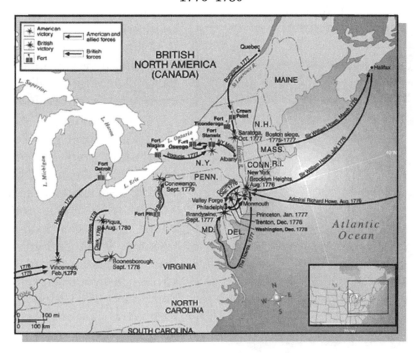

War on the Frontier

The British enlisted the help of Native Americans along the American frontier. Although most Native American groups tried to remain neutral, the majority of those involved in the war were loyal to Britain and posed a serious threat to the frontier regions. When the Iroquois Confederacy split, most groups sided with the British, while a few sided with the Americans. In 1779, Washington responded to British, Indian, and loyalist attacks in the frontier settlements in New York and Pennsylvania by launching raids that eventually ended with nearly 40 Iroquois villages being destroyed. The war's conclusion would see Native Americans scattered far from their familiar homelands when the Americans gained control of the area west of the Appalachians. Britain would eventually end up maintaining a few forts in the west under the guise of providing protection for the Native Americans.

War in the South

In 1778, France joined the war against Britain, as did Spain and the Dutch Republic in 1779 and 1780, respectively. Finding themselves in a larger war than anticipated, the British turned their attention southward, because America's southern ports provided the flexibility they needed to carry out a geographically broad conflict, and because Loyalist influences were far stronger there.

The British took control of the Continental garrison at Charleston, South Carolina, in May 1780. In August 1780, the British were again victorious when they crushed a group of poorly trained Continentals at Camden, South Carolina. The British troops continued to win battles between March and September 1781, though not without a significant cost to their forces.

War for Independence in the South, 1778–1781

At the same time, conflict was brewing in the South. Washington learned of a plot by **Benedict Arnold**, commander of West Point, to turn the outpost over to the British. Arnold escaped in September 1780 and received a commission as a brigadier general in the British army.

Lesson 5-3: Surrender and Victory

Britain's lack of supplies and troops led the colonial militia to lead the redcoats on wild chases throughout the region. The goal was to exhaust and deplete their supplies. During late 1780 and early 1781, the Continental Army won several more battles against the British, who were growing weary after eight years of conflict. Victories at King's Mountain, Cowpens, and the Battle of Guilford Courthouse gave the Continental troops a much-needed edge.

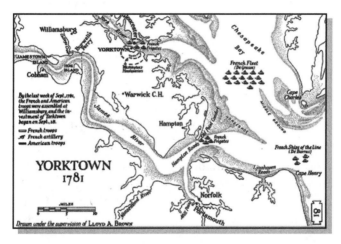

Washington moved his forces from New York toward **Yorktown**, Virginia, where the British had established a new base. Near Yorktown, Washington's 9,000 troops joined 7,800 French troops, outnumbering the British nearly two to one. Admiral de Grasse sailed his French battle fleet of 28 ships north toward Virginia in 1781. As Washington's troops marched south, Admiral de Grasse's fleet arrived at Chesapeake Bay, where they defeated the British fleet and won control of the river. On September 28, 1781, Washington, along with Lafayette's troops and 3,000 of de Grasse's men, arrived at Yorktown. In October, these troops besieged the British base until the British troops forced Cornwallis to surrender. The British defeat crushed their troops' fighting spirit and forced them to concede to the Americans.

King George III initially refused to admit defeat, but official peace talks finally began in June 1782. Benjamin Franklin, John Adams, and John Jay negotiated the **Treaty of Paris of 1783,** signed in September 1783. In the agreement, Britain recognized American independence and defined the new borders of the United States: the northern border along Canada, the western border along the Mississippi, and the southern border along Spanish Florida (a line disputed by Spain). The treaty recommended that the states return loyalist property seized during the war. After the war, about 100,000 loyalists left the country and ended up in Canada and Great Britain. Britain also agreed to evacuate its troops. The newly founded United States would now be faced with the great challenge of finding its economic and political place in the world.

Lesson 5-4: The Impact of the War on American Society

Despite economic problems, the war's length, battle defeats, and surprise victories, and a certain level of disagreement among the states, America emerged as the winner of the conflict. An estimated 25,000 American men died in the Revolutionary War (roughly one in 10 American soldiers). Most of the conflict was confined largely to direct engagements between armies, and the battles claimed very few civilians. A soldier described the war as "poor food, hard lodging, cold weather, fatigue, nasty clothes, and nasty cookery."

America now faced the challenge of producing and finding markets for goods. Inflationary prices and a weak currency threatened to undermine this newfound freedom. Because the Continental Congress simply printed money and circulated it without a sound tax base to support it, states were asked to tax their citizens to pay off war debt.

The Revolutionary War and Blacks

The British promised liberty to those slaves who joined the British cause, in an effort to undermine rebellious planters in the south. The British actively recruited slaves belonging to Patriot masters and, consequently, more blacks fought for the Crown during the war than fought on the American side. Although American military leaders were reluctant to allow former slaves to join their armed forces on a permanent basis, black men fought with the Continental Army since the beginning of the war at Concord, Lexington, and Bunker Hill. During the war, thousands of African-Americans fought for the freedom, and by the war's end, 5,000 had served in the patriot's war effort. Because of fears about slave rebellions, few slaves in the Deep South fought in the war, but thousands escaped to freedom during the chaos. After the war, northern states began pushing for abolition or the gradual emancipation of slaves. The southern states, however, didn't outlaw slavery; in fact, agriculture and slavery became the sole basis for economic growth in the South. Southerners found it inconvenient or difficult to live without slaves; the wealth of the South became dependent upon slavery.

The Revolutionary War and Women

Although women didn't gain any political rights from the war, they proved they were capable of serving their nation as more than just wives and mothers, which began to lay the groundwork for future women's rights efforts. In 1776, **Abigail Adams**, in a letter to her husband **John Adams**, encouraged her husband and other men working on the new frame of government for the country to simply "Remember the Ladies!" John Adams felt that women and poor landless males should continue to be excluded from extended participation in the new government on the grounds that they were "too little acquainted with public affairs to form a right judgment."

As men went off to fight the war on the frontlines, Martha Washington, Catherine Greene, Mary "Molly Pitcher" Hays, Deborah Sampson, and others followed the troops to do cooking, nursing, fighting, burials, spy missions, and other work. Other women took charge on the farms back home (Abigail Adams ran her own farm for years) or participated more publicly in women's associations. After the war, sympathy grew for women's property rights, petitions for divorce, and education, but there was little change in women's roles in society. Though the war didn't win major freedoms for American women, it did shape a new ideal of Republican womanhood—to rear the next generation of patriots.

The Revolutionary War and Native Americans

Many Native Americans fought for the British during the war, and casualty rates were high. But no Native Americans were present at the treaty negotiations in Paris, and they felt betrayed when Britain surrendered the land west of the Appalachians to the Americans. The war brought uncertainty for Native Americans, as postwar developments threatened their livelihood. They would find themselves in new conflicts over land as settlers continued their westward movement after the war.

Review Exam

Multiple Choice

1. In the events leading up to July 4, 1776, it became evident that:
   a) Britain was unwilling to make any concessions to the colonists
   b) the colonial militia began preparing for war
   c) delegates at the Second Continental Congress would sign the Declaration of Independence
   d) all of the choices on the list

2. During the Revolutionary War, this group of colonists (approximately 20 percent) remained sympathetic to the British cause:
   a) Whigs   c) women
   b) loyalists   d) free blacks

3. During the Revolutionary War, Americans enjoyed all of the following advantages *EXCEPT*:
   a) familiarity with the terrain
   b) widespread resistance to Britain
   c) an overwhelming majority of the population supporting the war
   d) France and Spain allied with America

4. The Battle of Saratoga was a major turning point in the Revolutionary war because:
   a) it prevented the British from taking control of New York City
   b) France joined the war effort as an ally of the United States
   c) it brought about a quick end to the war
   d) it prevented West Point from being turned over to the British

5. Britain's lack of supplies and troops led the colonial militia to:
   a) lead the redcoats on wild chases throughout the region
   b) exhaust and deplete the British army
   c) pressure the British to continue fighting to deplete their supplies
   d) all of the answers on the list

6. The American victory at Yorktown led to all of the following at the Treaty of Paris of 1783 *EXCEPT*:
   a) recognizing the independence of the United States
   b) Britain surrendering territory west of the Appalachians to the Mississippi River
   c) the surrender the territory of Florida to the United States
   d) Britain withdrawing its troops from the United States

7. In addition to facing the challenge of production and finding markets for goods following the end of the war, the American economy was faced with the challenge of:
   a) wartime inflation that threatened economic growth
   b) England agreeing to not flood the market with cheap imports
   c) dealing with a strong currency in most states
   d) other countries seeking aid from the United States

8. The American's victory over the British in the Revolutionary War led to:
   a) slavery being abolished
   b) voting rights and legal rights for women
   c) the spread of the ideas of liberty
   d) a stronger and larger Iroquois League

Matching

a. Abigail Adams
b. Martha Washington
c. Thomas Paine
d. France
e. Benjamin Franklin
f. Benedict Arnold
g. Lafayette

h. Republican womanhood
i. Valley Forge
j. Continentals
k. Tories
l. Hessians
m. General Horatio Gates
n. Cornwallis

_____ 9. British loyalists and sympathizers

_____ 10. the place where Washington and his troops spent a long, cold winter here in 1777–1778

_____ 11. he attempted to turn West Point over to the British

_____12. a major ally of the United States in the war

_____13. he surrendered to Washington at Yorktown in September 1781

_____14. before the war broke out, she asked that her husband simply "remember the ladies" in the new government that would be established

_____15. the colonial army commanded by George Washington

_____16. this person, along with other women, helped support her husband during the war (some by traveling to provide services and others actually engaging in conflict)

_____17. along with John Adams and John Jay, he helped negotiate the peace treaty

_____18. he hired German soldiers used by the British

_____19. encouraged the American troops with a new pamphlet stressing "these are the times that try men's souls"

_____20. the lofty goal of women in the new republic being responsible to raise the next generation of patriots

_____21. the French ally who served with distinction and helped Washington in the surrender of the British at Yorktown

_____22. he surrounded the British troops in the Battle of Saratoga, forcing Burgoyne to surrender his entire army

Short Response

23. Who were the Loyalists, and what impact did they have on the war? Why wasn't the war popular with all segments of society?

24. Why did Britain ultimately lose the war in America? Why did America finally win the war for independence? What did America gain by winning the war?

25. What role did *freedom, democracy, and independence* have in the war?

Answers begin on page 247.

Governing the New Nation

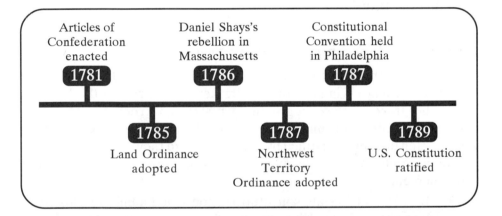

Articles of Confederation enacted **1781**

Daniel Shays's rebellion in Massachusetts **1786**

Constitutional Convention held in Philadelphia **1787**

1785 Land Ordinance adopted

1787 Northwest Territory Ordinance adopted

1789 U.S. Constitution ratified

Trends and Themes of the Era

▶ After the Revolution, the states joined in a loose federation under the Articles of Confederation, a result of their experience with the strong central government of Parliament.

▶ Because of the weakness of the Articles of Confederation, Americans held a constitutional convention to draft a new, stronger form of government.

▶ The goal of the Constitution was to create a strong central government that would balalnce the rights of the government and those of the individual states.

▶ The separate interests of the North and the South were becoming evident with ratification of the Constitution.

Rights, rights, and more rights! In 1781, the states ratified the Articles of Confederation to begin addressing which American rights would be guaranteed by the government. The meaning of liberty and power was hotly debated in the next few years as each state sought to manage its own affairs. It was becoming clear that regional conflicts and economic problems plaguing the states were insurmountable. Regional struggles continued to trouble the states, and an armed uprising by farmers in 1786 made it clear that a strong central government with the power to exercise control was needed. States' rights, personal rights, and sovereign rights became debate topics, leading to the meeting in Philadelphia in 1787. Only by forging a new government to "form a more perfect Union" would the states be able to secure the "blessings of liberty" they had gained by defeating the British.

Lesson 6-1: Governing the New States

Although the Articles of Confederation were adopted by the Continental Congress in 1777, during the Revolutionary War the 13 states began the process of creating their own state governments. The state constitutions differed from traditional British constitutions because they were written documents ratified by the people, and they could be amended by popular vote. These individual constitutions varied, but they shared some elements:

▶ By 1784, all 13 state constitutions contained a bill of rights that outlined the civil rights and freedoms of citizens.

▶ The constitutions generally established weak executive branches and gave most of the power to the legislature. Most states had bicameral legislatures and divided power between the governor and an elected assembly.

▶ Voting privileges were generally granted only to free white men, with some states still requiring voters and officeholders to own property.

▶ Most of the constitutions didn't establish an official state religion.

Lesson 6-2: The Articles of Confederation

After declaring independence, political leaders realized that they needed a unified national government, but several states feared a strong central government that was similar to the British system. John Dickinson submitted his draft of the **Articles of Confederation** to the Continental Congress in July 1776. Congress adopted the articles in 1777 and sent copies out for ratification by state legislatures; the articles became law in 1781 and provided for a loose confederation in which "each state retains its sovereignty, freedom, and independence" and "powers not delegated to the United States." The "firm league of friendship" of the 13 states would soon see its loose bonds severely challenged.

The Articles of Confederation favored the rights of each individual state, leaving the central government virtually powerless. The new central government consisted of a severely restricted unicameral Congress, with no executive branch or judicial department. Several states had their own armies and navies, and all the states had their own forms of currency. The economic status of each state was severely crippled by the new government.

Powers of the Articles of Confederation	Weaknesses of the Articles of Confederation
To declare war and peace	No authority to impose taxes
To make treaties with foreign nations	No authority to regulate interstate or foreign trade
A passing vote of nine out of 13 states for important laws	Could be amended only if all 13 states approved
To borrow and print money	No separate executive branch
To request funds from the states	No national court system to decide disputes
One member vote per state regardless of population	Lack of unity with 13 separate states
	Couldn't make binding treaties

Financial Crisis

The biggest economic challenge facing the new government was addressing the enormous debt from the war. By the end of the war, the Continental Congress had printed nearly $250 million in paper notes without being backed up by hard currency. At war's end, these notes were nearly worthless, and a postwar economic depression had spread to every state. Not only were citizens affected, but states also struggled to pay foreign debts. In 1781 and again in 1783, Congress proposed a tax on imports to finance the national budget and guarantee payment of war debts, but each time a state rejected the proposal. With the power only to "request" funding from the states, and no power to force taxation, Congress could do nothing to regulate the economy. The government was financially helpless.

A Lasting Legacy

The next challenge facing the government was westward expansion. Settlers, speculators, and state governments all pressed for expansion into the newly acquired territory. Many states claimed the same land in the territory. The government attempted to control this expansion with the **Land Ordinance of 1785**, which outlined the protocol for the sale of land and settlement. Land was to be plotted into townships of 36 square miles. Each square mile comprised 640 acres that could be divided into various section configurations for sale. Income from the sale of the 16th section was reserved for public school support.

Land Ordinance of 1785

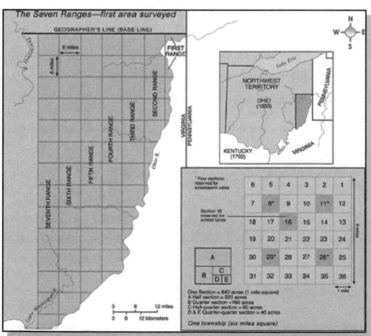

A second law, the **Northwest Ordinance of 1787,** provided for the territory above the Ohio River to be organized into three to five states and outlined the process for statehood. When a region had 5,000 adult males, it could organize a government in the territory by electing a legislature. Once a region had 60,000 inhabitants, it could draft a constitution and apply for statehood on equal footing with the original 13 states. This would solve land claims by various states in the region. In addition, it also forbade slavery in the territory above the Ohio River and included a settlers' bill of rights. These bills encouraged settlement in the region and reduced the prospect of secessionist movements. However, as the United States expanded further west, it faced opposition from the Native Americans and Spanish along the frontier.

Northwest Territory, 1787

Shays's Rebellion

The final challenge to the Articles of Confederation's limitations involved the government's ability to maintain law and order. Depression, inflation, and high taxes made life miserable for many Americans. The plight of farmers in western Massachusetts led to **Shays's Rebellion**, the first armed uprising in the new nation. In August 1786, Daniel Shays, a Revolutionary War veteran who was angered by high taxes and debt he couldn't repay, led about 2,000 men to close the courts in three western

Massachusetts counties, to prevent farm foreclosures. The Massachusetts government had increased taxes to pay off war debt, and creditors and sheriffs were hauling delinquent farmers into court, imposing high legal fees, and threatening them with imprisonment for failure to pay debts. Shays and his men dared to take control of the weapons arsenal at Springfield, Massachusetts, exposing the central government's inability to enforce order. The Massachusetts militia put down the rebellion, but it heightened a growing sense of panic around the nation and raised fears of rebellion.

Lesson 6-3: The Convention in Philadelphia

In September 1786, delegates from five states met at the **Annapolis Convention**. Originally concerned with interstate commerce, the delegates turned their focus to the shortcomings of the national government. They proposed a convention to consider amending the Articles of Confederation and asked the states to appoint delegates to meet in Philadelphia in May 1787. George Washington was elected to preside over the closed-door meeting for the next four months.

The original plan was just to revise the Articles of Confederation, but the major economic problems plaguing the country, along with the recent uprising, revealed the serious shortcomings of the national government. Adding to the problems were the British in the western states who refused to abandon forts until war debts were paid. In addition to British soldiers selling weapons to the Native Americans, Britain flooded the market with cheap goods, compounding the economic crisis. Spain closed the Mississippi River to travel, and Barbary pirates intimidated sailors and seized cargo in the Mediterranean.

A New Government Structure

In May 1787, 55 delegates (representing every state except Rhode Island) met in Philadelphia. The delegates to the **Constitutional Convention** included George Washington, John Dickinson, John Jay, Benjamin Franklin, Alexander Hamilton, and James Madison. The delegates were convinced of the need for a stronger national government and decided to create a new framework, embodied in a new constitution.

Difficulties in drafting the Constitution immediately became obvious. One challenge was balancing power among various branches of the new government. The second challenge was trying to achieve a balance between the needs of large and small states. **James Madison** presented the **Virginia Plan**, a framework of government that contained a potential solution to this problem. The plan called for a bicameral legislature with representation in both houses proportional to population. These houses of Congress would jointly name the president and federal judges. The smaller states opposed the Virginia Plan, arguing that representation by population would give more power to the larger states. The smaller states supported William Paterson's **New Jersey Plan**, which called for a unicameral Congress in which each state would have an equal number of seats.

Virginia Plan	New Jersey Plan
A bicameral legislature	A unicameral legislature
Representation based on population	One vote per state
A strong executive elected by Congress	A weak executive with little power
A separate judicial branch	A separate judicial branch
Power to pass taxes, regulate trade, and enact other measures	Power to pass taxes, regulate trade, and enact other measures

In June 1787, a committee assigned to resolve the conflict approved the Connecticut Compromise, or **Great Compromise**, which created a bicameral legislature where each state received an equal vote in the upper house (Senate), and representation in the lower house (House of Representatives) was proportional to population. The compromise also proposed an electoral process in which an **electoral college**, a group of competent leaders, would meet and choose the president. Members of the Senate would be appointed by state legislatures; the House of Representatives would be the only segment of the government in which the members were elected by popular vote. This compromise would allow the people some say in the new government while retaining a wide range of powers.

The power in the new government would be divided between three branches of government: (1) a strong executive, (2) a legislative body, and (3) a judicial branch. The process of checks and balances would be instituted among the three branches of the new government to keep their powers in check with one another so that one branch would not dominate the other two.

A second discussion about the issue of slavery threatened to deadlock debate on the compromise, as a sectional difference emerged. The solution came in the **3/5 Compromise**, which allowed 3/5 of "all other persons" (the word *slavery* was never mentioned in the Constitution) to be counted as people for the basis of representation and taxation in the southern states (this increased their representation by 20 percent). The only mention of slavery was that the slave trade itself would end in 20 years in 1808, and that runaway "persons in labor or service" be returned to their masters. The delegates rejected a proposal to abolish slavery. This solution would have lasting consequences, as Elbridge Gerry wrote in a letter to his wife: "They will...lay the foundation of Civil War." Madison warned that a great division lay between the North and South based on "having or not having slaves." In September 1787, the convention approved the new Constitution and sent it to the states for ratification.

The Constitution Completed

The document that emerged from Philadelphia represented a balance among a number of different interests:

▶   The need to strengthen the national government and the fear of government despotism and tyranny.

▶   The competing interests of the larger and smaller states.

▶   The differing interests of northern and southern states.

The powers of the new federal government rested on the Constitution as the "supreme law of the land." It also gave Congress the power to "make all Laws which shall be necessary and proper for carrying into Execution the foregoing Powers and all other Powers vested by this Constitution in the Government of the United States, or in any Department or Officer thereof" (Article I, Section 8). This section of the Constitution, known as the "elastic clause," would soon come under debate as the new government flexed its new power and authority.

The concept of federalism detailed the division of power between the national government and the state governments. The new federal government was granted the power to set and collect taxes, to regulate interstate commerce, and to conduct diplomacy in international affairs. The government also had the power to invoke military action against the states. The Constitution declared all acts and treaties made by Congress to be binding on the states. A system of checks and balances (in which each branch of the government holds certain powers over the others) protected against tyranny and was the cornerstone of the new framework of government. The 10th Amendment, added after ratification of the Constitution, further defined federalism by stating, "The powers not delegated to the United States by the Constitution, nor prohibited by it to the States, are reserved to the States respectively, or to the people." This argument of federalism versus states rights would lead to a heated debate over slavery and eventually lead to the outbreak of the Civil War in 1861.

The Constitution at a Glance

The Executive Branch	The Legislative Branch	The Judicial Branch
Signs bills into law	Passes bills into laws	Can declare a law unconstitutional
Has the power to veto acts of Congress	Can override a veto with 2/3 vote	Interprets the law
Enforces laws	Can declare war	
Appoints judges to the Supreme Court	Can impeach the president and other high officials	
Serves as commander in chief	Approves presidential appointments (Senate)	
Carries out foreign policy	Ratifies treaties (Senate)	
Appoints members to the cabinet (at first it was tradition started by Washington and then it became common practice)	Controls spending and regulates trade	

Lesson 6-4: The Ratification Debate

After its approval by the Constitutional Convention in 1787, the Constitution was sent to the states for ratification. In order for the Constitution to be implemented, nine of the 13 states had to ratify it.

The process of ratification began with two deeply opposed sides. The **federalists** came out in support of the Constitution. The **anti-federalists** opposed ratification of the Constitution, claiming that it granted too much power to the national government. They argued that, under the Constitution, the states could be dominated by a potentially tyrannical central government. The federalists defended the necessity of a strong national government and supported the Constitution as the best possible framework.

The federalists quickly pushed through ratification at eight state conventions, but Virginia and New York—crucial in terms of population and economics—remained undecided. In an effort to gain the support of the two most populous states, James Madison responded to objections to the Constitution by publishing *The Federalist Papers,* a series of 85 essays written by Madison along with Alexander Hamilton and John Jay. The essays argued in favor of ratifying the Constitution and cited a strong link between American prosperity and a powerful central government. Various essays dealt with the need for such a government and the separation of powers into three branches of government.

Letters from the Federal Farmer, written by Richard Henry Lee, was the most widely read anti-federalist publication. It argued for a **Bill of Rights** to protect certain freedoms. Samuel Adams and John Hancock, in fact, objected to the Constitution without a Bill of Rights. After the Constitution was ratified in 1791, Madison kept his promise and a Bill of Rights, the first 10 amendments to the Constitution, was soon adopted. These new provisions sought to protect individual freedoms from government interference. Freedoms such as speech, press, religion, the right to assemble peacefully, the right to bear arms, the protection against unreasonable searches and seizures of property, the right of due process of law in all criminal cases, the right to a fair and speedy trial, and the protection against cruel and unusual punishment were among the freedoms listed.

In June 1788, New Hampshire became the ninth state to ratify the Constitution, making the document effective as the framework of national government. Debate continued in still-undecided Virginia and New York.

In late June 1788, Virginia finally ratified the Constitution by a narrow 53-percent majority. In New York, debate went on for another month until Alexander Hamilton's federalists finally emerged victorious, by a margin only slightly greater than that in Virginia. By 1790, all of the states had ratified the Constitution, with Rhode Island being the last to sign.

Review Exam

Multiple Choice

1. The greatest weakness in the governing structure of the Articles of Confederation was that:
   a) the executive branch was too powerful
   b) it had no power to regulate trade between the states
   c) it had no power to engage in relations with foreign governments
   d) a two-house legislature was adopted

2. The Northwest Ordinance of 1787 stated that:
   a) all land confiscated from the Native Americans should be returned
   b) no more than three new slave states should be formed in the region
   c) the three to five new states formed in the region would be equal with the original 13 states
   d) no new states should be formed; they should remain as territories

3. Delegates to the Constitutional Convention originally met to:
   a) amend the Articles of Confederation
   b) empower the government under the Articles of Confederation
   c) write new state constitutions
   d) table the debate on slavery

4. The major premise of the Articles of Confederation was that:
   a) it favored the rights of individual states
   b) it created a weak central government out of fear of another government such as that of Britain
   c) it had no executive or judicial branch
   d) all of the answers on the list

5. The Great Compromise accomplished all of the following **EXCEPT**:
   a) establishing a two-house (bicameral) legislature
   b) equal state representation in the Senate
   c) electing the president by popular vote
   d) representation in the House based on a state's population

6. The new government structure under the Constitution allowed for:
   a) power to be divided between three branches of government
   b) slavery to be abolished after 1808
   c) freedom to be granted to runaway slaves
   d) term limits for the president

7. The new federal government was given an unprecedented amount of power with the elastic clause (Article I, Section 8 of the Constitution) which states that Congress could:
   a) make laws that only the states were in agreement with
   b) make all laws "necessary and proper" for carrying out the power of the federal government
   c) allow only 10 amendments to the Constitution
   d) override a presidential veto with a simple majority vote

8. Slavery became a hotly debated issue during the Constitutional debate and shortly thereafter with the adoption of the Bill of Rights by:
   a) not mentioning the word *slavery* in the constitution
   b) outlawing the slave trade in 1808 but still allowing slavery to exist
   c) allowing states to decide upon the matter of slavery as a states rights issue
   d) all of the choices on the list

9. Changes made to the Constitution with the Bill of Rights include all of the following **EXCEPT**:
   a) allowing women to vote
   b) allowing freedom of speech, religion, and the press
   c) guaranteeing the right to bear arms
   d) preventing the quartering of soldiers

10. As a safeguard to giving the people direct limited power in the new government, the members of the Constitutional Convention agreed to allow citizens to vote directly for:

a) senators

c) representatives in the House

b) Supreme Court justices

d) the president

11. In addition to flooding the market with cheap goods following the end of the Revolutionary War, problems in the years following the war included:

a) British soldiers who refused to abandon forts until war debts were paid

b) British soldiers selling weapons to Native Americans

c) closing the Mississippi for travel and the attacks of Barbary pirates on American ships in the Mediterranean

d) all of the answers on the list

Matching

a. 3/5 Compromise

b. 10th Amendment

c. John Dickinson

d. *Letters from the Federal Farmer*

e. Electoral College

f. Land Ordinance of 1785

g. federalism

h. George Washington

i. The Constitution

j. *The Federalist Papers*

k. Shays's Rebellion

l. James Madison

m. Bill of Rights

_____12. he drafted the original Articles of Confederation document

_____13. the set of amendments that guarantees certain rights of the people and to protect them from government interference

_____14. this outlined the protocol for the sale of land and settlement in the Northwest Territory

_____15. the supreme law of the land

_____16. this allowed for 3/5 of "all other persons" to be counted as 3/5 of a person for basis of representation in the House

_____17. the division of government power between the federal and state governments

____18. he is known as the father of the Constitution

____19. a series of essays written to counter the arguments for ratification of the Constitution (and argued for a Bill of rights to be added to the new Constitution)

____20. the "state's rights" amendment that delegates powers not expressly written for the federal government over to the states

____21. the armed uprising in 1786 that showed the country that the existing federal government was powerless

____22. under the structure of the new constitution, the group of competent leaders who would meet and choose the president (the members of this group equaled the total number of senators and representatives for each state)

____23. he was chosen to preside over the Constitutional Convention in 1787

____24. a series of essays written by Madison, Hamilton, and Jay to encourage the ratification of the new constitution

Short Response

25. Why did the Articles of Confederation prove to be weak in governing the new states?

26. What made the Constitution a radical document for its time? How did it seek to secure rights?

27. **Rights, rights, rights.** How did the Constitutional Convention and the states reach a series of compromises in order to preserve the Union?

Answers begin on page 249.

The Federalist Era

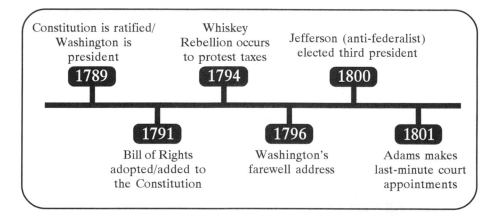

Constitution is ratified/ Washington is president
1789

Whiskey Rebellion occurs to protest taxes
1794

Jefferson (anti-federalist) elected third president
1800

1791
Bill of Rights adopted/added to the Constitution

1796
Washington's farewell address

1801
Adams makes last-minute court appointments

Trends and Themes of the Era

▶ George Washington's strong leadership began to define politics and the new government of the United States.

▶ A two-party system of politics soon emerged, based on differing viewpoints about policy and about how to interpret the Constitution.

▶ The federalists supported a strong central government, and the anti-federalists supported states' rights and local authority.

▶ Party politics were often defined by geographical regions and local interests.

Factions, frictions, and farewells! In 1789, George Washington began his first term in office as the first president of the United States. After the adoption of the Constitution, goodwill soon gave way to differing points of view. Political struggles would erupt during the decade as the United States dealt with challenges to peace at home and abroad. Despite the disagreement, Washington knew the nation would require strong leadership and a balance of opinion. After serving two terms as president, Washington decided to retire from public life, and John Adams succeeded him as president. Adams's term in office was marked by stark disagreements not only within his own party but also with the opposing political party and his friend and vice president, Thomas Jefferson. In 1800, the federalist's era in office ended with the election of a candidate from the opposing political party. The tumultuous decade of the federalists would soon cede to the Democratic-Republicans in the peaceful "Revolution of 1800."

Lesson 7-1: Washington's Vision of Leadership

George Washington, unanimously elected as the first president, took the oath of office in New York City on April 30, 1789. His vice president was John Adams. Washington's goal was to create a strong, independent presidency and firmly establish the new government.

The President and Congress Go to Work

The Constitution provided the new country with only a skeleton framework. The debate about civil liberties and the exact nature of the national government offered unique challenges to the new president. During Washington's two terms as president (from 1789 to 1796) Congress developed the nation's legal, bureaucratic, and military infrastructure.

The first Congress under the Constitution set out to establish a judicial branch, develop the executive branch, create a legislative agenda, and meet the popular demand for a bill of rights. Washington focused primarily on matters of finance, diplomacy, and the military, while Congress worked out the details of government bureaucracy and domestic policy. The new president interacted very little with Congress. He rarely spoke publicly about policy, suggested few laws, and vetoed only two bills during his presidency.

Presidential Advisors

The Constitution provided only the general framework of the executive branch, with no mention of executive posts. In 1789, Congress established what came to be known as the **cabinet**: three executive positions (Secretaries of State, War, and Treasury) and the office of Attorney General. Washington appointed Thomas Jefferson as Secretary of State, Alexander Hamilton as Secretary of Treasury, Henry Knox as Secretary of War, and Edmund Randolph as Attorney General. Vice President John Adams, whose duties were relatively undefined in the Constitution, was excluded from cabinet meetings, and by the end of his first term, the office of vice president was already in the backwater of political significance. The main duty of the vice president was to preside over the Senate, and if needed to break a tie vote. It was also assumed that the vice president would take over for the president upon his death.

The Bill of Rights

To dispel the fears of the anti-federalists, the **Bill of Rights** was proposed as a concession to demonstrate that a strong government could still guard the rights of individuals and states. James Madison led the group that drafted the first 10 amendments to the Constitution, seeking to safeguard personal and states' rights. The state legislatures ratified the amendments in December 1791, and they became an enduring part of the Constitution. The Bill of Rights listed certain liberties that the federal government would protect.

The Bill of Rights at a Glance

1. Freedom of religion, speech, press, assembly, petition.
2. Right to bear arms.
3. No quartering of soldiers.
4. Protection against unreasonable search and seizure.
5. Rights of the accused: no double jeopardy, due process.
6. Right to a speedy trial, knowledge of accusations, confrontation of witnesses, counsel for defense.
7. Right to a trial by jury in civil cases.
8. Protection against excessive bail and cruel and unusual punishments.
9. Rights not stated in the Constitution retained by the people.
10. Powers not delegated to the federal government nor prohibited by it to the states reserved to the states or to the people.

A National Court System

The **Judiciary Act of 1789** created a federal court system. The act established a Supreme Court with five justices and a chief justice, three circuit courts, and 13 federal district courts. State court decisions could be appealed to a federal court when constitutional issues were raised. To guarantee that federal laws remained the supreme law of the land, state laws could be nullified if they were found to be in conflict with the Constitution. The Supreme Court would have the final say in all cases that involved constitutional issues, but the states retained the right of original jurisdiction in civil and criminal cases.

Lesson 7-2: Federalists versus Anti-Federalists

The opposing viewpoints of conflict between the **federalists** and the **anti-federalists** shaped much of the nation's early political debate and policy. The federalists, led by Secretary of Treasury Alexander Hamilton, pushed for a strong central government and drew their greatest support from the mercantile interests of the New England and mid-Atlantic regions. The anti-federalists, led by Secretary of State Thomas Jefferson, advocated states' rights over central power and drew their greatest support from the agrarian interests in the South and West. Jefferson and others felt that the agricultural sector should be emphasized and that economic policy should focus on the economic resource of land. The differing viewpoints of Jefferson and Hamilton would shape party politics for many years.

The debate over national finances illustrated the growing divide between federalists and anti-federalists. Hamilton proposed in 1790 that the federal government assume the unpaid war debts of the states, to help stabilize the national economy and ensure economic support and credibility from foreign countries. Anti-federalists believed this plan granted the national government undue economic power over the states. Southern states also opposed the plan because they had already paid off nearly all of their debts, whereas the northern states lagged behind. Virginia and Maryland had paid their war debts and didn't want to be taxed to pay debts accumulated by other states. As a bargaining ploy in the process of getting the financial plan to pass, Hamilton proposed that the nation's capital be relocated from New York to present-day Washington, D.C., in return for securing enough votes for passage. The proposal passed, but political compromise would be short-lived.

The Bank of the United States

Hamilton's proposal to establish a national bank proved extremely controversial. He took bold steps to promote the fledgling commercial interests of the United States. Hamilton claimed the **Bank of the United States** would provide a secure depository for federal revenue, issue currency and federal loans, regulate the activities of smaller banks, and extend credit to U.S. citizens. He wanted people to invest in U.S. commercial ventures, believing that a sound economy would be beneficial to all. Opposing the proposal, anti-federalists such as Thomas Jefferson feared that the bank would tie private individuals too closely to government institutions.

Hamilton also argued that in order to strengthen the federal government's monetary policy, the federal government should fund the nation's debt, assuming the responsibility to repay creditors along with accrued interest. The federal government would also assume the debts that individual states incurred during the Revolutionary War. In order to reach a compromise to get enough votes for the program to pass in Congress, northern congressmen agreed to a southern location of the new capital for the country to be built on the Potomac River along the boundary of Virginia and Maryland in a newly created "District of Columbia."

The argument about the national bank centered on interpreting the Constitution. Anti-federalists and **strict constructionists** held to a strict interpretation of the Constitution by arguing that it didn't explicitly give the federal government the power to grant such charters. However, Hamilton didn't want action to be limited by the strict wording of the Constitution. Article I, Section VIII of the Constitution states that Congress shall have the power "to make all laws which shall be necessary and proper for carrying into execution...powers vested by this Constitution in the government of the United States." For loose constructionists such as Hamilton, this "elastic clause" gave Congress the power to establish policy not expressly forbidden by the Constitution, including founding a national bank.

After much debate between the two sides, Congress approved the bank, granting it a 20 charter in February 1791. Despite the disagreements over policy, Hamilton's financial program proved successful.

Tariffs

One final issue dividing Congress concerned protective tariffs. Under the **Tariff of 1789**, a high protective tariff of 5 to 50 percent was proposed to generate revenue for the national government and to foster industrial development in the United States. Northerners generally favored the tariff as a means of protection against foreign competition. Both Jefferson and Madison, however, opposed this protectionist economic policy, fearing that industries would become too dependent on government aid. Many congressmen also opposed the tariff because it favored industrial and merchant interests of the North over the more rural and agrarian South.

Lesson 7-3: The Rise of Political Parties

The framers of the Constitution considered political parties self-serving **factions** that would be detrimental to good government. But by the end of Washington's first term, differing viewpoints about constitutional interpretation had solidified into two distinct political parties: The loose constructionists formed the core of the **Federalist party**, and the strict constructionists made up the core of the anti-federalist or **Democratic-Republican party** or, simply, the Republicans. Remember to not confuse this Republican party with the modern Republican party that formed in 1854.

The birth of the Democratic-Republican party can be traced back to 1793, when Jefferson resigned from Washington's cabinet in opposition to federalist policy decisions, especially the financial decisions of Alexander Hamilton. Republicans attempted to arouse political awareness and spread criticism of federalist decisions through a media campaign centered on America's first opposition newspaper, *The National Gazette*. They also founded political societies and clubs across the nation. Washington clearly allied himself with the federalists in 1794 by accusing the Republicans of inciting the Whiskey Rebellion. The federalists, led by Washington and Hamilton, called for a strong central government. They represented the industrial and manufacturing interests, which were concentrated in the northeast.

The Democratic-Republicans, led by Jefferson and Madison, advocated state governments over centralized power, and represented the more rural and agrarian South, as well as the western frontier. Led by Jefferson and Madison, the Republicans fought for the expansion of states' rights while trying to limit the central government's power. They argued that liberty could be protected only if political power rested firmly in the hands of the people and government officials who were closest and most responsive to the people. That same year, the Republicans won a slight majority in the House of Representatives, signaling the arrival of the party as a powerful political movement.

Lesson 7-4: The Whiskey Rebellion

Frontier farmers in western Pennsylvania who produced whiskey from corn angrily protested in July 1794 against Hamilton's **excise tax** on domestically produced whiskey. This type of tax was generally imposed on the manufacture and distribution of non-essential consumer goods, and the farmers resented this tax because it lowered the profits they could make from selling whiskey. The conflict that became known as the **Whiskey Rebellion** was the first major test of the federal government's ability to enforce its laws within the states.

Tax collectors sent to western Pennsylvania were routinely threatened with tarring and feathering, making it impossible to collect the whiskey tax from that area. In June 1794, the farmers were further angered when local officials ordered the arrest of the leaders of the whiskey tax resistors. A month later, the commander of the local militia was shot and killed by federal troops defending a tax official. This enraged the local anti-tax settlers, who set fire to some outlying buildings.

In reaction, the president recruited a militia force in August 1794 from Pennsylvania, Maryland, New Jersey, and Virginia. After negotiations failed between federal commissioners and the rebels, Washington himself led the army of more than 12,000 troops into western Pennsylvania. The farmers quickly dispersed, and resistance faded. Most of the captured prisoners were later released due to lack of evidence, and Washington pardoned two of the rebels convicted of treason.

Washington's actions demonstrated the broad reach and commitment of the national government. When authority was openly challenged, the government was now prepared to use military force, if necessary, to compel obedience. Many anti-federalists condemned Washington's response, saying it was excessive and favored commercial interests over those of small-scale farmers. Overall, the rebellion strengthened the political power of the federalists, but many frontier farmers shifted their loyalty to the Democratic-Republican party. The uprising also raised the question of states' rights versus the powers of the federal government.

Lesson 7-5: Westward Expansion

During the 1790s, the United States attempted to expand its territory westward by admitting three new states: Vermont (1791), Kentucky (1792), and Tennessee (1796). Spain and Britain opposed this expansion. In addition, Native Americans, who inhabited much of this westward region, also resisted U.S. growth. Military efforts in 1790 and 1791, aimed at forcing peace with the Native Americans on U.S. terms, yielded little success. In 1794, U.S. troops (under the command of "Mad Anthony" Wayne) routed a group of Native American warriors at the **Battle of Fallen Timbers**. After this defeat, 12 Native American tribes signed the **Treaty of Greenville,** clearing the Ohio territory of tribes and opening it up to further settlement.

Lesson 7-6: France and U.S. Neutrality

Washington worked to preserve U.S. neutrality in international relations by keeping the country out of European conflicts. Foreign affairs, however, grew increasingly difficult to ignore. The French Revolution (1789 to 1799) inspired opposing loyalties within the federal government. Jefferson and other Republicans sympathized with the revolutionary cause, which championed individual rights against an aristocratic government. Hamilton and other federalists opposed the revolutionaries. In any case, the United States was in no condition to fight a prolonged war. The goal was to enhance U.S. domestic policy by remaining neutral and keeping trade open with both sides.

French Ambassador **Edmund Genet** came to the United States and began soliciting contributions. Crowds of supporters greeted him, and he tried to get the United States to raid British ships. Genet wanted Washington to call Congress into a special session to debate neutrality, but Washington wanted Genet recalled. Meanwhile, as France called for Genet's arrest, he opted to quietly settle in the United States rather than face the guillotine back home.

Loyalties in the United States were divided in 1793 when revolutionary France went to war with Britain and Spain. Northern merchants pressed for a pro-British policy, while southern planters pushed for an alliance with France. Refusing to be drawn into the war, Washington issued the Proclamation of American Neutrality. Although neutrality was the national policy, southwestern settlers offered some military support to the French against the Spanish in Florida and the Mississippi Valley, and 1,000 Americans enlisted with the French as privateers, terrorizing the British navy. It retaliated by seizing more than 250 American vessels during the winter of 1794, forcing their crews into service in the Royal Navy through a policy known as impressment. Tensions flared further when Canada's royal governor denied U.S. claims to the land north of the Ohio River and encouraged Native Americans in the region to resist expansion. War seemed almost inevitable as British and Spanish troops began building forts on U.S. territory.

Desperate to avoid conflict, Washington dispatched negotiators to the warring European nations. John Jay negotiated **Jay's Treaty** (1795) with Britain, securing the removal of British troops from American land and reopening limited trade with the British West Indies, but he didn't address British seizure of American ships or the impressment of American sailors. Although many Americans, especially anti-federalists, criticized Jay for helping Britain, Jay's Treaty did keep the United States out of a potentially ruinous war against a stronger and more established nation. When asked by Congress to disclose all the terms of the treaty, Washington cited executive privilege in not divulging certain matters of state to Congress.

Pinckney's Treaty (1795), negotiated with Spain, recognized the 31st parallel as the southern U.S. boundary and granted the United States free navigation of the Mississippi River with the right of deposit at New Orleans. Spain adopted a conciliatory note toward the United States in negotiating the treaty, attempting to protect its possessions in America and to secure recognition of its borders from foreign powers. These two treaties finally established American sovereignty over land west of the Appalachians and opened up U.S. commerce.

Lesson 7-7: Washington's Farewell Address

In 1796, Washington retired from office after deciding not to run for a third term, setting the precedent of presidents serving no more than two terms in office. In his farewell address, Washington appealed for national unity, warned against sectional and party loyalty, and argued for American disinterest in European affairs. He cautioned that the development of parties would destroy the government, fearing that special interest groups and foreign nations would come to dominate the two factions. Washington implored future generations to concentrate on the creation of "efficient government" at home: "The great rule of conduct for us in regard to foreign nations is, in extending our commercial relations to have with them as little political connection as possible. Why entangle our peace and prosperity in the toils of European ambition, rivalship, and interest."

Lesson 7-8: Continuing the Federalist Legacy

The election of 1796 was the first major political contest between the two political parties. John Adams, the Federalist candidate, ran against Thomas Jefferson, the Republican candidate. Republican strength remained strong in the South and West, and the Federalist stronghold continued in New England. Adams won the presidency by three electoral votes. Jefferson became vice president according to constitutional protocol, which stated that the person with the second-highest number of votes would become vice president. The friendship of these two men would soon be challenged by a tense rivalry.

Federalism Under Adams

The neutrality that George Washington had worked so hard to maintain was threatened as foreign affairs began to occupy Adams's agenda. The French saw Jay's Treaty as a signal that the United States supported Britain in its ongoing war against France. After Jefferson's loss in the election, France delayed no longer. It suspended diplomatic relations with the United States and began a tough policy toward American shipping, which included seizing more than 300 vessels, confiscating cargo valued at $20 million, and ordering that all Americans captured aboard British naval vessels be hanged. Britain began impressment of American sailors for evading the British blockade of Europe.

In response to such aggression, Adams dispatched a peace commission to Paris. In what would become known as the **XYZ affair**, the French foreign minister, Charles de Tallyrand, refused to meet with the commission and instead sent three anonymous agents to deliver a bribe: Tallyrand wouldn't negotiate with the United States until he received $250,000 for himself and a $12 million loan for France. In his report to Congress about the event, Adams labeled the three agents X, Y, and Z. This extortion attempt aroused public outrage among the American people, some of whom rallied for war. The XYZ affair actually boosted Adams's popularity when the American delegates refused the bribe.

Adams and the federalists began preparing the country for war in 1798. Citing the need for readiness should a war break out, Congress tripled the size of the American army in 1798. In what became known as the Quasi-War, Congress sent armed ships to protect Americans at sea. Although France and America never officially declared war, from 1798 to 1800 the U.S. navy seized 93 French privateers while losing only one ship. Despite Adams's possible desire to fight the war for his own political advantage (he was up for reelection in 1800), he decided to send a new minister to France, this time to be received by the French government.

The **Convention of 1800** was reached with Napoleon. France canceled U.S. debt and didn't pay for any attacks on American ships. In some respects, the Federalists were upset because war was avoided. Hamilton and others had favored a war, and this caused a split in the Federalist party in 1800.

Lesson 7-9: Silencing the Opposition

Riding the tide of anti-French sentiment, the federalists overwhelmingly won the 1798 Congressional elections. In an effort to protect national security if the country entered into war with France, Congress passed four measures called the **Alien and Sedition Acts** in 1798. The acts asserted the power of the central government over the liberty of individuals in an unprecedented way. They were also seen as a political move to squash mounting Republican opposition.

The Alien and Sedition Acts at a Glance

- **The Alien Enemies Act**—The first and least controversial act defined the prodedure by which, during wartime, U.S. authorities could deport a citizen of an enemy nation whom they deemed a threat to national security.

- **The Alien Friends Act**—This allowed the president to deport any citizen of any foreign nation whom he deemed a threat to the United States, even in the absence of proof.

- **The Naturalization Act**—This changed the residency requirement for becoming a citizen of the United States from five to 14 years.

- **The Sedition Act**—The final and most controversial act forbade any individual or group to speak, write, or publish anything of a "false, scandalous, and malicious" nature that brought the Congress and/or the president "into contempt or disrepute."

Americans across the country began to witness political repression. Of the four acts, two (the Alien Friends Act and the Sedition Act) were set to expire near the time of the 1800 elections so that they wouldn't be used against the Federalists if the party lost power. Just before the presidential election of 1800, four of the five major Republican newspapers were charged with sedition, arousing the anger of many who felt that the federalists were exploiting their political power to breach civil liberties and stifle their political opponents. Some felt that the Alien and Sedition Acts were unconstitutional because they violated the 1st Amendment's guarantee of free speech. However, the Supreme Court upheld the acts.

In opposition to the Alien and Sedition acts, both Kentucky and Virginia endorsed manifestos on states' rights written anonymously by Thomas Jefferson and James Madison, respectively. **The Virginia and Kentucky Resolutions (1798)** declared that state legislatures could deem acts of Congress unconstitutional, on the theory that states' rights superseded federal rights. They argued that the federal government was merely a representative of the compact of states, not an overriding power, and therefore states had the final say on federal laws. In 1799, Kentucky passed a further resolution that declared states could nullify objectionable federal laws. This doctrine of states' rights and nullification would emerge again in later political crises between the North and South about congressional authority on issues of tariffs and slavery.

Lesson 7-10: Changing of the Guard

The **election of 1800** marked the beginning of a 28-year period during which the party of Jefferson dominated national politics and the Federalist party's influence greatly declined. The Republicans won easily, in part because of public outrage over the Federalist Alien and Sedition Acts. In many ways, the acts proved the undoing of the Federalist party.

Although the Republican ticket of Thomas Jefferson and Aaron Burr easily won against the federalist ticket of John Adams and Charles Pinckney, all of the Republican electors had voted for both Jefferson and Burr, so both candidates earned the same number of electoral votes for president. Burr, who had been backed by the Republican party as vice president, now had as legitimate a claim to the presidency as Jefferson did. The task of choosing the president then fell to the House of Representatives. After seven days and 36 ballots, the House chose

Jefferson as president. To prevent future election deadlocks such as this, the 12th Amendment, ratified in 1804, changed the election process so that candidates must be clearly listed as running for either president or vice president.

Jefferson described his victory in the election of 1800 as the "Revolution of 1800." He believed the Republican win over the Federalists was "as real a revolution in the principles of our government as that of 1776 was in its form." Unlike the Federalists, who had pushed for a strong central government and who had favored industrial and commercial interests, the Jeffersonian Republicans (anti-federalists) aimed to limit central government in favor of states' rights and individual liberties, and preferred an agrarian republic over an urban, industrialized nation. This was the first time the government had experienced a dramatic change from one political party to another, and it had survived.

Midnight Judges and Judicial Review

In his last days in office, John Adams appointed a number of federalist judges to federal court positions as "midnight appointments" in an effort to extend the influence of the Federalist party. After the Senate confirmation hearings, Adams signed commissions for the **midnight judges** during his final few hours in office. The most influential appointment Adams made was naming federalist **John Marshall** to the Supreme Court as chief justice. Marshall would serve on the court for 35 years and, during his tenure, he authored more than half of the nearly 900 decisions handed down by the Court, securing the federalist influence on policy long after Adams left office.

Adams also appointed William Marbury as Justice of the Peace in the District of Columbia, but failed to deliver the commission by midnight. Jefferson's Secretary of State, James Madison, then refused to deliver it. In response, Marbury asked the Supreme Court for a writ of mandamus, an order requiring that a nondiscretionary government duty be performed, to force Madison to deliver the commission and accept the appointment. In February 1803, the chief justice and the Court denied Marbury's request, ruling that Congress had overstepped its constitutional bounds by giving the Supreme Court the authority to issue such a writ in the first place. (Congress had issued such authority in the Judiciary Act of 1789.) The *Marbury v. Madison* ruling was the first time the Supreme Court declared an act of Congress to be unconstitutional.

Review Exam

Multiple Choice

1. Alexander Hamilton attempted to give the federal government credibility abroad by:
    a) assuming state debts from the Revolutionary War
    b) increasing the whiskey tax
    c) abandoning tariffs
    d) opposing the formation of the Bank of the United States

2. In order to gain support for the new Constitution, James Madison worked to draft:
    a) tariff legislation
    b) the charter for the Bank of the United States
    c) the new bill of rights
    d) a list of duties for the vice president

3. Views on the interpretation of the powers in constitution centered on a debate about:
    a) judicial review
    b) loose interpretation
    c) strict interpretation
    d) choices *b* and *c* only

4. Washington's group of advisors to his cabinet included:
    a) Thomas Jefferson
    b) Alexander Hamilton
    c) Henry Knox
    d) all of the choices on the list

5. The responsibilities of the new role of the vice president included all of the following *EXCEPT*:
    a) offering advice to the president during cabinet meetings
    b) presiding over the Senate
    c) casting the deciding vote in case of a tie vote in the Senate
    d) assuming the role of the president if he died in office

6. The Bank of the United States created major disagreement between Jefferson and Hamilton over the issue of:
   a) the power of the state governments
   b) northern industrial interests over that of farmers in the South and in the frontier
   c) the limitations imposed on the bank
   d) the loose interpretation of the Constitution itself

7. Opposing viewpoints between the federalists and the anti-federalists can be seen in:
   a) the view of a strong central government
   b) the view of a strong state government in favor of states' rights
   c) economic policies
   d) all of the answers on the list

8. The Kentucky and Virginia Resolutions, written by Thomas Jefferson, argued that:
   a) the states themselves had the right to nullify or declare a federal law to be unconstitutional
   b) the Alien and Sedition Acts should be renewed
   c) any state in disagreement with the federal government could pursue secession
   d) states had to comply with all federal laws

9. The major purpose of the Alien and Sedition Acts included:
   a) squashing opposition from the anti-federalists
   b) individual rights could be curtailed
   c) gave more powers to the federal government
   d) all of the answers on the list

10. Before leaving office, Adams was able to secure his legacy by:
    a) planning a presidential library
    b) appointing John Marshall, a federalist, to the Supreme Court
    c) getting Jefferson to agree to continue the policies from Adams's term in office
    d) planning on running for president again in 1804

11. Washington attempted to formulate policy in regards to the United States's involvement in foreign affairs by:
   a) urging the United States to remain neutral in the conflict in France following the French Revolution
   b) negotiating Jay's Treaty with Britain to secure the removal of British troops from outposts in the American frontier
   c) using his farewell address in 1796 to urge the United States not to become entangled in foreign policy matters
   d) all of the answers on the list

12. Adams attempted to formulate policy and secure his legacy as president by:
   a) signing the Alien and Sedition Acts into law in 1798
   b) signing an informal declaration of war with France (while at the same time tripling the size of the U.S. navy)
   c) appointing a fellow federalist, John Marshall, to the Supreme Court
   d) *a* and *c* only

Matching

a. cabinet	j. Bank of the United States
b. Bill of Rights	k. protective tariff
c. anti-federalist	l. federalist
d. Washington, D.C.	m. midnight judges
e. impressment	n. Pinckney's Treaty
f. Alexander Hamilton	o. "Mad Anthony" Wayne
g. elastic clause	p. Whiskey Rebellion
h. Thomas Jefferson	q. excise tax
i. Judiciary Act of 1789	r. Ambassador Genet

_____13. the legislation that organized the Supreme Court and federal judges

_____14. the new site for the capital

_____15. the group that offers advice to the president

_____16. a tax on imports designed to generate revenue for the national government and to foster industrial development in the United States

_____17. he was Secretary of State for George Washington and later resigned this position

_____18. what gave Congress the power to establish policy that was "necessary and proper" for the federal government to carry out its functions

_____19. the political party that favored state power over that of the federal government and sought to represent the needs of the agrarian farmers in the South and the frontier

_____20. he came to the United States and began soliciting contributions in an attempt to draw the U.S. into the conflict in France

_____21. the tax that was imposed on the manufacture and distribution of non-essential consumer goods

_____22. the Secretary of the Treasury for George Washington who proposed the Bank of the United States

_____23. the policy where U.S. sailors were "kidnapped" by the British navy and forced into service

_____24. the political party that favored a strong central government and the needs of the industrial and manufacturing needs of the Northeast

_____25. a protest by western farmers in Pennsylvania over taxation policies and was put down by troops led by Washington

_____26. at the Battle of Fallen Timbers a group of Native Americans in the Ohio region were put down by U.S. troops under this commander

_____27. a last-minute appointment of a number of Federalist judges to federal court positions by John Adams

_____28. what was proposed by Hamilton to create a stable currency and financial policy for the United States

_____29. the first 10 amendments to the Constitution that sought to safeguard personal and states' rights

_____30. sought to get Spain to acknowledge the southern U.S. border with Spanish territory along the 31st parallel and to secure the right of deposit on the Mississippi River at New Orleans

Short Response

31. What role did party politics begin to play in government and sectional differences in the country? Make a T-chart labeled federalists and anti-federalists. List major points on where each party disagreed with the other on a variety of political issues.

32. How effectively did Washington and Adams deal with *factions, frictions, and farewells* in their administrations?

33. Using examples from Washington and Adams, how did each president attempt to extend his policy and influence upon leaving office?

Answers begin on page 251.

Jeffersonian Democracy

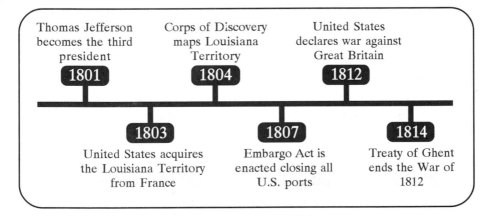

Thomas Jefferson becomes the third president
1801

Corps of Discovery maps Louisiana Territory
1804

United States declares war against Great Britain
1812

1803
United States acquires the Louisiana Territory from France

1807
Embargo Act is enacted closing all U.S. ports

1814
Treaty of Ghent ends the War of 1812

Trends and Themes of the Era

- Domestic and foreign affairs dramatically challenged and shaped the country during the terms of the Democratic-Republican presidents.

- Geographic and economic concerns began to dominate party politics.

- Actions taken during the era of the Democratic-Republican presidents continued to forge a national identity for the United States.

- Westward expansion became a unifying force in the country.

- Participation in politics began to increase during this period.

Transition, discovery, and challenge! During the first 15 years of the nineteenth century, the United States experienced a change in presidential leadership, doubled its size through land acquisitions, and fought another war with Great Britain. Through all of these changes, the resolve for independence grew, and the country became more confident. In his inaugural address in 1801, President Thomas Jefferson said, "We are all Republicans, we are all federalists." With this statement, he tried to conclude that regardless of political affiliation, all political leaders shared the same desire for the country's economic well-being, but federal authority would be called into question. During this time, the Democratic-Republican party, under Jefferson and Madison, gained a stronghold and promoted its agenda in the political arena, and the Federalist party was essentially swept aside. By the end of the War of 1812, there was an air of change and anticipation in the country. Political party affiliation became based on geographic and economic concerns. As the country grew, sectionalism became entrenched as each region debated its political agenda at the expense of other regions. As federal authority increased, it was not without question as politicians in the North, South, and West challenged the federal government during this time of economic growth and territorial expansion.

Lesson 8-1: Jefferson and the Democratic-Republicans

Once in office, Jefferson set out to establish his vision for the young country. The Revolution of 1800 saw the transfer of political power from the federalists to the Republicans. Despite the change, many Republican actions would have federalist overtones during the next few years.

One of Jefferson's first actions in office was to cut back on federal expenditures and bureaucracy. He persuaded Congress to cut almost all internal taxes, and balanced the cut with reductions in military spending and other government endeavors. At the same time, Jefferson responded to serious international problems. He launched a war against pirates in North Africa who were threatening U.S. trade interests, negotiated a treaty with France to gain the Louisiana Territory, and imposed an embargo to protect U.S. trade. He envisioned a nation of small family farmers, an agrarian republic. He also believed that the states were the most competent administrators for domestic concerns. While trying to limit the size of the federal government, Jefferson also saw it grow in power and influence.

Lesson 8-2: The Louisiana Purchase

In 1800, France gained control of the Louisiana Territory from Spain. Fearing that Napoleon had plans to build an empire in the Americas, Jefferson sent negotiators to France in an attempt to purchase the territory. The envoy of James Monroe and Robert Livingston found that Napoleon had abandoned his plan for a colonial empire, in part because of a massive slave revolt in Haiti, led by Toussaint L'Ouverture, that had severely depleted Napoleon's forces. Napoleon agreed to sell all of the Louisiana Territory to finance French efforts in the war in Europe. After some negotiations in 1803, the price was set at $15 million (roughly 13.5 cents per acre). With the **Louisiana Purchase**, the United States gained an enormous, uncharted piece of land, almost doubling the country's size and eliminating French (and remnant Spanish) control of New Orleans and the Mississippi River.

The Louisiana Purchase
Main Exploration Routes, 1804–1807

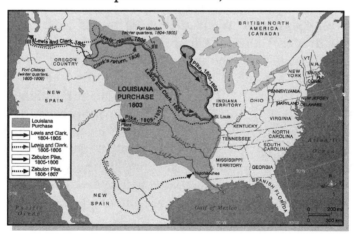

Many Americans questioned the purchase, especially New England federalists, who were alarmed at the increase in debt and unknown, empty land. Jefferson, always a strict constructionist, feared that the purchase would be deemed unconstitutional because the Constitution didn't explicitly grant such purchasing and expansionist powers to the federal government. Therefore, he drafted a constitutional amendment authorizing the national government to acquire new lands. Fellow Republicans, however, eventually persuaded him to drop the amendment and submit the purchase treaty directly to the Senate to prevent Napoleon from recanting his sale offer. The Senate speedily ratified the purchase. In spite of his overall aims to restrict the central government's power, Jefferson initiated a dramatic expansion of federal powers by backing the Louisiana Purchase. He claimed that the purchase would finally free the United States from European influence in the frontier.

Lesson 8-3: Westward Exploration

Jefferson was fascinated with the undiscovered frontier. Because he envisioned the United States as an agrarian republic, he sought to open up new farming along the vast and fertile frontier. Before the formal negotiations for the Louisiana Purchase, Jefferson had commissioned a team of explorers—including Meriwether Lewis, who was a captain in the army, and Lieutenant William Clark—to map the new territory. They were instructed to study the flora and fauna and to keep an eye out for mineral deposits and trading opportunities.

In 1804, the **Corps of Discovery** led by Lewis and Clark set off from St. Louis with 45 soldiers. While they were in the Dakotas, they met Canadian fur trader Toussaint Charbonneau and his wife, a Shoshone woman named **Sacajawea**, who proved indispensable as a guide. Their route followed the Missouri River, and after a winter at Fort Mandan, they continued through the Rocky Mountains to the Columbia River. During the winter of 1805 to 1806, they stayed near present-day Astoria, Oregon, and then returned to St. Louis in the spring after traveling nearly 3,000 miles in two and a half years. They brought back a large botanical collection, maps of the region, sketches and journals, and information about the valuable fur trade, and they laid the foundation for the American claim to Oregon. The success of the Lewis and Clark expedition inspired increasing exploration and settlement of the new territory.

In 1805, **Zebulon Pike** was sent to find the source of the Mississippi River. In 1806, he went to Colorado, where he explored the region and named Pike's Peak near Colorado Springs. He then traveled through the Rio Grande region, where he found the headwaters of the Rio Grande River. Soon thereafter in 1807, Spanish authorities intercepted his party's small fort near Alamosa, Colorado, and took him captive to Santa Fe, New Mexico, for a time. Although Spain thought Pike was a spy, he was escorted back to U.S. territory in July 1807. His later description of the southwest as "desert-like and inhospitable" endured for many years.

Lesson 8-4: The Aaron Burr Controversy

Aaron Burr became vice president after the House broke the tie vote in the 1800 election, making Jefferson president in 1801. During the next four years, Burr would be snubbed by the president and then dropped from the ballot in the next election. In 1804, while making a bid for governor of New York, Alexander Hamilton accused Burr of being a "dangerous man...one not to be trusted with the reins of government." After losing the election, Burr challenged Hamilton to a duel for his damaging remarks during the campaign. After Burr shot Hamilton at the dueling grounds of Weehawken, New Jersey, he faced murder charges in New York and New Jersey. Hamilton died the next day from the gunshot wound.

While fleeing from those charges, Burr began a conspiracy to detach Louisiana from the United States and join it with Texas and Mexico to create a new nation. Jefferson had Burr arrested and then captured in Pensacola, Florida, so he couldn't make an escape attempt. Burr was brought to trial in Virginia for treason. Jefferson refused to honor a deposition to testify in the Burr conspiracy trial, claiming executive privilege, and Burr was found not guilty by Chief Justice John Marshall. Jefferson hinted that he might seek to impeach Marshall, but he never did.

Lesson 8-5: Tension Overseas and American Trade

In 1803, France and Britain resumed war against each other. The United States continued trading with both nations while clinging to neutrality, but soon found herself drawn into the conflict as the French and British took aggressive measures that violated U.S. neutrality rights. The French policy, issued in the **Berlin Decree** by Napoleon, tried to diminish trade with Britain by subjecting to seizure any ship that first stopped in a British port. Through a series of countermeasures, known as **Orders in Council**, Britain blockaded French-controlled ports in Europe. The British also began searching American ships for goods from the French West Indies and threatened continued impressment of American crews into the Royal Navy. More than 200 American ships were seized in 1805 alone.

Tensions peaked in the **Chesapeake-Leopard Affair** in 1807, when the British frigate *HMS Leopard* opened fire on the American frigate *USS Chesapeake* off the Chesapeake Bay, after its request to board had been denied. The British killed three men, wounded 18, and took four men aboard the *Leopard*. Although he was outraged, Jefferson wanted to avoid war because of the downsizing of the U.S. army and navy, so he banned all British warships from American waters.

Congress then passed the **Embargo Act of 1807**, which prohibited any ship from leaving a U.S. port for a foreign port, targeting all imports and exports. Jefferson and Congress hoped that such a measure would so damage the British and French economies that the countries would be forced to honor U.S. neutrality. The goal was to reduce raw materials going to Great Britain, but the results were disastrous to the U.S. economy as commerce came to a virtual standstill. The United States was driven into a deep depression, and illegal trade began as merchants attempted to make profits.

Lesson 8-6: Madison and Preparations for War

Before leaving office, Jefferson repealed the Embargo Act of 1807. He then retired from office after serving two terms, continuing the two-term limit precedent set by Washington. James Madison, Jefferson's secretary of state, won the election of 1808. After becoming president on March 4, 1809, he immediately confronted the nation's deteriorating foreign relations.

Under Madison, Congress first replaced the Embargo Act with the **Non-Intercourse Act.** It prevented trade only with Britain and France, opening up all other foreign markets. The act did little to stimulate the struggling U.S. economy because the British and French were the largest and most powerful traders in the world. In 1810, Congress substituted **Macon's Bill No. 2** for the Non-Intercourse Act, as a ploy for either Britain or France to lift trade restrictions. Macon's Bill No. 2 resumed open trade with both Britain and France and stated that, if either nation repealed its restrictions on neutral shipping, the United States would start an embargo against the other nation. Napoleon seized the opportunity and repealed French restrictions, provoking an American declaration of non-intercourse with Britain. Despite Napoleon's promise, however, the French continued to seize American ships.

The War Hawks

As it became clear that peaceable coercion wouldn't ease the hostilities, Madison faced increasing pressure from **War Hawks** within Congress. These southerners and westerners, led by South Carolina's **John C. Calhoun** and Kentucky's **Henry Clay**, began asserting their power during

Madison's administration. They resented the recession that had plagued southern and western regions from 1808 to 1810. They advocated war rather than disgraceful terms of peace. They also hoped that, through war, the United States would win western and southwestern territories, annex Canada to eliminate the British and Native American threat along the frontier, and open up new lands to settlement. New England refused to cooperate with the looming war effort.

The War Hawks feared that the British were recruiting Native Americans along the Canadian border to fight American settlers. Heightening these fears, a Shawnee chief, Tecumseh, and his brother "The Prophet" attempted to unite a number of tribes in Ohio and Indiana under an anti-white government. In response, future president William Henry Harrison, then-governor of the Indiana Territory, crushed the Shawnees in the 1811 **Battle of Tippecanoe** by burning The Prophet's town to the ground, though his own forces also suffered heavy losses. Almost 30 years later, Harrison would run for president on his popularity as an Indian fighter, using the campaign slogan "Tippecanoe and Tyler too!" (John Tyler ran as his vice president.)

Although the Battle of Tippecanoe ended with an American victory over the Shawnee Indians, it didn't end the threat of an Anglo-Indian alliance. Tecumseh and the Shawnees later joined with British troops during the War of 1812. The War Hawks' resolve to crush Indian resistance remained strong.

Lesson 8-7: The War of 1812

In June 1812, convinced of the inevitability of war against Britain, Madison sent a message to Congress enumerating British violations of U.S. neutrality rights, including the presence of British ships in American waters and the impressment of American sailors. In a conciliatory measure, Britain repealed the Orders in Council, its aggressive naval policy, but it was too late. Congress had already passed a declaration of war, and the War Hawks pushed for full engagement. The federalists opposed the war, fearing it would further endanger trade.

The Americans were at a disadvantage when opposing the British troops on land and on sea. Although "the pride of the nation was at stake," the vote for war had been strictly on sectional lines. New England states opposed the war for fear that it would continue to hurt shipping. The South and West favored the war effort for economic reasons of trade.

Because of Jefferson's downsizing of the army and navy during his term, the United States was virtually weak throughout the entire war. Despite this fact, the United States managed a few significant victories. **Commodore Oliver Perry** cornered the British fleet at the Battle of Lake Erie on September 10, 1813, and captured a British squadron of warships. This victory allowed the United States to gain control of Lake Erie. Oliver Perry's victory over the British on Lake Erie in September 1813 came at a steep price. Less than a month later, Tecumseh, the Shawnee chief who had sided with Britain, was killed at the Battle of the Thames in October 1813 when General William Henry Harrison led militiamen in battle at the Thames River in Upper Canada. They returned to Kentucky with pieces of hair, clothing, and skin from the battle. These two victories not only provided a very important morale boost but also served to assist at the peace talks.

After the British captured Detroit in 1812, the war went badly for the Americans. The British instituted a strong blockade of the U.S. coastline. After the burning of the capitol building in the summer of 1814, the president and Congress were forced to flee. After the war, the president's house

War of 1812

was repainted white—hence the name "White House." Meanwhile, the Americans rallied against the British in Baltimore, inspiring Washington lawyer **Francis Scott Key** to write "The Star Spangled Banner" as he watched the battle over Fort McHenry. The song was later adapted as the national anthem in 1931. Late in 1814, Napoleon had begun to be defeated back in Europe by Britain, so Britain began to seek peace and trade with the United States.

Sizing up the Competition: America

Advantages	Disadvantages
The War Hawks strongly resolved to get Britain to recognize U.S. Rights.	Federalists opposed the war, calling it "Mr. Madison's War," and support for the conflict fell strictly along party lines.
"The pride of the nation is at stake" became a rallying cry for war.	The United States suffered from a downsized army and navy for war efforts.
Andrew Jackson's surprise victory at the Battle of New Orleans in 1815 instilled pride in the United States.	The British blockade of U.S. ports hurt trade.
	Threat of the New England states' secession at the Hartford Convention in 1814 undermined the war effort.
	The U.S. economy suffered from diminished trade with Europe.

Sizing up the Competition: Great Britain

Advantages	Disadvantages
The U.S. coastline was strongly blockaded.	Britain was still at war with France when the war in America began.
The British won major victories at Fort Niagara and Buffalo in 1813.	War in Europe delayed extra troops and warships for America until 1814.
The U.S. capitol building was burned on August 24, 1814, by British troops who set it on fire—a morale boost for British and demoralizing effect for the Americans (a rainstorm though prevented its complete destruction.)	The British failed to defeat American forces at Fort McHenry.
	They underestimated American resolve.
The Indians in the frontier supported them.	War disrupted trade with America.
They had a strong military with war experience.	

Nonetheless, the war ended in a stalemate, mainly because the British were also occupied with events in Europe. The signing of the **Treaty of Ghent** in December 1814 ended the war and restored the status quo. The treaty resolved almost nothing because no mention was made of impressment, blockades, or neutral rights. The treaty simply stopped the conflict and set up commissions to deal with lingering disputes after the war's end.

Two weeks after the signing of the Treaty of Ghent, but before news of it had reached America, U.S. troops won a decisive victory in the **Battle of New Orleans** on January 8, 1815. General Andrew Jackson's troops defended the city, killing more than 2,000 British troops while losing only 13 men. The timing of the Battle of New Orleans inspired the popular misconception that the United States won the war and forced the British to surrender and sign the treaty. Even without officially winning the war, the United States did succeed in protecting itself against one of the world's premier powers; in fact, the War of 1812 has been called the second war of independence. America was now free to pursue growth and freedom.

The Hartford Convention

In 1814, during the later stages of the War of 1812, a group of disillusioned federalists met at the **Hartford Convention**, where the party enumerated its complaints against the ruling Republican party. Some federalists threatened New England's secession, but cooler heads prevailed and called for a resolution summarizing New England's grievances, both general ones and those specifically relating to the War of 1812. These complaints included the charge that Republicans were neglecting the needs of New England industry and commerce. The war and its accompanying trade restrictions, in particular, hurt New England because of the region's concentration of seaboard manufacturers and merchants. The group at the Hartford Convention also drafted seven constitutional amendments intended to politically strengthen the northeast region and restrict federal power. The proposals included an amendment to abolish the 3/5 Compromise, one to change the policy by which Congress declared war and admitted new states, another to limit the president to one term, and a final amendment that would set a maximum time limit for trade embargoes.

The federalists had hoped to deliver their resolution to Madison as the United States struggled on in a deadlocked war and antiwar sentiment ran high. They arrived in Washington, D.C., however, just as news spread of the victory at New Orleans and the signing of the Treaty of Ghent. The federalists of their central complaints, and the threat of secession made them look to be traitors. Many Republicans accused the federalists of treason, weakening their power and influence as a party. The embarrassment of the Hartford Convention marked the end of the Federalist party, leading to its demise as a prominent influence in national politics by 1820.

The differences of opinion about the war illustrated the growing **sectionalism** within the expanding United States. This sectionalism would continue throughout the first half of the nineteenth century, eventually resulting in the Civil War.

Review Exam

Multiple Choice

1. The election of 1800 can be deemed "revolutionary" on the basis that:
   a) Jefferson quietly agreed to the Sedition Acts
   b) political power successfully passed from one political party to that of another
   c) Adams would now serve as Jefferson's vice president
   d) secret plans were already underway to purchase Louisiana Territory after the election

2. The Louisiana Purchase was important because:
   a) it more than doubled the size of the country in 1803
   b) it tested Jefferson's political beliefs about the power of the federal government to make such a purchase
   c) it gave the United States another chance to find the Northwest Passage
   d) all of the answers on the list

3. The controversy surrounding Aaron Burr is significant for all of the following *EXCEPT*:
   a) he served as an influential vice president for Jefferson in both terms
   b) he was charged with the murder of Alexander Hamilton in a duel in 1804
   c) he attempted to detach part of the Louisiana Territory in an effort to form a new nation
   d) he was brought to trial for treason but found not guilty

4. After 1803, American trade with Europe began to be hampered by:
   a) the impressment of U.S. sailors
   b) the declaration of war with Britain after Chesapeake-Leopard Affair in 1807
   c) fighting in Europe between Britain and France
   d) choices *a* and *c* only

5. The Embargo Act of 1807 was significant in that:
   a) it attempted to reduce raw materials going to Britain
   b) it closed all U.S. ports to trade
   c) although it aimed to protect U.S. neutrality, it crippled the economy by shutting down all commerce
   d) all the answers on the list

6. In June 1812, President Madison urged Congress to declare war against Great Britain on the basis that:
   a) the Embargo Act would end soon
   b) impressment was a flawed policy
   c) Britain had grossly violated the neutrality of the United States
   d) he needed to gain further support of the New England states

7. In preparation for war in 1812, the strongest political support in favor of declaring war against Britain came from this group of people in the United States:
   a) War Hawks in the West and South
   b) merchants in New England
   c) federalists
   d) southern farmers

8. All of the following were significant events during the War of 1812 **EXCEPT**:
   a) the burning of the capitol building in Washington, D.C., in the summer of 1814
   b) the last major battle of the war of 1812 was fought in New Orleans in January 1815
   c) the United States scored several significant military victories during the war
   d) the British instituted a successful blockade of U.S. ports

9. The Treaty of Ghent in December 1814 formally ended the War of 1812 by:
   a) ending the fighting and restoring the status quo
   b) reaching formal agreements about impressment
   c) reaching formal agreements about the blockade
   d) reaching formal agreements about trade and neutrality rights

10. The events of the Hartford Convention in 1814 were significant because:
   a) the New England states threatened secession over their opposition to the war
   b) they sought to restrict federal power with seven new constitutional amendments
   c) they sought to strengthen the states in the New England region
   d) all of the answers on the list

Matching

a. Orders in Council

b. Francis Scott Key

c. Zebulon Pike

d. Berlin Decree

e. Sacajawea

f. Lewis and Clark

g. Napoleon

h. War Hawks

i. Andrew Jackson

j. Commodore Oliver Perry

k. Chesapeake-Leopard Affair

l. Battle of Tippecanoe

m. William Henry Harrison

n. Macon's Bill No. 2

o. Non-Intercourse Act

_____11. he agreed to sell the Louisiana Territory to the United States for $15 million (at roughly 3.5 cents per acre)

_____12. a Shoshone Indian woman who accompanied Lewis and Clark on their expedition in the recently purchased Louisiana Territory from 1804 to 1806

_____13. prior to the War of 1812, the measure that allowed France to subject any ship stopping in a British port to seizure

_____14. he explored the Spanish regions of Colorado and New Mexico from 1806 to 1807

____15. prior to the War of 1812, the measure Britain used to blockade French-controlled ports in an attempt to hurt U.S. trade

____16. the policy Madison used to replace the Embargo Act of 1807 by opening trade with all countries except Britain and France

____17. the battle (in the Ohio region during the War of 1812) with the Shawnee Indians, during which the "Prophet" was defeated

____18. he wrote *The Star Spangled Banner* as he watched the battle over Fort McHenry in 1814

____19. he cornered and defeated the British fleet in a battle on Lake Erie in 1813

____20. the popular war hero general who emerged from the War of 1812 with battle victories at the Battle of Tippecanoe and Battle of the Thames River

____21. a group of southerners and westerners led by John C. Calhoun and Henry Clay who advocated going to war in 1812

____22. prior to the War of 1812, the legislation that opened trade with Britain and France when they repealed their restrictions on neutral shipping

____23. a popular war hero general who emerged from the War of 1812 victorious from the Battle of New Orleans in January 1815

____24. commissioned by Jefferson to head up the Corps of Discovery to explore the Louisiana Purchase Territory

____25. the naval event that occurred when the British fired upon an American ship of the Chesapeake Bay in 1807 and killed three men, wounded 18, and kidnapped four sailors

Short Response

26. How did *transition, discovery, and challenge* affect political developments during this period?

27. How did Jefferson's actions as president challenge his strict constructionist beliefs about matters that related to the Constitution?

28. How did the War of 1812 reflect the growing sectionalism in the country?

Answers begin on page 254.

The Era of Good Feelings

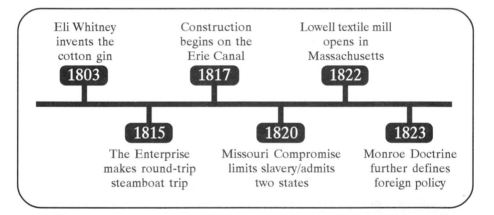

Eli Whitney invents the cotton gin
1803

Construction begins on the Erie Canal
1817

Lowell textile mill opens in Massachusetts
1822

1815
The Enterprise makes round-trip steamboat trip

1820
Missouri Compromise limits slavery/admits two states

1823
Monroe Doctrine further defines foreign policy

Trends and Themes of the Era

- Following the War of 1812, the United States enjoyed a period of optimism, growth, and general cooperation under a single political party.

- In this period the United States used the Monroe Doctrine to assert its dominance in the Western Hemisphere.

- Westward expansion gave rise to deepening sectional tensions. Slavery and regionalism would continue to play an increasing role in nineteenth-century politics.

- The economy of each region continued to reflect the country's growing sectionalism.

- John Marshall would lead the Supreme Court in establishing its strength through various rulings.

Idealism, improvements, and industry! Euphoria swept the nation after Jackson's victory at the Battle of New Orleans. Although the United States gained very little from the War of 1812, the conflict helped to shape the social, political, and economic lives of Americans. With the Democratic-Republicans firmly in control, the party sought to solidify its vision for America. In 1817, President James Monroe would refer to the "happy situation of the United States," and a Boston newspaper would write about an "era of good feelings." Many believed that America was fast becoming a great nation, spurred on by economic growth. The new market economy was quickly shaping the nation. Transportation advances helped spur economic growth, and a revolution in manufacturing was taking off. The country's good times would soon be tested by an economic crisis, a heated debate about slavery, threats from foreign nations, and conflict over the federal government's role and states' rights. The old adage that "all good things must come to an end" played itself out in the presidential election of 1824, when the Republican party began to splinter in favor of sectional issues. The **Era of Good Feelings** would give way to deeper challenges of nationalism and sectionalism that would impact the country profoundly.

Lesson 9-1: American Nationalism Takes Shape

The American "victory" in the War of 1812 ushered in an era of nationalism and cooperation and fueled a renewed sense of pride and purpose. Influenced by the post-war spirit (and no longer threatened by the federalists), the Republicans proposed their plan for the nation, which included openly embracing former Federalist policies.

The demise of the Federalist party was evident in the 1816 presidential election, which was easily won by James Monroe, the last president of the Revolutionary War era. This unifying nationalist spirit peaked in the election of 1820, also won by Monroe with 231 electoral votes to his opponent John Quincy Adams's one vote. Despite the apparent successes of the party in charge, without a viable second party to hold it in check, it would suffer much the same fate as the Federalist party.

Madison proposed plans for the nation that would be carried out by Monroe's administration. In Congress, Henry Clay fleshed out these nationalist economic policies in his **American System**, a policy program aimed at economic self-sufficiency. The major goal was to unite the country's economic interests, with the North producing manufactured goods, the South and West buying the manufactured goods, and the South and West raising grain, meat, and cotton needed by the North. The program included enacting a bill in 1816 to charter the **Second Bank of the United States**, pushing through a moderate tariff bill to protect America's growing industries, and urging federal funding for internal improvements, including a national system of roads and canals. Support was proposed for federal funding of internal improvements, though there was hesitation about authorizing direct federal involvement. A protective tariff was proposed to spur American manufacturing and to protect against foreign competition.

Although the tariff was enacted and the charter given to the Second Bank of the United States, disagreement arose over federal funding of internal improvements. Except for the national road project, funding for internal improvements was left up to local and state governments.

Lesson 9-2: Growth of the Market Economy

After the War of 1812, the country began to focus on strengthening the economy, building production and trade, and improving the transportation network. The acquisition of new territories continued to provide raw materials and energy sources. The country's population growth would provide not only a labor supply but also the consumers necessary for economic expansion. Transportation improvements helped move goods and people throughout the country. Local, state, and federal government projects aided economic ventures. The American economy was entering a new era of development as it focused not only on agricultural growth but also on industrial and technological advancements. This market revolution permanently altered the American economy and was aided by rapid improvements in transportation, commercialization of goods and services, and industrialization of factories.

Trade and Transportation

The transportation revolution began with the vast river system. Steamboats such as **Robert Fulton**'s *Clermont* on the Hudson River in New York, and the *New Orleans* and the *Enterprise* on the Mississippi helped boost two-way commerce along the rivers. In 1820, 69 steamboats were making their way along western waterways, becoming a great asset for farmers and merchants in the West. By the mid 1830s, more than 1,200 steamboats and their cargoes would find their way to New Orleans.

Principal Rivers, Roads, and Canals, 1840

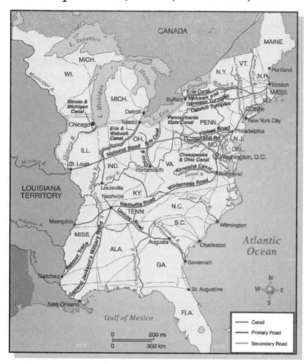

In 1817, 10 years after the invention of the steamboat, New York began constructing the **Erie Canal**, the first major canal project in the United States. When it was completed in 1825, the canal stretched 363 miles from Albany to Buffalo (much farther than any other American or European canal). A system of canals soon was created around the nation, linking waterways from the Northeast to the frontier. This would help increase commerce in the northeastern states.

The canals helped pump up economic growth by moving goods at a lower cost. Before the canals, shipping costs were approximately 19 cents per mile per ton of goods. Soon after canal construction, that cost dropped to around three cents, and by 1860 it was less than one cent per ton per mile. By 1840, nearly 3,300 miles of canals had been built in the United States at a cost of more than $125 million, half of which was financed by state governments. As a byproduct of this growth, New York City soon came to dominate trade with the West and became the commercial capital of the nation. The canal boom continued until the railroads began to compete for trade.

At the same time, the U.S. government invested in the **National Road**, which by 1818 stretched from Cumberland, Maryland, to Wheeling, Virginia. A system of privately owned toll roads also surrounded each major city, serving as the foundation for the growing national road system.

The Industrial Revolution

During the late eighteenth century, Great Britain launched the Industrial Revolution. Because of the embargoes before and during the

War of 1812, the United States began to change its focus from importing goods to manufacturing them. Both Britain and the United States relied on coal and water as cheap power sources for manufacturing. They also depended heavily on interchangeable parts, mass production, and inexpensive labor.

This shift in manufacturing would have a dramatic impact on the United States for the remainder of the nineteenth century. Although Great Britain was the world leader in the Industrial Revolution, the United States began to make great strides in this area. Not only did the North have a large labor force, but they were also ready to embrace new forms of manufacturing to help create new jobs. The North also enjoyed the advantage of an abundance of waterpower and coal for power supplies.

In 1793, Samuel Salter built the first successful mechanized textile factory in the United States. Later on, in 1813, three Bostonians, Francis Lowell, Nathan Appleton, and Patrick Johnson, built a weaving factory in Waltham, Massachusetts. Nine years later, in 1822, Appleton and Johnson built a bigger operation in Lowell, Massachusetts, that employed hundreds of young women. This textile mill would eventually employ hundreds of young women known as **Lowell Girls**. By 1839, Lowell would become the leading textile producer in the world. The rise of mills and industries in the North led to the development of a factory-working class of people: children, young single women, poor whites, and immigrants.

The South would also be impacted by the changes occurring in the American economy. **Eli Whitney**'s invention of the cotton gin in 1803 made it possible for southern farmers to grow short-staple cotton for a profit in the interior regions. The invention provided an efficient way to remove the seeds from the short-staple cotton so that more could be sold to the North and to Britain. By 1820, cotton was king in the South, and the southern economy became increasingly dependent on agriculture and slave labor. By 1857, nearly 60 percent of all U.S. exports was cotton, and the slave population reached four million by 1860. Whitney also pioneered the use of interchangeable parts in 1798, building a factory to produce standardized interchangeable parts for military muskets.

Lesson 9-3: Economic Boom and Bust

The economy dramatically expanded as a result of a postwar borrowing and buying frenzy. Banks lent money with little or no collateral to businessmen seeking to buy land, build factories, and develop industries.

The high protective tariff of 1816 promoted further domestic development. Accompanying this expansion were the steady rise of inflation and the increase in paper money and credit, leading to higher prices and less valuable currency.

In 1818, the global demand for American goods declined. As a result, the U.S. economy started to collapse and banks began contracting their lending practices. Many state banks folded, and many borrowers declared bankruptcy. Farmers suffering from installment credit for money owed on their land, equipment, seed, and housing materials had trouble making payments.

The speculative frenzy of the postwar era rested solely on profitable markets. When Europeans couldn't afford American goods, the international markets that fueled speculation in the U.S. market dried up. Cotton prices fell in Europe, with ripple effects throughout the U.S. economy. The government and the Second Bank of the United States tightened up credit policies, and they wanted immediate repayment of loans with hard currency. State banks followed their lead, and the tight credit and loan recalls drove the economy over the edge. In what became known as the **Panic of 1819**, land values fell 50 to 75 percent, rich land speculators lost fortunes, and homesteaders became mired in debt. This led to a panic, or depression, that lasted for nearly six years.

Lesson 9-4: Geographical Boundaries

During this period, the United States began to direct its attention to the vast territory out west. Tensions with the Spanish in Florida and the southwest region (along with the British claims in the Oregon) occupied the government's attention. Slavery concerns in the region raised political concerns, and potential threats from European countries in South America and the Pacific Northwest were seen as security problems.

Florida

Spain and the United States long debated whether or not the Louisiana Purchase included western Florida. In 1818, Andrew Jackson rushed into Florida to capture a Spanish fort, alarming Spain. In 1819, the matter was settled when Spain agreed to the **Adams-Onis Treaty**, also known as the Transcontinental Treaty. The United States assumed $5 million of debt owed to Spain, and Spain ceded eastern Florida to the United States, renouncing all claims to western Florida. Spain also agreed to a southern

U.S. border west of the Mississippi River that extended all the way to the Pacific Ocean, recognizing U.S. claims to the Oregon Territory. The treaty gave the United States its first legitimate claim to the west coast.

The Missouri Compromise

This period of cooperation and goodwill also saw political controversy between the North and South. Westward expansion spawned sectional conflict, as the North and the South feuded about the expansion of slavery into western territories.

In 1819, the Union consisted of 11 free states and 11 slave states. The Missouri Territory's application for statehood threatened to upset this balance, which was deemed crucial to the South. Because of its growing population, the North had approximately 60 percent of the seats in the House of Representatives. This gave it a distinct advantage over the South, despite the use of the 3/5 Compromise to count slaves for representation. The Senate remained equal at 22 senators for the North and 22 for the South.

Congress debated the issue heatedly until James Tallmadge, Jr., of New York proposed an amendment to the bill for Missouri's admission. It would prohibit further introduction of slaves into Missouri and mandate the emancipation at age 25 of slaves' offspring born after the state was admitted to the Union. The House approved the bill with the Tallmadge Amendment, but the Senate struck the amendment from the bill.

The Missouri Compromise

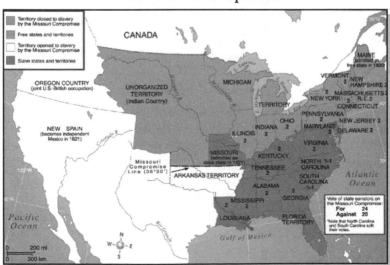

Maine's application for statehood allowed the Senate to escape the deadlock and to agree on the terms of the **Missouri Compromise:** Maine was to be admitted as a free state and Missouri as a slave state. In the remainder of the Louisiana Territory, slavery would be prohibited north of 36° 30′ latitude (the southern border of Missouri). With this statement, Congress asserted its right to restrict slavery. However, the compromise rapidly disintegrated when Missouri submitted a draft constitution that prohibited free blacks from entering the state.

Northern opposition blocked Missouri from statehood until 1821, when Speaker of the House Henry Clay designed a set of three agreements ending the controversy and allowing for the admission of two new states, one free, the other slave. The compromise temporarily cooled tensions. However, conflict would only increase in the years to come as discussions, debates, and votes followed strict sectional lines.

The Monroe Doctrine

During James Monroe's presidency, several revolutions against Spanish rule flared up in South and Central America, ousting the colonial governments and establishing independent regimes in the region. The United States, having broken away from colonial rule itself, officially recognized these new countries and established lucrative trading relations with many of them. Fearing that European governments—especially France and Russia—would intervene and try to reassert colonial dominance, Secretary of State John Quincy Adams composed the **Monroe Doctrine** in 1823. The doctrine declared American dominance in the western hemisphere and warned against European interference in the Americas.

The policy was an independent move after the United States refused to work on an agreement with the British to prevent any further intervention in the Americas by France and Spain. Although the United States had little military power to back up its claims, the declaration had immense symbolic importance because the country was declaring itself a world power equal to the great European nations. It served as a warning to Europe and demonstrated the growing strength and spirit of the United States.

The Monroe Doctrine, along with Washington's Farewell Address of 1796, would shape U.S. foreign policy for the next one hundred years. The Monroe Doctrine consisted of four principles shown on page 147.

The Monroe Doctrine at a Glance

• The Western Hemishpere was no longer open to colonization.

• Any attempt to establish colonies or gain political control would be considered an unfriendly act toward the United States.

• The United States was not to interfere in European affairs unless it involved the United States and/or U.S. interests.

• Europe was not to disturb the political status of any free country in the Western Hemisphere.

Lesson 9-5: The Marshall Court

John Marshall was appointed chief justice of the Supreme Court in 1801, and he remained in office until his death in 1835. Under his leadership, the Court increased its power to rival that of Congress and the president. A staunch federalist, Marshall delivered decisions that strengthened the central government at the expense of states' rights, and he upheld a broad interpretation of the Constitution.

Despite the demise of the Federalist party in the early 1800s, Marshall exerted a strong federalist influence on government. During his tenure on the high court, he authored more than half of the nearly 900 rulings the court issued. His rulings brought resistance from the Republican leadership and sparked political controversy, exposing issues of government authority, state versus federal rights, and trade regulation. Many Republicans condemned Marshall's rulings as too antagonistic toward states' rights.

Marshall's first significant decision came in the 1803 case of *Marbury v. Madison.* The ruling established the principle of judicial review, the Supreme Court's power to rule an act of Congress unconstitutional. The Court didn't invoke this power again until the Dred Scott case, 54 years later.

In 1819, the Supreme Court delivered two controversial decisions on the issue of state versus federal rights. In *Dartmouth College v. Woodward* (1819), Marshall ruled that New Hampshire couldn't convert Dartmouth College into a state university because the college's charter, issued by Britain before the American Revolution, qualified as a contract; the Constitution doesn't allow states to interfere with contracts. The grant of the college charter was a private matter and not subject to public regulation.

A month later, Marshall delivered an even more momentous decision in *McCulloch v. Maryland* (1819), which questioned whether Maryland could tax the Second Bank of the United States. Marshall argued that the federal government's power must be considered supreme within its sphere, and that states couldn't have the power to interfere with the exercise of federal powers. That made the Maryland tax unconstitutional. The ruling challenged states' rights by claiming that the states were subordinate to the Constitution and that the Union was created by the people and represented and acted for the good of everyone. The ruling also upheld the constitutionality of the Bank of the United States. Congress could pass laws "necessary and proper" for the functions of government.

The Marshall Court Cases at a Glance

Marbury v. Madison (1803)	**Judicial review**—The court can rule an act of Congress unconstitutional.
Dartmouth College v. Woodward (1819)	**Contracts**—New Hampshire couldn't convert Dartmouth College into a state university because the college's charter, issued by Britain before the American Revolution, qualified as a contract, and the Constitution forbids states to interfere with contracts.
McCulloch v. Maryland (1819)	**Power of the federal government**—The case questioned whether Maryland could tax the Second Bank of the United States. Marshall argued that the federal government's power must be considered supreme within its sphere and that states didn't have the power to interfere with the exercise of federal powers. A state couldn't tax the federal government—"the power to tax is the power to destroy." The constitutionality of the Bank of the United States was also upheld in this decision.
Gibbons v. Ogden (1824)	**Regulation of interstate commerce**—If a state law is in violation of the Constitution, then it is null and void.

The case of *Gibbons v. Ogden* in 1824 concerned interstate commerce. It involved a New York state steamboat franchise that had been granted a monopoly by the state legislature to run passenger ships between New York and New Jersey. The state license conflicted with a federal license, granted to another boat operator, to run the same steamboat route. Marshall ruled in favor of the federal license, arguing that a state can't interfere with Congress's right to regulate interstate commerce. Marshall interpreted "commerce" broadly to include all forms of business, not just the exchange of goods.

Review Exam

Multiple Choice

1. The wave of nationalism that spread across the country following the end of the war of 1812 and the Battle of New Orleans was evidenced in all of the following *EXCEPT*:
   a) the rise of Andrew Jackson as a war hero
   b) the political control of the Democratic Republican party
   c) the end of the debate about slavery
   d) the new market economy shaping the economy of the country

2. During this period of the "Era of Good Feelings" from 1815 to 1825, the American economy entered a new era of development as evidenced by:
   a) transportation improvements
   b) technological advancements
   c) industrial advancements
   d) all of the choices on the list

3. "The Lowell Girls" in Lowell, Massachusetts, were an example of:
   a) young women being hired to provide cheap labor for textile mills and to become part of a factory-working class
   b) young women being trained as steamboat operators
   c) young women being hired to work cotton gins
   d) none of the choices on the list

4. "King Cotton" came to symbolize:
   a) the significance of the cotton crop to the South's economic base
   b) the increase in the growth of cotton after the invention of the cotton gin
   c) an agricultural lifestyle built on the growth and expansion of cotton and slave labor
   d) all of the choices on the list

5. Canal building and steamboat travel along navigable rivers were important to the economic growth of the United States because:
   a) it allowed the manufacturing base of the South to grow
   b) it connected all three regions of the country (North, South, and West) together in trade and travel
   c) it allowed farmers and manufacturers to ships their goods quickly to a wide variety of markets
   d) choices *b* and *c* only

6. All of the following relates to the economic panic of 1819 *EXCEPT*:
   a) tightened credit policies in the United States
   b) the rise of cotton prices in Europe
   c) overspeculation in U.S. markets
   d) recalls on loan repayments

7. The Missouri Compromise was significant in that not only was Maine admitted as a free state and Missouri admitted as a slave state, but it also:
   a) ikept the balance of slave states and free states equal in representation in the House
   b) prevented the spread of slavery above the 36° 30′ line
   c) allowed for the limited spread of slavery below the 36° 30′ line
   d) established a 20-year limit on slavery

8. The Monroe Doctrine shaped U.S. foreign policy by:
   a) preparing for intervention in European conflicts
   b) allowing a limited time frame for European intervention in South America
   c) closing the Western Hemisphere to European influence
   d) agreeing to cooperate with European interests in the Western Hemisphere

9. John Marshall's influence as chief justice on the Supreme Court can best seen in:
   a) limiting the time a justice serves on the Supreme Court
   b) serving on the court for 35 years and authoring more than half of the rulings handed down by the Supreme Court during his tenure on the court

    c) ruling cases in such a way as to give more power to the states

    d) weakening the power and influence of the Supreme Court

10. One of the biggest political changes in the time period from 1815 to 1824 was evidenced in all of the following *EXCEPT*:

    a) the continuing rise of the Federalist party

    b) the rise of a political opposition with the growth of various political parties

    c) Madison running unopposed in his reelection as president in 1820

    d) the federalists nearly winning the presidency in 1820

Matching

a. Henry Clay

b. Erie Canal

c. John Marshall

d. James Monroe

e. Adams-Onis Treaty

f. *McCulloch v. Maryland*

g. protective tariff

h. Eli Whitney

i. the *Enterprise*

j. *Marbury v. Madison*

k. Federalist

l. National Road

m. *Gibbons v. Ogden*

n. Industrial Revolution

o. Second Bank of the United States

p. Era of Good Feelings

q. Robert Fulton

____11. a tax on imported goods meant to protect American industries against foreign competition

____12. a federalist who served as chief justice on the Supreme Court for 35 years

____13. a transportation system that connected Albany, New York, to Buffalo, New York

____14. the financial institution to which a 20-year renewal charter was given

____15. the time period immediately following the end of the war of 1812 that ushered in a wave of pride and nationalism

____16. one of many steamboats boosting commerce along the Mississippi River after 1815

____17. the court case that argued that the state could not interfere with the federal government's right to control interstate commerce

____18. by 1820 the party that had declined dramatically in its national influence

____19. the two-term Democratic-Republican president during the "Era of Good Feelings"

____20. the transportation system that stretched from Cumberland, Maryland, to Wheeling, Virginia

____21. the document that secured Florida as a U.S. territory and because of a new Spanish border recognized U.S. claims to the Oregon Territory and gave the United States its first legitimate claim to the west coast

____22. the court case that established the principal of judicial review (allowing the Supreme Court to rule a law unconstitutional)

____23. a time of economic growth due to the dramatic increase of manufacturing

____24. he proposed to Congress a series of economic policies of internal improvements that embodied the American System

____25. the court case that argued the supremacy of the federal government and that a state could not interfere with this power

____26. he developed the first steamboat, the *Clermont*, for travel on the Hudson River in New York in 1807

____27. he invented the cotton gin and developed the concept of interchangeable parts for manufacturing

Short Response

28. How did developments in **idealism, improvements, and industry** contribute to the growing sectionalism during the "Era of Good Feelings"?

29. What forces were at work to shape U.S. foreign policy at this time?

30. How did the Supreme Court begin to shape its judicial power and authority in this period?

31. How did the acquisition of territory impact the country's economy in this period?

Answers begin on page 257.

Jacksonian Democracy

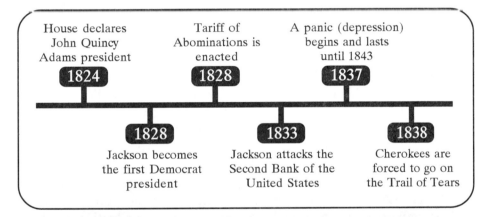

Trends and Themes of the Era

▶ The Republican Party split into two parties: the Democrats and the National Republicans. Soon, the National Republicans would give way to the Whig Party. The two-party system ushered in a newly democratic age, marked by more election choice and increased voter turnout.

▶ Andrew Jackson, the first man from the West to become president, won in large part on his appeal to the "common man." Politics increasingly began to be swayed by the public, rather than by the elites.

▶ The Nullification Crisis revealed deep regional differences in economic needs and attitudes about states' rights versus federal power.

▶ Jackson turned the presidency into a vastly more powerful office, using the presidential veto to assert his political and legislative will and embedding the government more deeply in party politics.

Corruption, bargains, and spoils! After the contested election of 1824, a second two-party political system emerged, resulting in greater voter participation. Elections focused not only on issues but also on promoting the candidates, and political parties deepened sectional rivalries. To survive, parties had to build coalitions from the different regions in the country. Political appointments and policy issues revealed the increasing influence a party could have, along with the growing differences in the country's regions. In this era of the common man, the office of the president and the Supreme Court grew in power and influence. Jackson emerged as one of the era's leading figures, and his response to westward expansion and the extension of suffrage would continue to change politics at national, state, and local levels. Despite differences of opinion, a strong sense of national consciousness began to form that would be challenged in the years ahead.

Lesson 10-1: A Two-Party System of Politics

From 1800 to 1824, the Republican party faced little political opposition and tried to foster a spirit of unity and cooperation. By the 1824 election, however, the two-party system of politics was back, intensifying sectional rivalries. Politics from 1820 to 1860 focused primarily on two issues: the growing rift between slave and free states, and the role of government in economic life. The explosive economic development and territorial expansion made increased demands on the political system, and personalities and sectional allegiances played a significant role in election outcomes.

By the end of the 1820s, most states had eliminated property ownership as the basis for voting requirements, resulting in universal white male suffrage. Voter participation rose dramatically from 1824 to 1840, nearly tripling to 78 percent. A democratic and egalitarian spirit filled the nation, prompting many historians to call the 1820s and 1830s "**the age of the common man**." Native Americans, women, and blacks, however, were still barred from political involvement.

Opposing Forces

The factions within the Republican party in the 1824 election became the foundation of a new political party. Jackson's supporters, led by Martin Van Buren and John C. Calhoun (who was also John Quincy Adams's vice president), rallied and formed what became known as the

Democratic party. This was the beginning of the modern Democratic Party. Angered over Jackson's loss in 1824, Democrats nominated Jackson for president in 1828. The opposition in the remaining Republican Party now called themselves the **National Republican party** and supported Adams for reelection in 1828.

The new two-party system reflected a sectional split within the United States. Democrats portrayed Jackson as a hero of the common man and states' rights, and portrayed Adams as a snobby aristocrat. The campaign tactic worked, and Jackson swept 56 percent of the popular vote. The South and West supported Jackson's Democrats, while the North sided with Adams and the National Republicans.

During Andrew Jackson's second term in office, leaders of the National Republican Party and other opponents of Jackson teamed up in 1834 to form the **Whig party.** Led by Henry Clay, Daniel Webster, and John C. Calhoun (who had split from Jackson and the Democratic party over issues of tariffs and nullification), the Whigs encompassed all different factions. Southern Republicans, northern Democrats, and social reformers united in their hatred of Jackson, whom many considered so tyrannical that they referred to him as "King Andrew I."

The Whig party opposed both Jackson's strong-arm political tactics and his policies. During his tenure in office, Jackson used his veto power an unprecedented 12 times. Southern Whigs disliked Jackson's handling of protective tariffs and the Nullification Crisis, among other issues, and Northern Democrats defected to the Whigs in part because of Jackson's anti-business stance. Jackson cultivated his image as friend to the common man and became increasingly hostile toward business and merchant interests, and toward all factions representing elite, privileged Americans. He used his position and power as the chief executive to shape the presidency and a powerful branch of the federal government.

By the election of 1836, the Whigs had become a national party with widespread popularity. On the strength of Jackson's common appeal, however, the Democrats maintained their hold on the presidenc. Jackson's chosen successor, Martin Van Buren, defeated William Henry Harrison and three other Whig candidates. The Whigs' attempt to split the vote, with each section running a candidate, so the election would be sent to the House of Representatives, backfired on them. Yet the Whig party continued to grow in popularity, and in 1840 the Whigs won the presidential election with William Henry Harrison.

Soon after, however, the party lost its national prominence. Although they were united in their dislike of Jackson, the Whigs were badly divided on other major issues, most notably slavery and protective tariffs. Southern Republican Whigs could never totally ally themselves with northern Democratic Whigs on these issues. The Whig alliance began to disintegrate, and by the 1850s it had disappeared from the political scene.

Political Party Development in U.S. History

1796–1824	1828–1850s
1st Party System	**2nd Party System**
• **Federalists**	• **Democrats** (faction group of the Democratic Republicans)
• **Antifederalists** (Democratic-Republicans)	• **Whigs** (also known as the National Republicans)
North—strong Federalist area	North—typically a strong Whig area
South—strong Democratic- Republican area	South and West—typically a stronghold for the Democrats

Lesson 10-2: The Election of 1824 and John Quincy Adams

Greater involvement in politics, along with in-party fighting, fragmented the Republican party. Before the election of 1824, party leaders chose a single presidential candidate in a centralized nomination system known as the congressional caucus. In the election of 1824, however, many states allowed their citizens to vote directly for presidential candidates; instead of one candidate representing the Republicans, four Republican candidates emerged on the ballot to compete for the presidency. Personalities and sectional interests would play key roles in this election.

These candidates reflected the divisions within American society and within the crumbling Republican coalition. John Quincy Adams (the son of John Adams) was New England's choice for president. William Crawford was from Virginia and appealed to the South, and Henry Clay and Andrew Jackson appealed to the West, the former drawing support from merchants and manufacturers and the latter from more rural groups. (John Calhoun withdrew from the race in hopes of becoming vice president.) Because of the demise of the congressional caucus system, the 1824 election is considered the first modern election. It was the first election in which party leaders no longer had exclusive control over the nomination process.

Andrew Jackson won more popular and electoral votes than any other candidate, but failed to win a majority, so the election was sent to the House of Representatives. Clay, the speaker of the House, backed Adams for president and helped ensure Adams's victory. In return, Adams rewarded Clay by making him secretary of state. Jackson and his supporters saw this backroom deal-making as a political conspiracy, denouncing it as a "corrupt bargain," and the 1828 election began in earnest. Jackson worried about "a corrupt power threatening to snuff out liberty."

Adams in Office

Adams's presidency proved unproductive, largely because of an uncooperative Congress. In December 1826, the Jacksonian Democrats won control of Congress, making it extremely difficult for Adams to carry out his agenda. By 1828, Congress hadn't acted on any of his original proposals (such as new roads, canals, a national university, a naval academy, and a national observatory). Unlike Adams, who advocated a loose interpretation of the Constitution, most congressmen were strict constructionists, favoring states' rights over central power. Many thought Adams was unpleasant because he refused to engage in political maneuvering, such as trading favors and distributing patronage. Adams, in turn, failed to participate in the give and take of politics that was necessary to build a coalition for support. In his campaign bid for reelection in 1828, not only was Adams criticized for his continued references to Jackson's private life, but he also didn't actively campaign. "If my country wants my services, she must ask for them," he said.

Lesson 10-3: Jackson and the Era of the Common Man

Jackson's inauguration after the 1828 election was symbolic of a new age. He saw himself as the spokesman of the people. Andrew Jackson came to Washington in 1829, saying he intended to rule according to the will of the people and not the Washington select. His wife, Rachel, fell ill and died shortly before his inauguration. Jackson blamed her death on the personal attacks waged against him by Adams during the 1828 campaign. He stated, "May God Almighty forgive her murderers as I know she forgave them. I never can."

During the campaign, both parties sought to challenge the moral character of the candidates. Adams's supporters portrayed Jackson as having married a divorced woman whose divorce was not finalized and said that Jackson's mother had married a mulatto man. Jackson's supporters countered those arguments by attempting to portray Adams as a Sabbath breaker and said that he had used government monies to buy gambling devices.

Once in office, Jackson created a strong presence in the White House by exerting tough control over his administration and being the first president to use the **veto power** extensively. His 12 vetoes were more than the total vetoes of all the previous presidents, and he took a heavy hand with Congress and other government departments. Jackson also broke with many traditions and created new ones that continue to affect American politics.

Jackson's administration is credited with the creation of a strong executive power. In addition to Jackson, other prominent national political figures with sectional interests emerged, including Senator Daniel Webster of Massachusetts, Senator John C. Calhoun of South Carolina, and Speaker of the House Henry Clay of Kentucky.

The Kitchen Cabinet and the Spoils System

Past presidents had used the cabinet as a policy forum, selecting men of different backgrounds to represent the varied allegiances and interests of the country. Jackson, in contrast, appointed each cabinet member based on his political loyalty and his value as a political ally. Instead of using his cabinet members for advice on setting policy, Jackson turned to an informal group of friends and advisors that became known as the **Kitchen Cabinet.** This group of advisors, which didn't include the vice president, was made up of newspaper editors, the treasury department head, and the secretary of state. They offered advice on setting national and party policies.

For all government appointments, Jackson openly favored an office rotation known as the spoils system, under which the winning party removed officeholders who belonged to the opposing party and then filled the open positions with its own supporters—"to the victor belongs the spoils." Jackson reasoned that ordinary party members could easily fill government positions as well as any trained officials. During his term, Jackson placed people loyal to his party in nearly 20 percent of federal jobs. This process allowed the political party in charge to continue to solidify its base and promote its programs.

The Eaton Scandal

One of the biggest challenges facing Jackson's group of advisors was a scandal involving **Peggy Eaton.** She had grown up as a tavern keeper's daughter in the Washington area. The so-called "affair" involved the refusal of the cabinet members' wives to receive Peggy at formal socials. Peggy O'Neale Timberlake's 1829 marriage to Secretary of War John Eaton had raised eyebrows because of her previous marriage to John Timberlake, a naval officer who had recently died at sea. Rumors of John Eaton marrying Peggy included references to him marrying his mistress, who had also been the "mistress of nearly a dozen others." Vice President John Calhoun's wife, Floride, led the anti-Peggy crusade, because Eaton was considered to be a "fallen woman" and "unfit for polite society."

The fallout of this scandal was serious. It created a rift between Jackson and his vice president Calhoun. After two cabinet members (Eaton and Van Buren) resigned, Jackson asked his entire cabinet to resign, including many who were supporters of Calhoun. New members loyal to Jackson were appointed, especially men allied with Martin Van Buren, who was being groomed for the presidency in 1836. When Calhoun blocked Van Buren's nomination for minister to Great Britain, Jackson put Van Buren on the ticket in 1832 as his vice-presidential candidate. When it was revealed that Calhoun favored having Jackson censured for his 1819 invasion into Florida, Calhoun was openly rejected by Jackson.

Lesson 10-4: The Nullification Crisis

The most important problem that Jackson faced in office was the **Nullification Crisis.** Congress had raised protective tariffs steadily over the previous decade: in 1816, in 1824, and again in 1828, a year before Jackson's presidency. These tariffs protected western farming interests, New England manufacturers, and Pennsylvania miners, but they hurt farmers in the South. South Carolina felt that, if British imports continued to be taxed at a high rate, then Britain would raise its taxes on imports, preventing cotton from being sold fairly on the open market. Southern politicians grew so angry at the trade imbalance that they named the 1828 tariff the **Tariff of Abominations.** South Carolina reacted particularly strongly, flying its flags at half-mast when the 1828 bill was passed, and the state threatened to boycott New England's manufactured goods. The tariff supporters aimed to discredit Adams in his reelection bid. Because the tariff was unpopular with a large segment of society, all of the blame could be placed on the president.

Led by John C. Calhoun, a South Carolina native, the state denounced the tariff as unconstitutional, arguing that Congress could levy only tariffs that raised revenue for common purposes, not tariffs that protected regional interests. Calhoun contended that federal laws must benefit all equally in order to be constitutional and urged southern states to nullify, or void, the tariffs within their own borders.

Calhoun's justification for nullification, published in his *South Carolina Exposition and Protest* (1828), was largely derived from Jefferson's and Madison's arguments in the Virginia and Kentucky Resolutions (1798). Calhoun, as had Jefferson and Madison, argued that the states were sovereign over the central government, and the states should have the final authority to judge the constitutionality of laws affecting their regions. Calhoun saw the Constitution as a compact of states, with the states independent and sovereign even before the Constitution was approved. States had created the federal government and endowed it with strictly limited powers, so a state had the right to nullify a federal law.

Jackson came into office in 1829, after the publication of Calhoun's protest. Southern interests hoped that Jackson would modify the Tariff of Abominations, especially because Calhoun served as Jackson's vice president. Although Jackson did push through a modified, milder tariff in 1832, the changes did little to satisfy many southerners. At the Jefferson Day dinner in 1830, Jackson offered a toast, saying, "Our Federal Union, it must be preserved." Calhoun's response to that toast was his comment: "The Union—next to our liberty most dear...may we always remember that it can only be preserved by distributing equally the benefits and burdens of the Union." Now the president and vice president were in open conflict with each other and permanently split over the issue. Calhoun later resigned and returned home to South Carolina.

In November 1832, the South Carolina legislature approved Calhoun's Ordinance of Nullification, which nullified the tariffs of 1828 and 1832 and ordered state officials to stop collecting duties at South Carolina's ports. The state threatened to secede if the national government intervened to force tax collection. Jackson responded swiftly and decisively, denouncing the nullifiers and sending a token military and naval force to intimidate them.

The following March, Senator Henry Clay brokered a compromise bill that Jackson signed into law. The Tariff of 1833 provided for a gradual lowering of duties over the next decade. The second measure, the **Force Bill**, authorized the president to use the army and navy, if necessary, to force the collection of customs duties in South Carolina. South Carolina at first nullified the Force Bill, but under threat of force, reconsidered and rescinded its previous nullifications. This would be the most serious threat to the Union until South Carolina led the secession movement in December 1860.

Lesson 10-5: The Indian Removal Act

The Cherokee and Creek Indian tribes in Georgia and Alabama, the Chickasaw and Choctaw tribes in Mississippi, Alabama, and Tennessee, and the Seminole Indians in Florida had remained in the South and in control of large enclaves, often with federal protection guaranteed by previous treaties. But Jackson was determined to secure Native American lands for settlement. He favored removing all American Indians west of the Mississippi, claiming that Native American treaties were absurd and that Indians were blocking advancement. He also claimed that Native Americans were "barbarians who could never become part of American society, that they were inferior, and that removal was the humane thing to do."

After gold was discovered in Georgia, the state tried to oust the American Indians by claiming that the Cherokees weren't an Indian nation, but tenants on state property. The **Indian Removal Act**, passed in 1830, granted Jackson the funds and the authority to move Native Americans to assigned lands in the West, using as much force as necessary. U.S. officials began aggressively clearing out the Cherokee tribe from the Southwest, and Georgia took control of the formerly Cherokee territory. Jackson favored moving the Native Americans far beyond the reach of injury or oppression because "the paternal care of the general government will hereafter watch over them and protect them."

Removal of American Indians
1830–1838

In 1831 and 1832, the Supreme Court under Chief Justice John Marshall delivered rulings against Cherokee removal. In *Cherokee Nation v. Georgia* (1831) and *Worcester v. Georgia* (1832), the Court ruled that the Indian self-governing bodies were "domestic independent nations" under the authority of the U.S. government rather than under the authority of the states. Because of that status, the states had to defer to the federal government with regard to the welfare and governance of Indian affairs. This meant the Indians couldn't be forced to give up its lands by the state of Georgia. Jackson opposed the ruling and proceeded with removal, purportedly commenting in defiance, "John Marshall has made his decision; now let him enforce it."

Without the president, the Supreme Court couldn't protect the Cherokees, and the aggressive Cherokee removal continued unabated. Between 1835 and 1838, the U.S. army forced bands of Cherokees to move west on a journey known as the **Trail of Tears**. General Winfield Scott, with an army of 7,000, was sent to enforce the treaty. The Indians were rounded up and relocated to government camps in Oklahoma. Along the 1,200-mile journey, nearly 25 percent of the 16,000 migrating Cherokees died.

Lesson 10-6: Opposition to the Bank

In 1816, the **Second Bank of the United States** received a 20-year charter from Congress. In 1832, four years before the charter expired, the bank sought a recharter. Congress approved the recharter, but Jackson vetoed the bill, denouncing the bank as a privileged monopoly that was unfriendly to the interests of the West. He felt that the bank damaged the humbler members of society, claiming, "The bank...is trying to kill me, but I will kill it!"

Bank president **Nicholas Biddle** intended to use the bank to regulate the amount of credit available in the economy and to provide the nation with a sound credit system. Nevertheless, after Jackson easily won reelection in 1832, he effectively destroyed the bank by removing its federal deposits and placing the money in state banks. Jackson's critics called these "pet banks" because they seemed to be chosen solely for their allegiance to the Democratic party. In 1836, Jackson further enhanced the state banks' power by signing the Deposit Act, which increased the number of state banks serving as depositories and loosened federal control over the banking system.

Jackson's policy included distributing federal government surpluses to states, which stimulated spending and inflation. To check the inflationary spiral, Jackson issued the **specie circular,** which required gold and silver for land purchases. Before the panic of 1837, English bankers called in loans to states and investors, which depleted gold supplies, and prevented banks from making payments, which forced failures. Many of the policies Jackson used to destroy the bank created major economic problems.

Lesson 10-7: Martin Van "Ruin" and Economic Crisis

Martin Van Buren, Jackson's handpicked successor, won the 1836 election largely because of Jackson's support. Unable to escape from the shadow of his charismatic predecessor, Van Buren ruled mostly in obscurity, simply continuing the Jacksonian tradition. He would also be blamed for the economic crisis of the impending panic and would earn the nickname of Martin Van "Ruin."

The Panic of 1837

Van Buren assumed office in the middle of a severe economic depression. During 1835 and 1836, Andrew Jackson's policy of removing federal deposits from the Second Bank of the United States and placing them in state banks promoted an economy of speculative buying, risky lending, and unregulated banking practices. Prices increased and land sales multiplied rapidly from 1835 to 1837. Attempting to stabilize the currency in 1836, Jackson issued the specie circular, which required that land payments be made in gold and silver rather than in paper money or with credit. This move forced prices to drop and left speculators with enormous debts. Many banks failed, and the economy fell into a depression called the panic of 1837.

The depression that had begun in Great Britain spread to the United States and lasted until 1843. The overheated economy, the high prices, the abundant credit, and the buying frenzy ended when the bubble burst into what would be the most severe depression until the 1870s. By 1843, prices had fallen by 50 percent, investment had declined by 25 percent, canal construction had declined by 90 percent, unemployment averaged 10 to 20 percent, and wages had fallen 30 to 50 percent.

Van Buren spent his time in office trying to solve the nation's economic woes. He called for the creation of an Independent Treasury that would hold public funds in reserve and prevent excessive lending by state banks, thereby guarding against inflation. Van Buren and his Democratic supporters hailed the Independent Treasury Bill, signed in 1840, as a second Declaration of Independence, using it as a rallying cry to battle against the entire banking system. In Louisiana and Arkansas, Democrats succeeded in prohibiting banks altogether.

By 1840, the Democrats had firmly established themselves as an anti-bank party. Van Buren's failure to effectively deal with the depression gave the Whigs an opportunity to take over the White House. Van Buren also cut government spending, but the Whigs demanded a protective tariff and continuation of state improvement projects.

In the election of 1840, the Democrats were blamed for the depression, opening the way for the Whigs to nominate William Henry Harrison. He was a hero from the Battle of Tippecanoe in 1812, but Harrison lacked executive ability and had virtually no opinions or views on national issues. Whigs narrowly won the election in the popular vote, but took 80 percent of the electoral college votes. At 78 percent, voter turnout was high and would remain so until the Civil War.

Harrison died of pneumonia one month into his term in office, and his vice president, John Tyler, took over. As a Whig, Tyler betrayed his party and blocked its reforms. But by now, the two-party system was firmly in place, and it continued to deepen sectional differences.

Review Exam

Multiple Choice

1. From 1820 to 1860 politics in the United States focused primarily on the role of the federal government in regulating the economy and on:

   a) slavery; and slave and free states

   b) the role of the president setting an agenda for his term in office

   c) using the elastic clause for new legislation

   d) internal improvements

2. One of the major differences between the Jacksonian Democrats and the National Republicans was that the Democrats:

   a) supported the Bank of the United States

   b) overwhelmingly supported the tariff

   c) did not favor the federal government becoming involved with the economy

   d) typically ignored the interests of the common man

3. John Quincy Adams's one term in office was characterized by:
   a) opposition mounting from the newly formed Democratic party
   b) Jackson claiming that a "corrupt bargain" had been struck by the House, declaring Adams the winner in the 1824 election
   c) Congress not acting on any of the president's proposals for legislation
   d) all of the answers on the list

4. The outcome of the presidential election in 1824 focused on all of the following *EXCEPT*:
   a) Andrew Jackson failing to have the majority of the electoral college votes needed to win the election
   b) candidates from two parties appearing on the ballot
   c) Clay agreeing to support Adams for the presidency in return for being appointed secretary of state
   d) the sectional interests of New England, the South, and the West became key factors in the election

5. Andrew Jackson is best known as ushering in the "era of the common man" as evidenced by:
   a) his policies as a National Republican
   b) his support of the merchants and business leaders
   c) his support of farmers in the South and West
   d) his support of his vice president, John Calhoun

6. The Nullification Crisis that resulted from the Tariff of 1828 was significant because:
   a) South Carolina argued that a state could nullify the tariff within its state borders
   b) it would give states authority over the federal government
   c) it brought to light the argument of states' rights in the 10th Amendment
   d) all of the answers on the list

7. The Indian Removal Act granted Jackson the authority to:
   a) move Native Americans from their homeland to parts out West
   b) purchase disputed territory from American Indians in Georgia and Florida

c) temporarily relocate certain Native Americans from their homeland for a period of up to five years

d) fully comply with the recent ruling from the Supreme Court that ruled in favor of American Indians not being forced from their homelands in Georgia

8. In the court cases of *Cherokee Nation v. Georgia* and *Worcester v. Georgia* the Supreme Court ruled that:
   a) the Indian self-governing bodies were independent nations
   b) the governing bodies of the Indians were under the authority of the state government instead of the federal government
   c) the states had to defer to the federal government with its governance of Indian affairs
   d) choices *a* and *c* only

9. As a result of the election of 1840:
   a) the Democrats lost their influence as a major political party
   b) the Whigs capitalized on the mistakes of the Democrats in winning the election
   c) low voter turnout began to occur in presidential elections
   d) personal popularity was no longer a major factor in the outcome of an election

10. Speaker of the House Henry Clay (Kentucky), Senator (and former vice president) John C. Calhoun (South Carolina), Senator Daniel Webster (Massachusetts), and Andrew Jackson (Tennessee) were important political figures who:
    a) represented strong sectional interests
    b) were strong political allies
    c) were all members of the Democratic party
    d) represented weakening sectional interests

11. During its process to secure a recharter, the Second Bank of the United States was:
    a) granted a last-minute reprieve
    b) denied its renewal by Congress
    c) denounced by Jackson as a "privileged monopoly" favoring the interests of the business elite
    d) denounced by the state banks for having too much authority

Matching

a. Kitchen Cabinet

b. Democratic party

c. Rachel Jackson

d. National Republicans

e. veto power

f. John C. Calhoun

g. Whig

h. House of Representatives

i. Floride Calhoun

j. Nicholas Biddle

k. Martin Van Buren

l. Trail of Tears

m. pet banks

n. Tariff of Abominations

o. William Henry Harrison

p. Force Bill

q. South Carolina Exposition and Protest

r. spoils system

s. Panic of 1837

t. specie circular

u. Peggy Eaton

_____12. the practice of the winning party filling government jobs with its supporters (making appointments based on political loyalty)

_____13. she caused a scandal in Jackson's cabinet because of her reputation and marriage to John Eaton

_____14. Jackson's vice president who left the Democratic party and helped form the Whig party (to oppose Jackson and his policies)

_____15. the 1824 election was the beginning of this political party; they campaigned to elect their first president in 1828

_____16. the forced relocation of the Cherokees from their land in Georgia to government camps in the Oklahoma region

_____17. decided the final outcome of the election of 1824 by declaring John Quincy Adams the winner

_____18. the political party that formed out of the remnants of the old Democratic-Republican after the 1824 election

_____19. what the president uses to override a measure and prevent it from becoming a law

_____20. Andrew Jackson's wife, whose death in 1829 he blamed on the attacks from his political opponents during the 1828 campaign

_____21. the political party that was formed out of opponents of Andrew Jackson and his Democratic party

_____22. this authorized the president to use the army and navy, if necessary, to collect duties in South Carolina

_____23. the vice president's wife who fueled the debate in the "Peggy Eaton affair" by refusing to include her in social functions

_____24. the president of the Second Bank of the United States who attempted to use the bank to regulate the amount of credit available (and who was opposed by Jackson)

_____25. the economic crisis that was brought on in part by Jackson's financial policies

_____26. Jackson's successor in 1836 who received the blame for the panic in 1837 and who lost reelection in 1840

_____27. these institutions were state banks chosen by Jackson for the deposit of federal monies

_____28. an old war hero from the War of 1812 at the Battle of Tippecanoe who was nominated by the Whigs in 1840

_____29. the nickname in South Carolina associated with the unpopular Tariff of 1828

_____30. a money policy requiring gold and silver for land purchases and resulted in paper money being devalued

_____31. argued that because the states were sovereign over the central government that the states would have the final authority in laws affecting the states

_____32. a group of informal advisors to president Andrew Jackson

Short Response

33. How did Jackson and his policies help redefine the office of the president?

34. How did the emergence of the Democrat and Whig parties reflect the growing sectional interests in the country?

35. How was the period from 1824 to the early 1840s marked by *corruption, bargains, and spoils*?

Answers begin on page 259.

The Era of Reform

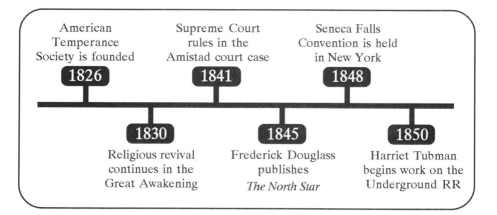

American Temperance Society is founded
1826

Supreme Court rules in the Amistad court case
1841

Seneca Falls Convention is held in New York
1848

1830
Religious revival continues in the Great Awakening

1845
Frederick Douglass publishes *The North Star*

1850
Harriet Tubman begins work on the Underground RR

Trends and Themes of the Era

- Women were extremely active in reform movement causes involving women's rights and abolitionism.
- Reform movements of this period had measured success but laid important foundations for later reforms.
- Reform measures reflected the growing sectionalism in the country.
- Reform measures included moral and social reforms.

Goals, accomplishments, and setbacks! To protest being shut out from the political process, many of the "forgotten" groups and their sympathizers organized reform movements to heighten public awareness and to influence social and political policy. Many reformers believed they were doing God's work, and the Second Great Awakening encouraged them in their missions. Reformers in this period were optimistic about creating lasting change in society, and many felt it was truly an age of progress. New England and Midwestern areas were most likely to be reformist; Southerners generally opposed attempts at social reform. Most reformers operated with a sense of urgency, and many of them saw their reforms played out on the national stage. As regional interests began to be stressed, sectionalism came to dominate economic, political, and social arenas. In 1847, Daniel Webster commented in a speech at the opening of a Northern Railroad section that, "It is an extraordinary era in which we live...it is altogether new...the progress of the age has almost outstripped human belief." Yet as sectionalism became more entrenched in the antebellum period and the issue of slavery moved to the forefront, many reform attempts had limited success and ended up taking a backseat to the slavery issue and the "impending crisis" facing the country by late 1860.

Lesson 11-1: The Abolitionist Movement

Perhaps the most prominent and controversial reform movement of the period was **abolitionism**, the antislavery movement. Although abolitionism had attracted many followers in the revolutionary period, the movement lagged during the early 1800s. But by the 1830s, the spirit of abolitionism was surging again, especially in the Northeast.

In 1831, **William Lloyd Garrison** launched an abolitionist newspaper called *The Liberator*, earning himself a reputation as the most radical white abolitionist. Past abolitionists had suggested blacks be shipped back to Africa, but Garrison worked with prominent black abolitionists, including Frederick Douglass, to demand equal civil rights for blacks. Garrison's battle cry was immediate emancipation, but he recognized that it would take years to persuade enough Americans to oppose slavery. To spread the abolition fervor, he founded the **American Anti-Slavery Society** in 1833, vowing to end the immoral practice of the "peculiar institution" of slavery in the United States. By 1840, these abolitionist organizations had more than 1,500 local chapters and were distributing literature throughout the North. Garrison's newspaper spoke for the most extreme abolitionists.

Frederick Douglass soon became outspoken in his opposition to slavery. His 1845 autobiography (*The Narrative of the Life of Frederick Douglass*) and his speeches were compelling firsthand accounts of slavery. He also began publishing an antislavery paper called *The North Star* in Rochester, New York, in 1847. Douglass decided that political reforms should be used to end slavery. He realized that blacks would have to pay a heavy price to win their freedom, and that they "must do this by labor, by suffering, by sacrifice, and if needs be, by our lives and the lives of others."

The abolition movement began appealing to a wide audience. **Sarah and Angelina Grimke**, sisters from South Carolina who had moved north to Philadelphia, were the first women in the United States to publicly argue for the abolition of slavery. They traveled throughout the North and lectured extensively about their first hand experiences with slavery on their family plantation. Although they were often harshly criticized for their abolitionist activity, they insisted on the importance of equality for both women and blacks. The attacks continued, in large part because they were women seeking to operate in the public sphere.

The controversy over slavery continued when **Cinque** and 52 other slaves commandeered the slave ship *Amistad* off the coast of Cuba in 1839. The ship eventually ended up off Long Island. President Van Buren wanted Cinque and the slaves returned to Spain. The judge in the original case announced his decision in January 1840 and ruled that, because the *Amistad* captives were born free and kidnapped in violation of international law, they should be allowed to return to Africa. This ruling was appealed to the Supreme Court, where former president John Quincy Adams argued for the slaves by quoting the Declaration of Independence: "The moment you come to the Declaration of Independence, that every man has a right to life and liberty, an inalienable right, this case is decided. I ask nothing more in behalf of these unfortunate men than this Declaration." Once again, the court ruled in favor of the kidnapped slaves—they were free. This Supreme Court case became the most important decision about slavery until the Dred Scott ruling in 1857.

Harriet Tubman gained her freedom in 1849 when she escaped to Philadelphia and began working as a domestic servant in order to save money and to make plans to rescue several family members. In 1850, she began the first of 19 trips back into the South to guide more than 300 slaves to freedom in the North and Canada. This former slave became a conductor on the secret, shifting routes of the **Underground Railroad.** Outraged slaveowners in Maryland even placed a $40,000 bounty for her capture. Another significant purpose of the Underground Railroad was that it provided an opportunity for abolitionists, including Quakers such as Levi and Catharine Coffin, to play an active role in openly resisting slavery by providing assistance to escaped slaves as they traveled from one destination to another in their pursuit of freedom. Tubman was nicknamed "the Moses of her people" for her daring exploits, and during the Civil War she aided the Union Army by working as a guide, spy, nurse, and cook.

Opposed to abolitionism, Southern congressmen succeeded in pushing the **gag rule** through Congress in 1836. The rule tabled all abolitionist petitions in Congress, serving as a preemptive strike against all antislavery discussions. The gag rule wasn't repealed until 1844, when it came under increased pressure from Northern abolitionists and others concerned about restricting the right to petition granted by the Constitution.

The abolition movement succeeded in bringing slavery to the forefront of public awareness. Northerners attacked slavery on moral and social grounds, as Southerners continued to grow more vocal in defending the institution of slavery. On moral and legal grounds, slavery would become the predominant issue in the country in the 1850s.

Lesson 11-2: Women's Issues

The position of American women in the early 1800s was legally and socially inferior to that of men. Women couldn't vote, and if they were married, they couldn't own property or retain their own earnings. The reform movements of the 1830s, specifically abolition and temperance, served as a catalyst for women's involvement in the public arena. Women reformers soon began to speak out not just for temperance and abolition, but also for women's rights. Some women even spoke to mixed audiences of men and women, but they were often rebuffed for their departure from accepted women's roles.

Activists such as the Grimke sisters, **Elizabeth Cady Stanton**, **Susan B. Anthony**, and **Lucretia Mott** argued that men and women were created equal and should be treated equally under the law. These advocates worked with abolitionist William Lloyd Garrison, also an ardent feminist, merging the powers of the abolitionist and the women's rights movements. Other advocates of both movements included **Sojourner Truth**, a former slave, outspoken abolitionist speaker, and advocate of women's rights, who gave her famous speech, "Ain't I a Woman?" in 1850, and Frederick Douglass, a former slave, speaker, and author of *The North Star*.

In 1848, Mott and Stanton organized a women's rights convention in Seneca Falls, New York. The Seneca Falls Convention issued a **Declaration of Sentiments**, modeled on the Declaration of Independence, stating that all men and women were created equal. The activists argued that women should be given the right to vote and should be freed from unjust laws that gave their husbands control of their property, persons, and children.

The declaration and other reformist strategies, however, affected little change. Though some states passed Married Women's Property Acts to allow married women to retain their property, women would have to wait until the 19th Amendment gave them the right to vote in 1920.

The "Cult of Domesticity" had long promoted the doctrine of separate spheres of influence for men and women. By the early nineteenth century, the "cult of true womanhood" had taken hold in the United States. Its message was widely portrayed through novels, religious writings, and advice books written by and for middle-class women. It created a highly restrictive series of roles for women. The attributes of "true womanhood," by which a woman judged herself and was judged by her husband, her neighbors, and her society could be divided into four simple virtues: piety, purity, submissiveness, and domesticity. By having these virtues, a woman was promised happiness and power. She must be confined to the home, devoted to husband and children, and shun productive labor and involvement in politics. But even while the women's magazines and related literature encouraged this ideal of the perfect woman, forces were at work to impel women to change and to play a more active role in society. The movements for social reform, westward migration, missionary activity, utopian communities, and the growth of industrialism beckoned responses from women. This differed greatly from the expectations of society. When women participated actively in reform movements, however, they were openly challenging the belief in separate spheres of influence for men (the public realm) and women (the realm of home and family).

Lesson 11-3: American Literature

Transcendentalism emerged during the 1830s, arguing that knowledge didn't come exclusively through the intellect but also through the senses, intuition, and sudden insight. It promoted the belief that concepts such as God, freedom, and absolute truth were inborn and could be accessed through inner experience and emotional openness.

The authors Ralph Waldo Emerson and Henry David Thoreau were prominent transcendentalists. Their works emphasized spontaneous, vivid expression of emotion rather than logic and analysis. In his essays "Nature" and "Self-Reliance," Ralph Waldo Emerson claimed that all people were capable of seeing the truth if they relied on their inner selves and trusted their hearts. In *Walden*, Henry David Thoreau recounted his two years in a cabin in the woods, away from civilization and materialism. He advocated living simply, according to one's conscience rather than society's repressive codes. One of Thoreau's most important works, his essay "**Civil Disobedience**" (1849), was inspired by his conscientious refusal to pay a poll tax that supported the Mexican War. After an overnight stay in prison to protest paying a tax that he felt also represented an effort to extend slavery, Thoreau published his thoughts on civil disobedience as a means for an individual to protest unjust government actions. Thoreau's work would later have a wide-ranging impact on the British Labour movement, the passive resistance independence movement led by Mahatma Gandhi in India, and the nonviolent Civil Rights movement led by Martin Luther King, Jr., in the United States.

Margaret Fuller was also a member of the transcendentalist group. Her major work, *Woman in the Nineteenth Century* (published in 1845) made a dramatic impact on the women's rights movement by advocating equal status for women. She also promoted education for women and women's colleges. American literature continued to develop through works from other major authors of the period. Edgar Allan Poe, a poet, short-story writer, and critic, became one of the most important original writers in American literature in the nineteenth century. Nathaniel Hawthorne set out to explore moral and spiritual conflicts in his novel *The Scarlet Letter,* which was set in a Puritan community. Hawthorne wrote about the moral dilemmas of personal responsibility, and the overwhelming emotions of guilt, anger, loyalty, and revenge. In *Moby Dick*, Herman Melville described the classic struggle of Captain Ahab's obsessive voyage to find and destroy the great white whale that had ripped off his leg. The sea story novel was a symbolic look at the nature of good and evil, and of man and his fate.

Lesson 11-4: Education

The nineteenth-century movement to reform public schools began in rural areas, where one-room schoolhouses provided only minimal education. School reformers hoped to improve education so that children would become responsible citizens who shared common cultural values. Extending the right to vote to all free males no doubt helped galvanize the movement, because politicians began fearing the effects of an illiterate, ill-educated electorate.

In 1837, **Horace Mann** of Massachusetts became secretary of that state's board of education. He reformed the school system by increasing state spending on schools, lengthening the school year, dividing the students into grades, instilling strict discipline, using standardized textbooks, and introducing professional teacher training. Mann stated that education was "the great equalizer of the conditions of men" and that it promoted the acquisition of basic knowledge and skills necessary for success. Noah Webster's dictionary, along with William McGuffey's *Reader* series, helped teach reading, writing, and morals.

Education also promoted American values of hard work, punctuality, and sobriety. Much of the North reformed its schools along the lines dictated by Horace Mann, and free public schools spread throughout the region. The South, however, made little progress in public education, partly because of its low population density and a general indifference toward progressive reforms. Slaves weren't allowed to learn to read or write, and southern women were generally perceived as not needing an education.

In other areas of education, Thomas Hopkins Gallaudet promoted deaf education by cofounding the first American school for the deaf. While Gallaudet was in France, he became interested in educating the deaf and learned sign language. Back in America, Gallaudet's new school trained most of the country's teachers of the deaf, and Gallaudet himself raised enormous amounts of money for the disabled. In Massachusetts, Samuel Gridley Howe became director of the state school for the blind and received much attention for teaching braille. Although the disability civil rights movement didn't reach full swing until the late twentieth century, reformers in the nineteenth century had begun to gain some ground.

Lesson 11-5: Crime and Criminals

Beginning in the 1820s, social activists pressed for prison reform. These reformers argued that instead of simply confining criminals, prisons should provide them with instruction, order, and discipline so that they would be rehabilitated rather than just punished. Contending that crime was largely the result of childhood neglect and trauma, prison reformers hoped that such instruction would counteract the effects of a poor upbringing and effectively purge criminals of their violent and immoral tendencies. The reformers believed that criminals could be morally redeemed.

Additional rehabilitative efforts were directed at the poor and the insane. To combat poverty, almshouses were built for poor invalids. Workhouses were built for the able-bodied poor in the hopes that a regimented environment would turn them into productive citizens.

Until the early 1840s, the insane were also confined in these kinds of poorhouses or in prisons, living in miserable conditions that often exacerbated their illnesses. In 1843, **Dorothea Dix**, a Massachusetts schoolteacher, described to the state legislature the conditions of the insane in prison and encouraged the construction of insane asylums to better treat the mentally ill. In the following years, asylums opened throughout the United States.

Lesson 11-6: Temperance

Alcohol production and consumption in the United States rose markedly in the early 1800s. The **temperance movement** emerged as a backlash against the rising popularity of liquor. Founded in 1826, the American Temperance Society advocated total abstinence from alcohol. Many advocates considered drinking immoral or sinful and thought that it caused poverty or mental instability. Others saw it as a male indulgence that harmed women and children, who often suffered abuse at drunkards' hands.

During the 1830s, an increasing number of workingmen joined the movement, concerned about alcohol's effects on job performance. By 1835, about 5,000 temperance societies were affiliated with the American Temperance Society. Largely because of this association's impact, liquor consumption began to decrease in the late 1830s and early 1840s, and many states passed restrictions or bans on the sale of alcohol.

It would take a lot of effort to change old forms of social behavior. The work that had been accomplished by the 1850s paved the way for the temperance movement to continue in the late 1800s and early 1900s, ultimately ending with the adoption of the 18th Amendment in 1919.

Lesson 11-7: A Religious Revival in America

About 70 years after the First Great Awakening, the **Second Great Awakening** emerged during the early 1800s, partly as a backlash against the spread of rationalism, and partly in response to calls for an organized religion more accessible to the common man. As in the First Great Awakening, revivalist ministers urged followers to reach a personal, emotional understanding of God. Women, blacks, and young men participated in the revival meetings.

The revivals began in Connecticut in 1790. Unlike the revivals during the First Great Awakening, which were emotionally raucous and neared hysteria, these revivals were often calm and quiet, as gatherers respectfully observed believers in prayer. In New England, the revivals spawned a movement to educate and reform America. Social activists with renewed religious spirit founded all sorts of evangelical and reform groups: the American Bible Society (1816), the Society for the Promotion of Temperance, abolition groups, and groups urging educational reform and women's rights. Moral issues such as drunkenness, idleness, breaking the Sabbath, and slavery were often topics of sermons at revival meetings.

Religious fervor quickly spread to the West, where revivals more closely resembled the earlier, more animated events. In Kentucky and Tennessee, camp meetings were rowdy gatherings filled with dancing, singing, and shouting. The Methodists, who emphasized that religion was a matter of the heart rather than an issue of logic, came to dominate frontier revivals. By 1845, Methodists and Baptists were among the fastest-growing denominations of Protestantism in the United States.

The Second Great Awakening gathered momentum and made big strides toward converting a secularized American public. After his conversion in 1821, Charles Finney, a former lawyer, became the most sought-after preacher. His message of salvation, repentance, and belief in Christ appealed to many in his audiences. The singing of hymns and modern music, along with prayers and sermons, was the focus of long revival meetings in towns and villages across the country. The area of New York from Lake Ontario to the Adirondack Mountains was one of the major focal points of the revival movement. In fact, it had been the scene of so many religious revivals in the past that it was known as the "Burned-Over District."

Lesson 11-8: Utopian Communities

The most extreme reform movement in the United States during the first half of the 1800s was the utopian movement, founded on the belief that humans could live perfectly in small experimental societies. Though utopian communities varied in their philosophies, most were designed and founded by intellectuals proposing alternatives to the competitive market economy. Utopian communities aimed to perfect social relation-ships, to reform the institutions of marriage and private property, and to balance political, occupational, and religious influences. They attempted to pursue human perfection while following separatist religious practices.

The Church of Jesus Christ of Latter-Day Saints, also known as **Mormonism**, was the most controversial challenge to traditional religion. Its founder, **Joseph Smith**, claimed that God and Jesus Christ appeared to him and directed him to a buried book of revelation in 1830. The Book of Mormon, similar in form and style to the Bible, tells of the descendents of a sixth century B.C. prophet whose family founded a civilization in South America.

Violent religious persecution forced the Mormons to move steadily westward in search of land upon which to establish a perfect spiritual community. The Mormons considered themselves a reformed Christian movement, but found that they were rejected by many Christians as an illegitimate religion. After Smith's murder in Illinois, a new leader, **Brigham Young**, led the Mormons to Utah to the Great Salt Lake Basin in 1847 (present-day Provo and Salt Lake City), where they prospered.

Most utopian communities didn't last beyond the early 1850s, but the **Oneida community** in New York survived from 1848 to 1881. Its leader, John Humphrey Noyes, believed that the Second Coming had already occurred and promoted "free love," denouncing traditional marriages in favor of a practice called complex marriage. The community stressed two basic values: self-perfection and communalism. They translated their values into everyday life through shared property and work benefiting the community at large.

English Quakers in the United States established the first **Shaker community** under the leadership of Mother Ann Lee in 1774. She believed that she was the female incarnation of Christ, and her new religion was based on sexual equality. The group believed in universal salvation and practiced celibacy while living apart from the rest of the world. Followers were dubbed "Shakers" because of their movements in the ritualized dances at their meetings. They promoted a simple lifestyle and had minimal contact with the outside world while awaiting the Second Coming of Christ. By the late 1840s, 6,000 Shakers lived in more than a dozen northern communities.

Other utopian groups sprang up around the country during this time. George Ripley founded **Brook Farm** near Boston in 1841, an economic community that became famous with its connection to the transcendentalist movement. A Welsh social reformer, Robert Owen, founded **New Harmony** in 1814 in Indiana and became a village of cooperation that ultimately disbanded because of disharmony. Nearly 100 such communities with about 100,000 members were established in the United States between 1820 and 1860.

Review Exam

Multiple Choice

1. Abolitionism gained momentum during the reform era because of:
   a) William Lloyd Garrison's work on his abolitionist newspaper *The Liberator*

b) Frederick Douglass and his work as abolitionist with his newspaper, *The North Star*, and his speeches speaking out against the horrors of slavery

c) abolitionists such as the Grimke sisters who spoke out against the cruelty of slavery

d) all of the answers on the list

2. The Seneca Falls Convention in upstate New York in 1848 was significant for its role in the women's rights movement because:

a) it denounced the abolitionist movement

b) women began to speak out not only for equality but also the right to vote

c) women did not see the need for the right to vote

d) they succeeded in securing a motion for the creation of a constitutional amendment giving women the right to vote

3. The "cult of domesticity" was significant for all of the following reasons *EXCEPT*:

a) it promoted the doctrine of separate spheres for men and women

b) it promoted the attributes of "true womanhood" by stressing the virtues of piety, purity, submissiveness, and domesticity

c) it created several new roles for women in society

d) being confined to the home to be a good wife and mother

4. The temperance movement attempted to focus on the need for:

a) gradual abolition of alcohol

b) total abstinence from alcohol

c) temporary bans on the sale of alcohol

d) responsible drinking habits

5. The importance of the Supreme Court case involving the *Amistad* in 1840 was:

a) that it became the most important court case involving the issue of slavery until the Dred Scott case in 1857

b) the ruling was in favor of Cinque, the kidnapped African

c) former president John Quincy Adams argued the case before the Supreme Court, stressing every man has a right to life and liberty

d) all of the answers on the list

6. All of the following are true about the Declaration of Sentiments authored by Lucretia Mott and Susan B. Anthony *EXCEPT*:

   a) it was modeled after the Declaration of Independence

   b) it stated that all men and women were created equal

   c) women should not be allowed to own property

   d) women should be given the right to vote

7. Transcendentalism was a literary movement characterized by:

   a) knowledge that came through the intellect and insight that came through the senses, intuition, and sudden insight

   b) the reliance on only absolute truth

   c) logic and analysis

   d) the denial of emotion

8. This group proved to be one of the most active groups in promoting reform during the Reform Era:

   a) business leaders from the North and West

   b) women from the North

   c) plantation owners and political leaders in the South

   d) political leaders in the North

9. Education reform was important, as evidenced by Horace Mann's statement of "education being the great equalizer of the conditions of men" and by:

   a) McGuffey's *Reader* being used to teach reading, writing, and morals

   b) education being accessible for all children

   c) education being made available only to boys

   d) education being expanded to include children of slaves

10. As a result of the Second Great Awakening:

    a) women, blacks, and young men responded to the message in large numbers

    b) revivals that included hymns, prayers, and sermons swept across large segments of the country

    c) several denominations, including Methodists and Baptists, grew in large numbers

    d) all of the choices on the list

11. Characteristics of utopian communities often included:
   a) alternative lifestyles of simple living
   b) the pursuit of human perfection
   c) denial of separatist religious practices
   d) choices *a* and *b* only

Matching

a. gag rule	j. Herman Melville
b. "Civil Disobedience"	k. Horace Mann
c. Charles Finney	l. peculiar institution
d. "Self-Reliance"	m. Edgar Allan Poe
e. Dorthea Dix	n. American Anti-Slavery Society
f. Margaret Fuller	o. Joseph Smith
g. Quakers	p. Nathaniel Hawthorne
h. John Humphrey Noyes	q. Shakers
i. Harriet Tubman	r. Brigham Young

_____ 12. an advocate for education reform that included spending more money on education, focusing on curriculum, using strict discipline, and training teachers

_____ 13. a former slave who became the conductor along the secret routes of the Underground Railroad and helped rescue 300 slaves by bringing them north to freedom

_____ 14. she promoted a focus on mental health by encouraging the building of asylums to treat the mentally ill

_____ 15. the religious group that helped provide safe houses along the route of the Underground Railroad

_____ 16. Thoreau's most important work, in which he wrote about obeying his conscience in refusing to pay taxes that supported the Mexican War

_____ 17. the author of *Moby Dick* who described the classic struggle between the forces of good and evil

_____ 18. Emerson's famous work in which he claimed that people should rely on their inner selves and trust their hearts rather than relying on logic and analysis

____19. the measure in Congress in 1836 that tabled all abolitionist petitions, effectively shutting down any discussion of slavery in Congress

____20. an outspoken advocate for equal status for women and men

____21. he led the Mormons to Utah and helped establish a thriving community

____22. he was the leader of the Oneida community from 1848 to 1881

____23. founded by William Lloyd Garrison to combat the immoral practice of slavery

____24. an American author who sought to explore moral and spiritual conflicts in his writings

____25. Southerners' reference to the "uniqueness" of slavery in the South (they believed that slavery was actually beneficial for the blacks)

____26. a popular revival preacher with his message of repentance and salvation during the second Great Awakening

____27. the founder of the Mormon religion who claimed that God appeared to him and directed him to a book of revelation

____28. a famous author and creator of the American short story

____29. a utopian community led by Mother Ann Lee and believed in universal salvation and celibacy

Short Response

30. To what extent did the reform movement in this period experience *goals, accomplishments, and setbacks* success? What were the limits to reform in the antebellum period?

31. What were the political characteristics of abolitionism?

32. What influences drew women into the reform movement?

33. To what extent did the reform movement of this period lay the foundation for future reforms?

Answers begin on page 261.

Manifest Destiny

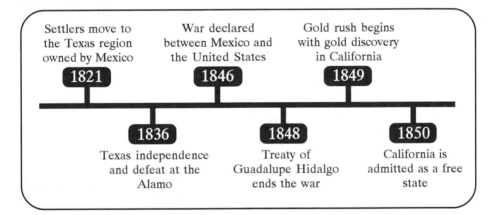

Settlers move to the Texas region owned by Mexico
1821

War declared between Mexico and the United States
1846

Gold rush begins with gold discovery in California
1849

1836
Texas independence and defeat at the Alamo

1848
Treaty of Guadalupe Hidalgo ends the war

1850
California is admitted as a free state

Trends and Themes of the Era

❯ Economic and demographic challenges would encourage westward movement.

❯ Manifest destiny promoted the belief that it was the United States's fate to extend from coast to coast.

❯ Annexation of new territories would heighten the debate over expanding slavery.

❯ Brief compromises relieved tensions from time to time, but no compromise would be able to resolve the fundamental differences between the North and South.

❯ Political parties developed platforms and supported candidates in response to the growing sectional concerns of expansion and slavery.

Destiny, riches, and expansion! In the mid-1800s, Americans spread westward across the Mississippi River. As settlers migrated toward the Pacific Coast in their overloaded wagons, the West became the fastest-growing area of the country. This expansion helped to not only fuel economic and territorial growth, but regional passions sparked intense sectional debate as the nation considered the extension of slavery into the new territories. As Americans moved west in pursuit of land and adventure, new technological advances and expanded trade made expansion easier. Despite fierce resistance from Native Americans, Mexicans, and the British, Americans eventually claimed the entire region west of the Mississippi. The West became the focal point of the country, with the battle cry of Manifest Destiny. This movement didn't come without a cost, however. The United States's expansion into the West reopened a controversy that had been temporarily settled by the 1820 Missouri Compromise: the balance of slave-holding versus free lands. Settlers, Native Americans, Mexicans, politicians, and even the Union's integrity were all affected to some extent in this "era of American greatness."

Lesson 12-1: Settling the West

Fueling the expansion westward was the popular belief that it was America's **Manifest Destiny** to expand through Texas, and toward the Pacific coast. In 1839, **John L. O'Sullivan**, a New York journalist, wrote that America "is destined to be the great nation of futurity...the far-reaching, the boundless future will be an era of American greatness." During the election of 1844, James K. Polk's Democratic party platform promoted the annexation of Texas and the claim for all of Oregon, and the Whigs campaigned as anti-expansionists.

After Polk's narrow victory, O'Sullivan continued to tap into the expansionist mood spreading across the country in 1845, by writing about "our Manifest Destiny is to overspread and to possess the whole of our continent which Providence has given us for the development of the great experiment of liberty." This notion of Manifest Destiny appealed to America's nationalist spirit, which had been growing since the War of 1812, and echoed Protestant beliefs that America was a "called nation" chosen by God as a haven from which Protestants could spread their faith. Manifest Destiny supporters believed that free development allowed democracy to grow, and that more land was needed for the booming population.

However, Manifest Destiny was not without its critics. As America continued to expand across the Mississippi River into Texas and the

Southwest (and into the territories of California and Oregon) Native Americans and Mexicans were forced to submit to new authorities amid strained political tensions and heightened sectionalist interests.

Lesson 12-2: Texas and the Alamo

After Mexico gained its independence from Spain in 1821, the country lured people to Texas for settlement and economic gain. **Stephen F. Austin** brought 300 families into the region and established a colony along the Brazos River. During the decade of the 1820s, Americans streamed into the Mexican territory of Texas, often receiving land grants from the Mexican government. Mexico gave these grants to promote trade and development.

When people settled in the Texas region, Mexico placed only three restrictions on them:

1. They were to adopt the Catholic religion.

2. They must become residents of Mexico.

3. They weren't allowed to have slaves.

By 1830, more than 30,000 Americans and 5,000 blacks had settled in the region, compared with only 4,000 Mexicans. The settlement rules were all but ignored. The Mexican government was alarmed about the growth and potential problems this situation presented, as settlers largely ignored Mexico's restrictions. More than 90 percent of the settlers were from the South, and they were looking for fresh land on which to grow cotton. As settlers continued to move into the area and bring slaves with them, they simply called them lifelong indentured servants.

In 1833, Stephen Austin went to Mexico City to present a list of grievances to the Mexican government. When he left Mexico City, he was arrested and thrown in jail for a short time for promoting Texan independence from Mexico. The following year, Santa Ana proclaimed himself dictator of Mexico and dissolved the Mexican congress. These actions threatened settlers in the Texas region. Rebel Texan leaders, most of them American, declared their independence from the Mexican dictatorship on March 2, 1836, and created a written constitution.

After the Texan army seized Goliad and San Antonio, skirmishes between the Texan and Mexican troops continued. Mexico retaliated with an attack on the Spanish mission at the **Alamo**, in which 186 Americans were killed (including Davy Crockett, Jim Bowie, and William Travis).

Sam Houston, commander of the Texan troops, met Santa Ana at the San Jacinto River in April with the battle cry of "Remember the Alamo!" The Texans defeated nearly half of Santa Ana's army in fifteen minutes: While Santa Ana's army was resting, Houston's troops made a surprise attack. A treaty was signed on May 14, 1836. declaring Texan independence and creating the Lone Star Republic, but the Mexican government refused to officially acknowledge the new country's independence. Houston was elected the first president of the new Lone Star Republic.

The Texas Revolution, 1835–1836

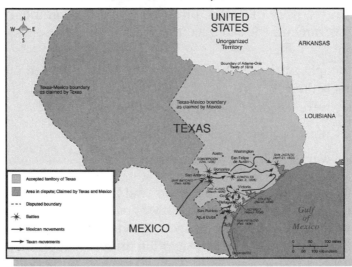

Because most Texan settlers were American, the question of Texas's potential statehood immediately arose. John Tyler, who became president in 1841 after William Henry Harrison died in office, broke with the Whig party and favored annexing Texas and admitting it to the Union. Northerners opposed annexing Texas because it might spread slavery. In 1844, Democrat James K. Polk won the presidential election with a slogan of expansion: "Re-annex Texas and re-occupy Oregon." Days before Polk's presidency began in 1845, Congress voted in favor of annexation, making Texas the 28th state in the Union. Mexico, however, never officially recognized Texan independence, and threatened war over the annexation.

Lesson 12-3: The Mexican-American War

When Polk assumed office in 1845, he was an avowed expansionist who coveted the region west of Texas. He sent a force of 3,500 troops to the Nueces River to defend Texas in case of an invasion, and he secretly sent John Slidell to Mexico with an offer of $2 million to buy the Rio Grande border, $5 million for New Mexico, and $25 million for California. Tensions escalated when Mexico broke off diplomatic relations with the United States during the summer and officials refused to meet with Slidell when he reached Mexico City in December.

In preparation for war, Polk secretly sent a message to the Pacific naval squadron to seize the California ports if Mexico declared war. John Fremont arrived in California in the winter of 1845 to 1846, and Stephen Kearney was dispatched to Santa Fe to take possession of New Mexico. On April 25, 1846, Mexican troops crossed the Rio Grande River border at Matamoros and killed 11 Americans. On May 11, 1846, in a war message to Congress, Polk made the accusation that "American blood had been shed on American soil."

War finally erupted, with the United States insisting that the southern Texas border lay along the Rio Grande River; Mexico claimed that the border lay much further north at the Nueces River. The Mexican American War ranged throughout Texas, New Mexico, and California, and into the Mexican interior.

Whigs in Congress were uneasy about Polk's actions and accused the president of misleading Congress and maneuvering the United States into an unnecessary war. Many people referred to it as "Mr. Polk's War" and accused him of wanting to expand slavery. Furthermore, several politicians questioned the president, including Lincoln, by issuing his "Spot Resolution"

The Mexican War, 1846–1848

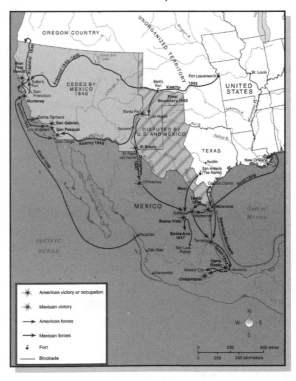

in Congress, demanding to know the "exact spot" where American blood had been shed.

Journalists were soon caught up in the excitement of the country being at war. This was the first popular war in which citizens could follow the progress of the war on a daily basis, thanks in large part to the telegraph. The penny press mass-circulated newspapers that simply fueled the public's appetite for war news. News of the war stirred up excitement in the public's mind and maintained a deep hold on the popular imagination.

Despite the arguments, Polk continued to direct the war, and a blockade was established along the eastern coast of Mexico. Zachary Taylor was sent south into northeastern Mexico (and later replaced by Winfield Scott). The Kearney expedition went to New Mexico and, after a peaceful surrender by the Mexicans at Santa Fe, went on to California. John Fremont staged the **Bear Flag Revolt** for California's independence in the summer of 1846. Santa Ana attacked American troops at Buena Vista in February 1847 but failed to defeat Scott's forces. General Winfield Scott launched an amphibious attack on the coastal city of Veracruz, and by September of 1847, Scott had succeeded in taking Mexico City.

With the **Treaty of Guadalupe Hidalgo**, signed in February 1848, the war was over and Mexico ceded Texas, New Mexico, and California to the United States for $15 million. The ceded territory encompassed present-day Arizona, Nevada, California, Utah, and parts of present-day New Mexico, Colorado, and Wyoming.

The treaty secured the West for American settlement, and American land stretched continuously from the Atlantic Ocean to the Pacific Ocean. Interest now began to grow in Congress over the proposal for a transcontinental railroad. To facilitate a southern railroad, the United States acquired parts of present-day southern Arizona and New Mexico for $10 million from Mexico in the **Gadsden Purchase** (1853).

Sectional debate heated up again in 1846 when David Wilmot, a northern Democrat, proposed an amendment to a war appropriation, known as the **Wilmot Proviso,** banning slavery in all territories acquired from Mexico. Slavery would be allowed to remain where it already existed, but it wouldn't expand into territorial regions. Sectional interests triumphed over party loyalty when Northerners and Southerners voted along sectional lines, reopening the national debate about the place of slavery in the country. The final vote was delayed until the end of the Mexican American War. Threats were made and fistfights broke out on the floor of the House of Representatives. The amendment was defeated, but a newly formed political party, the **Free-Soil party**, eventually adopted its provisions. This new party vowed to keep the territories free with its platform of "free soil, free speech, free labor, free men."

The Mexican American War at a Glance

- From the beginning the war was politically divisive with opposition from the North.

- Whigs accused the president of misleading Congress and maneuvering the United States into an unnecessary war, and many referred to it as "Mr. Polk's War."

- As the war continued, casualties, cost, and opposition mounted (13,000 American and 50,000 Mexican casualties; war costs—$97 million).

- Whigs accused Polk of wanting to expand slavery with the war.

- Many of the U.S. commanders in the war were West Point graduates and would later see action in the Civil War.

- This was the first popular war that citizens could follow on a daily basis, thanks to the telegraph.

- Technology would play a huge role in the war through railroad and steamboat transportation for troops and supplies, telegraph communication, and the six-shot revolving pistol invented by Samuel Colt.

- The penny press mass-circulated newspapers fueled the public's appetite for war news.

- The territory gained by the Treaty of Guadalupe Hidalgo increased the size of the United States by 20 percent.

Lesson 12-4: Internal Expansion

The concept of Manifest Destiny and the territorial growth that accompanied it fueled Americans' imaginations. Land, adventure, and the dream of striking it rich motivated thousands to embark westward on perilous journeys.

Trails West

The 900-mile **Santa Fe Trail** opened up the New Mexico region in 1822 for lucrative trade with the United States. It extended from

Oregon Trail

Independence, Missouri, to Bent's Fort in Colorado, where the trail turned to the southwest and on to Taos and Santa Fe. The trail served as a profitable trade route until the Santa Fe Railroad ended trade along it in 1880.

Settlers also began traveling west along the **Oregon Trail** from 1842 through the 1850s. The route began at Independence, Missouri, and then turned northward at the South Platte River. It extended through Wyoming, down to the Colorado River, across the Salt Lake Basin, over the mountains, and finally to the Columbia River and the Willamette Valley. More than 150,000 people made the arduous trek west, hoping to shape a new future for themselves despite the possibility of hardship, disease, and death.

Oregon Territory

By 1845, more than 5,000 settlers had made the journey to Oregon and the Willamette Valley region. The second half of Polk's campaign slogan in 1844, "Re-annex Mexico and re-occupy Oregon," referred to territory in the Northwest held jointly by the United States and Great Britain. This territory included present-day Oregon, Washington, and Idaho; parts of present-day Montana and Wyoming; and much of western Canada. Expansionists pressured Congress to annex the entire Oregon Territory with their motto, "**54° 40′ or fight**," along the border of Russian Alaska and British Canada. Northerners also pushed for acquisition, because the admission of Oregon, a free state, would balance the admission of slave-holding Texas.

Despite President Polk's expansionist aims, he couldn't commit to acquiring the territory. Already caught up in border disputes with Mexico, Polk didn't want further conflict and instead proposed a compromise with Britain. The 1846 compromise divided the Oregon Territory along the **49th parallel** after settling the issue of Vancouver Island and the Puget Sound. The United States received the land south of the line, and Great Britain received the land north of the line, with British rights of navigation along the Columbia River. Oregon was then admitted as a state in 1859.

"California or Bust"

In 1846, Lansford Hastings made a claim about finding a shortcut that would save time in traveling to California. The **Donner-Reed party**, led by George Donner and James Reed, trusted Hastings and agreed to use this new shortcut. They got a late start from Independence, Missouri, in May 1846. When they reached Utah, they joined Hastings group and attempted to reach California along the new route. The traveling party got lost, fell behind schedule, ran low on provisions, and soon were trapped by early winter snows in the Sierra Nevada Mountains. There are rumors that the survivors were forced to resort to cannibalism to make it through the winter. The survivors were rescued in the spring of 1847.

In January 1848, an American carpenter named James Marshall struck gold at **Sutter's Mill** in California's Sierra Nevada Mountains. News of the discovery sparked a gold rush by the fall of 1848, drawing thousands to the West Coast, including Americans from the East Coast, Mexicans, Europeans, and Chinese. California attracted more than 100,000 immigrants, known as "forty-niners," in a single year. San Francisco was the main port of entry, and it grew from a settlement of about 1,000 in 1848 to a city of more than 35,000 by 1850. People rushed to California to mine for riches in the gold fields or to "mine the miners" with goods and services. Many would claim that they had "seen the elephant," meaning they had endured hardships along their arduous trek to California in their quest for riches and a new life.

California Trail

The influx of settlers created pressure for California to organize its own government. After being admitted as a free state in 1850, California saw its population surge to more than 260,000 by 1852. Its population was extremely diverse, including a 40-percent minority population consisting of Hispanics, Chinese, and blacks. In addition to the great population influx, the mining boom in the California and parts of the West would continue over the next few decades, setting up a **boom-and-bust** cycle as minerals were discovered, mining towns were established, mines played out, and ghost towns were left behind.

Lesson 12-5: Slavery in the South

As the debate about Manifest Destiny and territorial expansion continued, slavery began to take center stage in the political arena. The South was out to protect its investments and maximize profits on its land and slaves. By 1860, the slave population was estimated at four million. More than 90 percent of slaves worked on farms and plantations, and cotton made up 57 percent of all U.S. exports. James Henry Hammond of South Carolina, in a speech before the Senate in 1858, declared, "No you dare not to make war on cotton; No power on the earth dares to make war upon it—Cotton is King." The South was deeply concerned about its economic investment in slavery and cotton because Britain bought 75 percent of its cotton from the South, and the plant provided 20 percent of the jobs in Britain. The profitability of slavery also depended on opening up new land for agriculture and expanding slavery.

The South greatly needed to diversify its economy prior to the Civil War, but warnings went unheeded. Cotton diverted energy and resources away from southern cities, and the South's large rural population lagged behind the North in industrialization and transportation. Plantation owners, however, saw no reason to risk capital in new areas. By 1860, the South contained only 15 percent of the nation's factories and 35 percent of the nation's railroads. Less than 40 percent of the U.S. population lived in the South, and only 13 percent of the southern population was urban, compared with 33 percent in the North. The South lagged behind the rest of the nation in education and had a high rate of illiteracy.

Slavery, the "peculiar institution," was a forced labor condition meant to keep white southerners in control because they believed they were superior human beings who could best care for the needs of blacks. Although the perception was that all whites owned slaves, more than 2/3 of all southerners didn't own slaves. Although less than 1 percent of southern families owned more than100 slaves, this elite hierarchy kept the planter class in control of political, economic, and social life in the South. As the soil became depleted, the large growers moved on to better land, and because the plantations owned the most productive land, this left the landowners with the poorest land in the South. Southerners developed an elaborate defense system to help protect their "peculiar institution." They claimed they were superior, noble, born leaders, hospitable, courageous, loyal, and chivalrous, while blacks were inferior and permanently unsuited for freedom. The legal defense of slavery claimed it was protected by the Constitution, because it wasn't specifically forbidden by name. Slavery's legal defenders also cited the use of the 3/5 Compromise and believed that slavery was a state-protected right according to the 10th Amendment, to be managed by the states. John Calhoun referred to slavery in a paternalistic manner by calling it a "positive good," claiming that slavery was actually beneficial to blacks.

Some southerners even believed Josiah Nott's work called *Types of Mankind*, in which he claimed that blacks and whites were different species and should not intermarry. He claimed that blacks were degraded, suffered from retarded mental and moral development, were created separately, and were inherently inferior. He tried to support his work with a study of cranial shapes, claiming that the animal parts of the brain dominate over the moral and intellectual areas, making blacks deficient in reasoning and judgment and leaving them childlike all their lives. These ideas have since been disproven by doctors and scientists around the world.

Southerners topped off their arguments with a biblical defense, citing passages in both the Old and New Testaments about slaves and servants needing to "obey their masters" and to accept their lot in life. Jews owned slaves, Jews had once been slaves themselves, and no prophet or apostle condemned slavery. Closely related to this was the historical defense, which referred to Egypt, Greece, and Rome and these civilizations' use of slave labor. Aristotle had even spoken of men of superior talents ruling over the inferior.

Slaves weren't evenly distributed throughout the South. More than half of the slave population lived in the Deep South, and by 1850, more than half of the populations of Mississippi and South Carolina were slaves. Elsewhere in the Deep South, 40 percent or more of the population was enslaved. The fear of slave rebellions dominated life in the South. In 1800, **Gabriel Prosser**, a slave blacksmith, carefully recruited several hundred slaves in hopes of marching on Richmond, Virginia. Bad weather postponed the plot, and, after its discovery, Prosser and 25 others were executed. In 1822, **Denmark Vesey** planned to take over Charleston and then flee to Haiti. After two domestic servants disclosed the plan, Vesey and more than 35 conspirators were hung. **Nat Turner**, a Virginia slave preacher who could read and write, began planning a slave rebellion in 1831 in Southampton County. Turner claimed he was an instrument of God's wrath. He and several others were lynched after killing 55 white men, women, and children. Southerners continued to enact and enforce laws and punishments aimed at keeping rebellions and uprisings in check.

Lesson 12-6: The Politics of Expansion

The **Liberty party** was founded in 1840 by abolitionists who wanted to draw attention to the increasingly important issue of slavery. Even though their candidate, James Birney, didn't win the 1840 presidential election, the party helped draw attention to the issue of ending slavery. Third-party politics had a significant influence in the 1844 election when the Liberty party candidate received 62,000 votes, allowing James Polk, the Democratic candidate, to narrowly defeat Henry Clay, the Whig candidate.

In 1848, the **Free-Soil party** grew out of this third-party sentiment. This new party tried to shift the focus away from the morality of slavery to the question of expansion. They supported allowing slavery to exist where it was established, but preventing the extension of slavery into any new territory. The party platform was based on the premise of "Free soil, free speech, free labor, and free men." Many Free-Soilers meant "anti-black" when they said "anti-slavery" and proposed banning all black people from the new territories. The Free-Soil party was denounced by some as a racist effort to make the territories all white.

In an effort to keep the slavery issue alive, the Democrats proposed the concept of **popular sovereignty**—leaving the decision about slavery to the citizens of each territory. Meanwhile, the Whigs avoided establishing a platform in an attempt to avoid the issue of slavery altogether. The 1848 presidential race among Martin Van Buren (Free-Soil), Zachary Taylor (Whig), and Lewis Cass (Democrat) was won by Taylor, the Whig's war hero, but the campaign established a new third-party threat. It also made the future of slavery the dominant political issue of the day.

Review Exam

Multiple Choice

1. Manifest Destiny promoted the belief that the United States was destined to be a great nation because:
   a) slavery would be abolished by the federal government
   b) God had ordained the spread of the United States from the Atlantic to the Pacific
   c) slavery would continue to expand in new territories acquired by the United States
   d) new states would ban slavery

2. Texas became a focal point of significant events during this time as a result of:
   a) the fall of the Alamo in 1836
   b) the independence of the Lone Star Republic
   c) the spread of slavery into Texas
   d) all of the choices on the list

3. Polk's desire to expand the territory of the United States led to:
   a) Polk's campaign in 1844 focusing on the annexation of Texas
   b) the failed attempt to acquire Texas
   c) outgoing president Tyler urging Congress to pass a joint resolution admitting Texas to the union as a slave state
   d) choices *a* and *c* only

4. The start of the Mexican-American War in May 1846 occurred when:
   a) Mexico agreed but then backed out of the United States's offer to buy territory near the Rio Grande border
   b) Mexico killed U.S. diplomat John Slidell
   c) Mexico crossed the Rio Grande border and killed 11 Americans
   d) Americans crossed the Nueces River border and killed a dozen Mexican soldiers

5. The role of journalists in the Mexican-American War was to:
   a) report events from the war several weeks after the incident occurred
   b) use the telegraph to report back on events from the war as they occurred
   c) fuel the public's appetite for news about the war
   d) choices *b* and *c* only

6. The importance of the Wilmot Proviso was that:
   a) it tried to ban slavery in territory acquired from Mexico
   b) slavery would be banned in states where it was already in existence
   c) it delayed the start of war with Mexico
   d) it became law shortly after the end of the Mexican War

7. As a result of the war with Mexico ending in 1848:
   a) new territory was acquired
   b) the United States emerged victorious from the war
   c) the debate on slavery heated up
   d) all of the choices on the list

8. Travel to areas west of the Mississippi River was made possible by all of the following *EXCEPT*:
   a) the Santa Fe Trail from Independence, Missouri to Santa Fe, New Mexico
   b) the Oregon Trail from Independence to the Willamette Valley in Oregon
   c) shortcut trails from Utah to California shortening the travel time
   d) the California Trails leading people to areas around Sutter's Mill and other places of settlement

9. Expansionists interested in the Oregon Territory were successful in:
   a) acquiring a new boundary at the 54° 40′ mark
   b) compromising with Britain for a new boundary between the United States and Canada along the 49th parallel
   c) going to war with Britain for a brief time to secure new boundaries between the United States and Canada
   d) having Oregon admitted as a state after the Civil War

10. The Southern defense of slavery included:
    a) a biblical defense of slaves being mentioned in both the Old and New Testaments
    b) a historical defense of slaves being mentioned in Egyptian, Greek, and Roman societies
    c) slavery being treated as a "positive good" that actually benefited the slaves
    d) all of the choices on the list

11. Slave rebellions frightened many Southerners because:
    a) the majority of states in the Deep South had large percentages of their population that was made up of slaves
    b) slaves used communication networks in their tight-knit communities to plan rebellions

c) weapons were readily available to slaves

d) slave rebellions might cut into their profits from the sale of cotton

12. Popular Sovereignty was the concept that:
   a) slavery would be limited to certain regions of the country
   b) the people of a particular territory could vote and decide for themselves whether or not to permit slavery in their boundaries
   c) slavery would be prohibited in all territories
   d) the federal government could decide on the status of slavery in new territories

Matching

a. "Mr. Polk's War"	j. Sam Houston
b. Donner party	k. King Cotton
c. Abraham Lincoln	l. Gadsden Purchase
d. "seeing the elephant"	m. California
e. Free-Soil party	n. boom and bust cycle
f. Gabriel Prosser	o. Sutter's Mill
g. Treaty of Guadalupe Hidalgo	p. Denmark Vesey
h. Nat Turner	q. John Fremont
i. "forty-niners"	r. Stephen F. Austin

_____13. he fought Santa Ana after the attack at the Alamo in 1836 and defeated the Mexican troops

_____14. a Whig Congressman who issued the "Spot Resolution" demanding to know the exact spot where American blood had been shed on American soil sparking the beginning of the war with Mexico

_____15. the political party whose platform aimed at keeping slavery out of territory recently acquired from Mexico after the Mexican war ended in 1848

_____16. he planned a slave revolt to take over Charleston and flee to Haiti (this slave and 35 others were hung)

_____17. the Whig's reference to President Polk, a Democrat, leading the country into war with Mexico on the veiled premise of expansionism

_____18. symbolic of enduring hardship along the way on trails leading to California

_____19. this acquired land in southern Arizona and New Mexico in 1853 for a possible southern route for a transcontinental railroad

_____20. a slave blacksmith who recruited several hundred slaves in hopes of marching on Richmond, Virginia (but was executed once the plot was discovered)

_____21. the belief that no one dare make war on cotton because of its economic importance to the entire country

_____22. this formally ended the Mexican War in 1848 with Mexico ceding the territories of Texas, New Mexico and California to the United States for $15 million

_____23. he staged the Bear Flag Revolt in California in 1846

_____24. mining towns would be established as soon as minerals were discovered, and when the mine played out, the mining town became a ghost town

_____25. where gold was discovered in 1848

_____26. this state was admitted as a free state in 1850

_____27. he brought 300 families into the Texas region in 1821 to establish a colony along the Brazos River

_____28. this Virginia slave preacher planned a slave revolt, but was lynched after 55 white men, women, and children were killed

_____29. more than 100,000 immigrants who made their way to California in search of gold in 1849

_____30. became trapped in the Sierra Nevada Mountains in 1846 along their trip to California

Short Response

31. *Destiny, riches, and expansion!* How did westward expansion add to the growing sectionalism in the country?

32. What were the political implications of the issues raised by the Mexican American War?

33. What effect did expansion and the debate on slavery have on the country from 1820 to 1850?

Answers begin on page 265.

The Road to Civil War

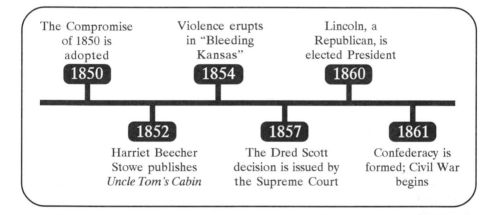

1850	1854	1860
The Compromise of 1850 is adopted	Violence erupts in "Bleeding Kansas"	Lincoln, a Republican, is elected President

1852	1857	1861
Harriet Beecher Stowe publishes *Uncle Tom's Cabin*	The Dred Scott decision is issued by the Supreme Court	Confederacy is formed; Civil War begins

Trends and Themes of the Era

▶ A series of compromises failed to settle the ongoing debate about the existence and expansion of slavery.

▶ Political parties and their platforms were becoming increasingly sectional in their focus.

▶ As the country continued to expand with the addition of new territories in the West, the debate about slavery escalated.

▶ Presidential candidates, members of both houses of Congress, and the Supreme Court weighed in on the issue of slavery.

▶ From the Compromise of 1850 to the presidential election of 1860, the country was on a course toward civil war.

Challenges, threats, and secession! The 1850s would prove to be a turning point for the United States. The decade began with a great compromise aimed at stemming the conflict over slavery. Instead, the compromise ignited a furious debate across the country that resulted in heated arguments, impassioned speeches, and physical confrontations from new territories all the way to the floor of the Senate. In addition, the country ushered in a new set of leaders who would guide it over the next decade as the nation headed toward civil war. Southerners continued to claim that slavery was a states' rights issue and that the federal government had no say in the matter. Northerners grew increasingly alarmed at the expansion of slavery and some sought to have it curbed. Others fought for total abolition of the institution. Throughout the decade, the issues of the spirit of freedom and the spirit of slavery divided the nation. Lincoln warned that "A house divided against itself cannot stand.... I believe this government cannot endure permanently half slave and half free." By the end of the 1850s, the country had reached a point of no return. War was inevitable. The country would now become engaged in battle to resolve the conflict.

Lesson 13-1: The Compromise of 1850

In 1850, President Zachary Taylor encouraged California's request for admission to the Union as a free state, angering the South, because adding a free state would upset the balance between free and slaveholding states in Congress. Southern Congressmen tried to block California's admission. Because the territory above the Missouri Compromise line was likely to remain free, Southerners hoped the line would be extended westward so slavery could expand into new states and territories admitted to the Union. The challenge before Congress focused on how to best preserve the Union. Senator Henry Clay stepped forward in May 1850 to present a compromise, much as he had 30 years earlier when Missouri sought statehood.

Clay's five-point proposal (summarized on page 203) threw Congress into an eight-month discussion known as the Great Debate. Proponents of each side criticized Clay's compromise for being too lenient toward the other side. Most prominent among the debaters were Henry Clay, Daniel Webster, and John C. Calhoun. Calhoun's goal was states' rights; he felt that slavery should remain a state rather than a federal issue. That arguing point would later lead to disunion. Calhoun blamed the sectional crisis on the North, contending that the South had no concession to make on the issue of slavery.

The Compromise of 1850 at a Glance

· California would be admitted as a free state.

· The remainder of the Mexican cession would be divided into two separate territories, New Mexico and Utah, and they would decide by **popular sovereignty** whether to be slave holding or free.

· Texas would cede its claim to parts of the New Mexico territory, and, in exchange, the government would cover Texas's $10 million war debt.

· The slave trade would be abolished in the District of Columbia, but slavery itself would continue.

· Congress would strengthen the Fugitive Slave Act by requiring citizens of any state, slave or free, to assist in the capture and return of runaway slaves.

Webster appealed to Congress by urging a compromise to appease both North and South. He agreed with Northern Whigs that slavery shouldn't be extended into the territories and endorsed Clay's compromise to preserve the Union and to keep the South from seceding. In the midst of the ongoing debate, President Taylor died on July 9th and was succeeded by Vice President Millard Fillmore. **Stephen A. Douglas** took over for Henry Clay as Speaker of the House and divided the compromise bill into separate components, each of which passed. Together, the separate bills became known as the **Compromise of 1850.**

Growth of the United States to 1853

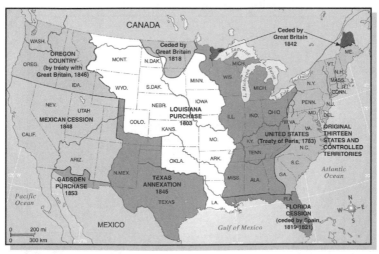

Lesson 13-2: The Fugitive Slave Act

During the Great Debate, one particular point of contention was strengthening the **Fugitive Slave Act**. The act denied alleged fugitives the right to a trial and didn't allow them to testify in their own defense. It also granted court-appointed commissioners higher payments of $10 for every slave returned. Fines and jail time could be imposed on those who failed to cooperate with the commissioners. In addition, the law authorized federal marshals and Southern bands to enter the North and search for runaway slaves who had escaped decades earlier. All of these actions gave slave owners increased power to capture escaped slaves, while reminding Northerners of their longstanding complicity with the institution of slavery.

Some Northerners worked vigorously to undermine the Fugitive Slave Act through legal tactics, organized social protest, and violent resistance. During the 1850s, nine northern states passed personal liberty laws to counteract the Fugitive Slave Act. These state laws guaranteed all alleged fugitives the right to a trial by jury and to a lawyer, and they prohibited state jails from holding alleged fugitives. Northern Vigilance Committees worked hard to protect escaped slaves, at times in conjunction with the **Underground Railroad**, a network of safe houses and escorts throughout the North that helped escaped slaves travel to freedom. Others wrote and lectured about the evils of the Fugitive Slave Act, including Frederick Douglass. The Northerners' protests against the act fueled suspicion and encouraged Southerners to continue thinking about secession.

Underground Railroad, 1860

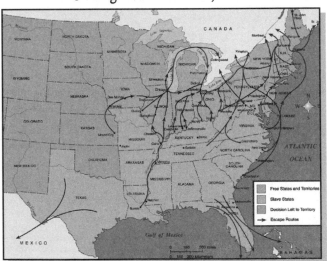

Lesson 13-3: Harriet Beecher Stowe

Anger continued to grow over the enforcement of the Fugitive Slave Act. The strong-armed resistance against the act showed how Northern abolitionist sentiment was rising. No event did more to encourage Northern abolitionism and sympathy for runaway slaves than the 1852 publication of *Uncle Tom's Cabin*. **Harriet Beecher Stowe**'s book became a runaway bestseller, selling 300,000 copies within the first year of publication and more than two million in the next decade. Its depictions of the corruption of slavery was turned into a play and, along with the book, it was praised by large audiences in the North, who saw it as a graphic depiction of the horrors of slavery. The work was condemned in the South for its "falsehoods" of slavery. In the midst of the Civil War in 1863, President Lincoln invited Stowe to the White House and commented, "So you are the little woman who wrote the book that made this Great War."

Lesson 13-4: The Ostend Manifesto

President Franklin Pierce was interested in obtaining Cuba from Spain in order to allay Southern fears about the spread of free states. Some Southerners began to be interested in the purchase of Cuba for an additional slave state and as another way of extending Manifest Destiny for their purposes. Not only could they then turn it into a slave state, but, by taking it away from Spain, they could avoid a potential slave uprising in Cuba. The president dispatched three American diplomats along with the secretary of state to discuss Cuba at a meeting in Ostend, Belgium, in 1854. It was stated that the United States would make an offer to buy Cuba from Spain, but if the offer were rejected, the diplomats warned of military action to "wrest it from Spain." When details of the meeting became public, Southerners applauded the move, though many Free-Soilers in Congress were outraged and the president was greatly embarrassed. The document was repudiated, the secretary of state resigned, and the debate over expanding slavery continued.

Lesson 13-5: Bleeding Kansas

In January 1854, Senator Stephen Douglas of Illinois proposed a bill to organize Nebraska (part of the Louisiana Purchase) as a territory, to make it easier to build a transcontinental railroad along a northern route from Chicago westward. Douglas was from Illinois and wanted Chicago to be the first stop along the transcontinental railroad, but first, the territories had to be organized. Because the Nebraska Territory lay above the 36° 30' line set by the Missouri Compromise to prohibit slavery, Nebraska would automatically become a candidate for admission as a free state. Southerners planned to oppose the bill unless Douglas made some concessions.

In an effort to make the measure acceptable to Southerners, Douglas added a provision that the territorial legislature would determine the status of slavery. According to the concept of **popular sovereignty,** a territory or state would be able to decide for itself on the issue of slavery. When Southern Democrats demanded more, Douglas agreed to two changes in the bill. He wrote an additional clause explicitly withdrawing the antislavery provision in the Missouri Compromise, and he added an adjustment creating two territories in the region, Nebraska and Kansas, so that the new Kansas Territory might become a slave state. In its final form, the measure was known as the **Kansas-Nebraska Act** and gained the support of President Pierce. After a lengthy debate, it became law in May 1854, with the unanimous support of the South and the partial support of Northern Democrats.

However, the Kansas-Nebraska Act didn't prevent further sectional conflict. Because Nebraska was likely to prohibit slavery as a territory above the 36° 30' line, Kansas became a battleground for sectional interests. The Kansas-Nebraska Act produced many immediate, far-reaching changes. It led to the demise of the Whig party, which disappeared almost entirely by 1856. It divided the Northern Democrats (many of whom were shocked by the repeal of the Missouri Compromise) and drove many of them from the party. Most important, it encouraged the creation of a new party that was openly sectional in its composition and beliefs.

People in both major parties who opposed Douglas's bill began to call themselves Anti-Nebraska Democrats and Anti-Nebraska Whigs. In 1854, they formed a new organization: the **Republican party.** In the elections of that year, the Republicans won enough seats in Congress to be able to organize the House of Representatives, and they also won control of several Northern state governments.

Both Northern abolitionist groups and Southern interests rushed into the Kansas Territory to try to control the local elections, making it a battleground between anti- and pro-slavery forces. In March 1855, during the first election of the territorial legislature, thousands of pro-slavery citizens of western Missouri crossed into Kansas to tilt the vote in favor of slaveholding interests. The election fraud perpetrated by these "border ruffians" swept a pro-slavery government into power. The new government immediately ousted antislavery legislators and set up a proslavery constitution known as the Lecompton Constitution.

In opposition to the new legislature, abolitionist John Brown, together with his four sons and two helpers, went to Lawrence armed with broad swords, murdering five proslavery settlers. The **Pottawatomie Massacre** provoked reprisals and initiated a guerrilla war that cost about 200 lives, earning the territory the nickname Bleeding Kansas.

The violence even extended to the floor of Congress, where Massachusetts **Senator Charles Sumner**, a staunch abolitionist, insulted South Carolina Senator Andrew Butler, while calling for the admission of Kansas to the Union as a free state. Butler's cousin Preston Brooks, a member of the House, used a cane to attack Sumner in the head and then kept beating him after he fell to the floor. The cane broke in three pieces, knocking Sumner unconscious. Attempts to expel or censure Brooks in the House failed. Brooks became a Southern hero and was invited to dinners and receptions and given souvenir canes, one of which was engraved with the phrase, "Hit him again!" Sumner was re-elected in 1857, but he was out recovering from the inflicted wounds until 1860. His empty seat became a symbol of Southern brutality and further inflamed the slavery debate.

In addition to the slavery and statehood issues in Kansas, proponents of a transcontinental railroad saw interest in the territory because it would become part of an eventual route for the railroads. So, adding to the conflict in Kansas, in 1856, Illinois lawyer Abraham Lincoln agreed to take a case that argued the right of the Chicago and Rock Island Railroad to construct a bridge across the Mississippi. Two weeks after the first train had run across the newly constructed bridge, a steamboat, *Effie Afton*, was navigating the river when attempting to clear the drawspan on an upstream journey. Suddenly, after clearing the drawspan, the steamboat went out of control and drifted backward, striking the span and setting it ablaze. The draw portion of the bridge was destroyed. This started court action in which Abraham Lincoln defended the railroad's right to bridge the river. Steamboat owners feared the coming of the "iron horse" and the potential damage it would have on their trade on the Mississippi. Railroad companies fought for their rights to expand trade. In the second trial of the case, the court order this time resulted in an order to remove the bridge. But when the case found its way to the Supreme Court in 1862, the Supreme Court ruled in favor of the railroad and their right to build a bridge across a navigable stream. Later, as president, Lincoln signed the Pacific Railway Act in 1862 to provide government support for the building of the transcontinental railroad.

Status of Slavery in the Territories, 1850–1854

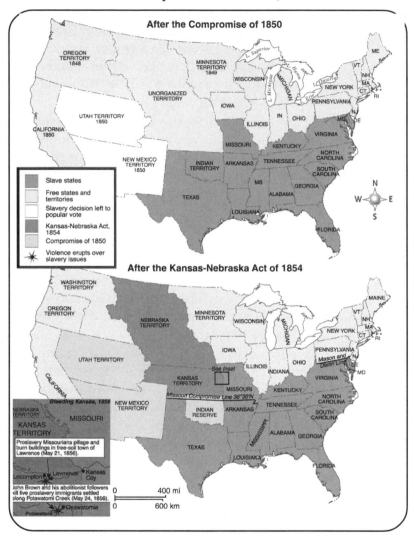

After the Compromise of 1850

After the Kansas-Nebraska Act of 1854

Lesson 13-6: The Birth of the Republican Party

The Whig party (an alliance between Southern Republicans and Northern Democrats) disintegrated in the 1850s over the increasingly contentious issue of slavery. In its place, the **Republican party** arose as the chief political opposition to the Democrats. This was the beginning of the modern-day Republican Party. The Republican Party's major platform centered around an opposition to slavery. The Kansas-Nebraska Act divided the Whigs Southern pro-slavery and Northern antislavery components. The fractures ran so deep that even Northern Whigs were divided, between antislavery "Conscience Whigs" and conservatives who supported the Compromise of 1850.

One alternative was the American Party, which became known as the **Know-Nothing party** because the members met secretly and refused to identify themselves. The party was a nativist organization that spread anti-German, anti-Irish, and anti-Catholic propaganda. Many members also favored temperance and opposed slavery. The party remained divided on the issue of slavery, and in 1855 the Know-Nothing party found itself weakened and near ruin. Despite dissension about slavery, the party managed to gain a sizeable percentage of the popular vote with presidential candidate Millard Fillmore in 1856.

In the Know-Nothing party's place, the Republican party emerged in the North in 1854 as Northern Democrats, antislavery Whigs, and former Free-Soil party members united to oppose the Democratic party. The Republican platform included stances on temperance, abolitionism, and Protestantism. The influence of Northern Whigs also added protective tariffs and cheap land out West. Although all Republicans disapproved of the Kansas-Nebraska Act, some merely wanted to restore the Missouri Compromise, some were Free-Soilers, and still others were ardent abolitionists. In spite of the members' differences of opinion, opposition to expanding slavery united the party and gave it focus. Abraham Lincoln became the rising star of the new political party and faced the challenge of making the Republican party a national rather than a sectional party. (See the chart on page 210.)

Lesson 13-7: The Dred Scott Decision

Distraught by the violence of Bleeding Kansas, President James Buchanan (who was elected in 1856) sought a judicial resolution to the issue of slavery's extension. He saw the Dred Scott case as a potential source of such a resolution. **Dred Scott**, a Missouri slave, sued for his freedom on the basis that his owner had taken him to live in a free state (Illinois), and later a free territory (Wisconsin).

In March 1857, two days after Buchanan was sworn into office, **Chief Justice Roger B. Taney** delivered the majority opinion in *Dred Scott v. Sanford.* In the 7–2 ruling, the five Southern justices concurred with Taney's decision that Scott, as a slave, had no right to sue in federal court, and furthermore claimed that no black, slave or free, could become a citizen

Political Party Development in U.S. History

1850–1860

3rd Party System

- **Democrats**
- **Republicans**
- **Know-Nothings**
- **Free-Soilers**

North

▶ **Democrats** begin to distance themselves from the Southern Democrats.

▶ **Know-Nothing party** in 1854 became an anti-immigrant, anti-Catholic party with a major stronghold in the North.

▶ **Republican party** formed out of the old Whig party in 1854 and, although they favored some of the ideals of the Know-Nothings, they also promoted their opposition to the extension of slavery in the territories. Lincoln ran for president as this party's candidate in 1860.

▶ **Free-Soil party** formed from splinter groups of the Liberty, Whigs, and northern Democrats who vowed to keep the territories free—"free soil, free speech, free labor, free men." Their goal was to oppose slave labor in the territories.

South

▶ **Democrats** began to distance themselves from Northern Democrats over the issue of slavery. After 1854 the Democrat party became predominately Southern.

▶ **Know-Nothing party** in 1854 became an anti-immigrant, anti-Catholic party with some limited strongholds in the South. They split with the northern wing of the party in the 1856 presidential election.

▶ **Republican party** was not even included on the ballot in the southern states in the 1860 election.

of the United States. Slaves were property only, according to Taney, and would remain so even if they resided in free territory. In addition, Taney ruled that Congress couldn't forbid slavery in any U.S. territory because doing so would violate the 5th Amendment's protection of property, including slaves, from being taken away without due process.

The decision rendered the Missouri Compromise unconstitutional. Taney further suggested that the Compromise of 1850 and the Kansas-Nebraska Act were unconstitutional, because they enforced popular sovereignty, which allowed territorial governments to prohibit slavery and therefore violated the 5th Amendment as interpreted by the Court. Taney's arguments supported the states' rights position favored by John Calhoun years earlier. Though Buchanan initially had hoped that the *Dred Scott* ruling might resolve the debates about extending slavery, it actually provoked further sectional tensions. The ruling divided the Democratic party with Southerners celebrating as Northerners condemned it. The media and Republicans assailed the Court's ruling by attacking individual justices and by questioning the Supreme Court's integrity at a time when a compromise on slavery was becoming impossible.

Lesson 13-8: The Lincoln-Douglas Debates

In the 1858 midterm elections, Republicans and Democrats faced off for the first time. Lincoln was running as a Senate Republican to oppose Democrat Stephen Douglas in Illinois. Lincoln challenged Douglas to a series of debates to discuss one issue: slavery and the future of the Union. In a series of seven events known as the **Lincoln-Douglas Debates**, Douglas advocated popular sovereignty while Lincoln promoted the Free-Soil argument.

Lincoln was attacked as being a "Black Republican." He stated that a "house divided against itself cannot stand." Lincoln pledged the Republican party to the ultimate extinction of slavery, but also stated, "I am not nor ever have been in favor of bringing about the social and political equality of the white man and the black man." Lincoln condemned slavery as a moral, social, and political wrong. In attacking his opponent, Lincoln contended that Douglas's belief in popular sovereignty, in particular his Freeport Doctrine, was incompatible with the *Dred Scott* decision. In the Freeport Doctrine, Douglas stated that territorial governments could effectively forbid slavery by refusing to enact slave codes, even though the *Dred Scott* decision had explicitly deprived Congress of the authority to restrict slavery in the territories.

In the end, neither candidate emerged from the debates as the clear victor. Although Douglas won the Senate seat, he alienated Southern supporters by encouraging disobedience of the *Dred Scott* decision with his Freeport Doctrine. Lincoln, meanwhile, lost the election but emerged with national prominence as a spokesman for antislavery interests. This Republican loss helped set the stage for the 1860 presidential election.

Lesson 13-9: John Brown's Raid

In October 1859, John Brown followed "a leading by God" to instigate a slave rebellion in Virginia, attempting to seize the federal arsenal at **Harpers Ferry**. After Brown and 22 men seized the arsenal and armory, they took some local citizens hostage and issued a call through the countryside for other slaves to join the rebellion. However, slaves failed to answer the call to rebel, and Brown and his survivors were taken prisoner after two days of battle. Brown was indicted for treason and criminal conspiracy to incite a slave insurrection. His trial ended with a conviction, and he was hanged along with four of his band on December 2nd. Many Northerners mourned his death as a martyr, and Southerners reacted with fear to the possibility of further slave rebellions.

Lesson 13-10: The Election of 1860

In 1860, Buchanan announced he wouldn't run for re-election. The Democratic party split over whom to nominate in Buchanan's place. Northern Democrats defended the doctrine of popular sovereignty and nominated Stephen Douglas for president; Southern Democrats nominated Vice President John Breckenridge for president. Southern moderates from the lower South walked out of the Democratic Convention and formed their own party, the Constitutional party, which nominated John C. Bell for president. These three candidates faced Republican nominee Abraham Lincoln.

The highly contested election drew the second-highest voter turnout in U.S. history at 81 percent. Lincoln emerged as the winner of the contest with a majority of the electoral votes, but he received only 40 percent of the popular vote. He carried all 18 free states, but didn't even appear on the ballots of the slave states. Lincoln's election so alienated the South that secession seemed imminent. Although South Carolina had threatened earlier to secede from the Union over the Tariff of Abominations in 1828, the current threat was much more serious.

Lesson 13-11: Secession

After the 1860 election, the state governments of South Carolina, Alabama, and Mississippi set special state conventions to call for secession. On December 20, 1860, South Carolina led the way in seceding from the nation. The outgoing president, James Buchanan, did nothing. Mississippi, Florida, Alabama, Georgia, Louisiana, and Texas followed South Carolina's lead, and together formed the **Confederate States of America** and swore in **Jefferson Davis** as its president on February 18, 1861.

Map of Secession

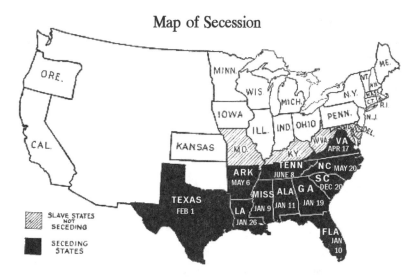

The **Crittenden Compromise** was a last-ditch attempt to resolve the slavery question peacefully. In December of 1860, Senator John J. Crittenden of Kentucky, backed by the National Union party, proposed six constitutional amendments and four resolutions that made major concessions to Southern concerns. They forbade the abolition of slavery on federal land in slaveholding states, compensated owners of runaway slaves, and restored the Missouri Compromise line of 36° 30′ (which had been repealed in the Kansas-Nebraska Act). The last amendment guaranteed that future constitutional amendments couldn't change the previous amendments or the 3/5 Compromise and fugitive slave clauses of the Constitution.

Crittenden's proposals also called for the repeal of Northern personal liberty laws. Because of the deep division in Congress, Crittenden urged that his plan be submitted to a nationwide vote. The proposed compromise was supported by the border states and acceptable to the South, but Lincoln and the Republican party opposed it. The Crittenden Compromise was defeated in both the House and Senate, making clear the inevitability of the Civil War.

When Jefferson Davis assumed the presidency of the newly formed Confederacy, he claimed that secession was a legal and peaceful step to resolve the crisis. He also contended that the American idea of government rests "on the consent of the governed and that it is the right of the people to alter or abolish them at will whenever they become destructive of the ends for which they were established."

Lincoln's inauguration took place on March 4, 1861, under guard, for fear of a Confederate attack. By April, the states of Virginia, North Carolina, Tennessee, and Arkansas had joined the ranks of the Confederate rebels. Days later, on April 12, 1861, General Beauregard, under orders from Confederate president Jefferson Davis, led the attack on **Fort Sumter**, a federal military installation at the entrance to Charleston Harbor. The Civil War had begun.

Review Exam

Multiple Choice

1. The Compromise of 1850 stated all of the following *EXCEPT*:
   a) California being admitted as a free state
   b) New Mexico and Utah territories would be allowed to decide upon the issue of slavery themselves with popular sovereignty
   c) admitting another slave state in the near future to restore the equal balance of slave and free states
   d) enforcing a strict fugitive slave law allowing for the capture and return of runaway slaves to their masters in the South

2. The work on the Underground Railroad and the new Fugitive Slave Act were both significant in that:
   a) they fueled Northern protest against the act and added to their antislavery sentiments
   b) Southerners were encouraged to continue thinking about the issue of secession
   c) several Northern states passed personal liberty laws to counteract the measures of the Fugitive Act
   d) all of the answers on the list

3. Harriet Beecher Stowe was able to add to the lingering debate about slavery with the publication of her novel, *Uncle Tom's Cabin,* because it:
   a) resolved the debate about slavery
   b) enraged Northerners because of its depiction of the cruelty of slavery
   c) became a bestseller in Southern states
   d) was received and highly praised by audiences in both the North and South

4. The violence over the issue of slavery was evidenced in all of the following **EXCEPT**:
   a) Representative Preston Brooks defended the honor of his cousin Senator Butler by violently attacking Senator Sumner on the Senate floor over the issue of slavery
   b) the demise of the Underground Railroad with the capture and hanging of Harriet Tubman
   c) proslavery citizens of Missouri crossing the border into Kansas to attempt to tilt the vote in favor of slaveholding interests in Kansas
   d) the violent attack known as "Bleeding Kansas" that ended with the deaths of 200 people over the issue of slavery in Kansas

5. Slavery and property rights became hot topics in the 1850s debate about states rights, as illustrated by:
   a) Justice Taney ruling that popular sovereignty violated the 5th Amendment protection of property
   b) the end of popular sovereignty as a way to let territories decide upon the issue of slavery themselves
   c) the Fugitive Slave Act allowing for the capture and return of runaway slaves
   d) choices *a* and *c* only

6. Opposition to the Kansas-Nebraska debate centered on:
   a) Nebraska becoming a slave territory and state because of the provisions of the Missouri Compromise
   b) allowing the concept of popular sovereignty to be used by territorial and state legislatures to decide upon the status of slavery in their borders

c) Kansas becoming a free territory and state because of the provisions of the Missouri compromise

d) the federal government abolishing slavery in all new territories

7. While campaigning for the Senate seat in Illinois in 1858, Lincoln and Douglas held a series of debates in which:

a) Douglas proposed the end of slavery in the South

b) Lincoln argued the extension of slavery into limited territories

c) Lincoln favored the "free soil" theory for new territories

d) Douglas advocated limits on popular sovereignty

8. South Carolina was the first of several Southern states to secede from the Union as a result of:

a) the 1860 election in which Abraham Lincoln was elected president

b) the federal government was proposing new legislation abolishing slavery

c) the support of President Buchanan and the Compromise of 1850

d) the rejection of the Missouri Compromise

9. The Republican party was able to capitalize on the antislavery sentiment in the North by:

a) allying themselves with the Southern Whigs and Northern Democrat factions

b) not opposing the secession of Southern states after the 1860 election

c) selecting Abraham Lincoln as their presidential candidate in the 1860 election

d) applauding the execution of John Brown in 1859 for the failed attempt to seize the federal arsenal at Harpers Ferry

10. Although defeated in both the House of Representatives and the Senate, the Crittenden Compromise after the election of 1860 attempted resolve the debate over slavery by proposing legislation that would:

a) forbid the abolition of slavery on federal land in slaveholding states

b) compensate owners of runaway slaves

c) restore the Missouri Compromise line that was repealed in the Kansas-Nebraska Act

d) all of the choices on the list

11. The Confederate States of America was formed in response to:
    a) secession being a legal and peaceful step to resolve the states rights issue concerning slavery
    b) the Crittenden Compromise
    c) the contested election of 1860 because Lincoln was not on the ballot in any of the slave states
    d) the failed policy of popular sovereignty

Matching

a. Harriet Beecher Stowe
b. Republican party
c. Know-Nothing party
d. Ostend Manifesto
e. Dred Scott
f. Stephen Douglas
g. Jefferson Davis
h. Kansas-Nebraska Act

i. Fort Sumter
j. James Buchanan
k. Abraham Lincoln
l. Fugitive Slave Act
m. John Brown
n. Charles Sumner
o. Roger Taney

_____12. he was sworn in as president of the Confederate States of America on February 18, 1861

_____13. he worked on a series of compromise bills that collectively became the Compromise of 1850

_____14. a new political party that started in 1854 with its party platform based on antislavery and elected its first presidential candidate in the 1860 election

_____15. the author of *Uncle Tom's Cabin* (Lincoln commented, "so you are the little woman who wrote the book that made this Great War")

_____16. the site of the outbreak of the Civil War when the Confederates led the attack on the federal military installation on April 12, 1861

_____17. this denied runaway slaves the right to a trial and allowed Southern men to enter the North to search for runaway slaves

_____18. a somewhat-secret attempt to purchase Cuba from Spain in 1854 in another attempt to spread slavery and fuel the slavery debate

____19. the senator who was brutally beaten on the floor of the Senate for his insults of a South Carolina Senator and for his stance on the admission of Kansas as a free state

____20. an Illinois lawyer who in 1856 defended the right of the Chicago and Rock Island Railroad to build a bridge across the Mississippi River (raising fear in steamboat owners with the potential damage to their trade along the Mississippi)

____21. the abolitionist who, along with his four sons, was responsible for the Pottawatomie Massacre in Lawrence, Kansas

____22. the chief justice of the Supreme Court who ruled against Dred Scott in 1857 by claiming that blacks were not citizens and therefore could not sue in court

____23. a nativist party that not only opposed immigration but also opposed slavery

____24. a legislative attempt to allow the Kansas territory to become a slave state

____25. after the election result of 1860, he did nothing to stop the Southern states from seceding

____26. a former slave who attempted to sue for his freedom on the basis that having been in free territory made him a free man

Short Response

27. How did slavery dominate issues throughout the decade of the 1850s with *challenges, threats, and secession*?

28. How did both Southerners and Northerners defend their positions on slavery?

29. Why were compromises no longer feasible in addressing the issue of slavery?

30. How can the election of 1860 be seen as a point of no return in the sectional crisis facing the nation?

Answers begin on page 267.

A Nation Divided

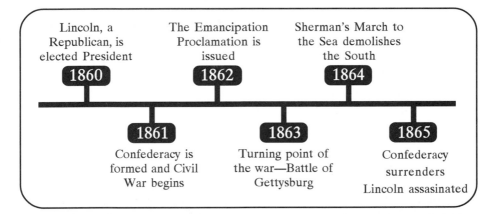

Lincoln, a Republican, is elected President
1860

The Emancipation Proclamation is issued
1862

Sherman's March to the Sea demolishes the South
1864

1861
Confederacy is formed and Civil War begins

1863
Turning point of the war—Battle of Gettysburg

1865
Confederacy surrenders
Lincoln assasinated

Trends and Themes of the Era

▶ Sectional differences over slavery and the question of states' rights versus federal power finally erupted in the Civil War.

▶ What began as a war to preserve the Union expanded to also end slavery.

▶ Presidents and military commanders in both the Union and the Confederacy were greatly challenged as they demonstrated leadership throughout the war.

▶ The end of the conflict secured the supremacy of the federal government over states' rights.

▶ Political conflict would continue after the war as the Republican party in Congress and the president debated the terms of Reconstruction.

Conflict, victory, reconstruction! The nation endured four long years of battle that would ultimately bring about tremendous political, economic, and social changes. War would attempt to resolve the question of slavery and the power of the federal government. Lincoln carried the Union through the years of conflict only to have his own life and plans for Reconstruction cut short by an assassin's bullet. Davis, who was chosen to lead the South, was equally confident that his cause would prevail on the battlefields, but he suffered humiliation with the surrender of the Confederacy. Not only were countless soldiers' lives lost on battlefields from Antietam to Fort Wagner to Gettysburg, but families and prisoners were forever affected by the ravages of war. The conflict finally ended with both the nation and the Constitution intact. Slavery was abolished, and the power of the federal government was solidified for the first time since the ratification of the Constitution. The Union's victory in the war, however, also left many unresolved problems. The challenges that confronted the country at the end of April 1865 were left to politicians and political parties debating postwar Reconstruction and how to bring the South back into the Union. The grand experiment of democracy had endured a civil war and would now have to meet the challenges of Reconstruction.

Lesson 14-1: The Blue and the Gray

In December 1860, soon after Lincoln's victory in the presidential election, a special South Carolina convention led the charge and voted unanimously for **secession**. By February 1861, six more Southern states had followed suit: Alabama, Mississippi, Florida, Georgia, Louisiana, and Texas. Delegates from all seven states met to establish the **Confederate States of America** and chose **Jefferson Davis** as the Confederacy's first president. War was now inevitable between the Union (whose soldiers wore blue uniforms) and the Confederacy (whose soldiers wore gray uniforms).

Lincoln refused to recognize the Confederacy and declared the secession "legally void." His goal was to preserve the Union first and foremost, by whatever means necessary, even if that meant freeing no slaves at all. He once said, "If I could save the Union without freeing *any* slaves I would do it, and if I could save the Union by freeing *all* the slaves I would do it." In contrast, the South's uncompromising goal was intent on preserving slavery. The Southern states would have to decide if they were unified in their desire for secession from the Union.

Lincoln hoped that loyal Unionists in the South would help him over-turn secession. Nevertheless, the nation's rift only widened in the early months of Lincoln's presidency. In April 1861, Confederate troops opened fire on the federal army base at Fort Sumter, forcing federal troops to surrender. Lincoln proclaimed the South in rebellion and called for an army to suppress the insurrection. The threat of incoming federal troops prompted four more states—Virginia, Arkansas, Tennessee, and North Carolina—to secede and join the Confederacy. Maryland, Delaware, Kentucky, and Missouri, all slave states, remained in the Union and dem-onstrated a rift with Southern states willing to leaving the Union for the cause of preserving slavery and their way of life as it existed prior to the beginning of the Civil War.

Soon after the fighting started at Fort Sumter, Lincoln began to as-sume a broader range of executive powers and strengthened his leader-ship and control of the war effort. His first move was to expand the army and the advancement of money without congressional approval. He then declared martial law, enabling the military to arrest anyone suspected of aiding the enemy. Lincoln also suspended the writ of habeas corpus, allowing Confederate sympathizers to be arrested and held without trial. Supreme Court Chief Justice Roger Taney challenged the president on this matter. Lincoln argued that the suspension of certain civil rights was necessary to suppress rebellion and it was in the best interest for national security during a time of conflict. Some newspapers in the North were also shut down for a brief time for publishing false information or mili-tary secrets. During the war, a few politicians were arrested for pro-Confederate activities.

Although many thought that a war would only last a few months, by the summer of 1861, the North had imposed a blockade of the Confederacy. Southerners feared the blockade would not only interrupt the valuable cotton trade with Great Britain but would also keep Britain and France from recognizing the Confederacy. At first, the blockade proved unsuccessful because of the lack of ships from the North to patrol the blockade runners in the South. But as the war progressed, the North was able to build more ships. As more blockade runners were captured and fewer supplies reached the South, the blockade began to have a devastating impact on the South.

In 1861, most Northerners believed that the war was being fought to restore the Union, not to end slavery. Most anticipated a quick Union victory with little bloodshed. The first major battle occurred at Bull Run just south of Washington, D.C., in July as journalists, politicians, and picnickers observed the battle. The decisive Confederate victory dashed Union hopes that the war would end quickly. By 1862, as fighting in various battles continued and casualties began to mount, Confederate soldiers were required to serve for the duration of the long and bloody war. At war's end, more than three million men had fought and 620,000 men lay dead. Truly, as **General Sherman** said, "War is hell."

The war was not without opposition, however. Lincoln faced it not only from Northern Democrats but also within his own Republican party, with the Radical Republicans questioning his war aims and his views on slavery. Many of the Radical Republicans, including Secretary of the Treasury Salmon Chase, were still pushing the president for total abolition of slavery. An extreme wing of the Northern Democrats, known as the Copperheads, questioned Lincoln's approach to the war and favored an end to the fighting.

Jefferson Davis was not without his detractors in the South. He had to confront the rights of each independent state with the powers of the new Confederate government. Davis defined his powers very narrowly and left much of the decision-making process up to the Confederate Congress. However, states were reluctant to cede much power to the centralized government. Davis ultimately failed to take the initiative in dealing with the serious economic problems on the home front, and as the war dragged on his popularity began to wane.

Sizing up the Competition: The Union
Initial Advantages/Disadvantages

- Larger population—18 million (71 percent of total U.S. population) in 23 states.

- 71 percent of railroad mileage.

- 90 percent of nation's industrial output.

- 94 percent of iron production.

- 75 percent of farm acreage.

- 75 percent of wealth produced in the country.

- 44 percent of eligible men in military service by the end of the war.

- Strong leadership with President Lincoln.

- Biggest disadvantage—Union troops invading the South perceived as the aggressors.

Sizing up the Competition: The Confederacy

Initial Advantages/Disadvantages

- The South had to establish a government and chose a loose confederacy that closely resembled the states in 1776.

- Fighting occurred on familiar terrain; guerrilla war tactics

- The South was fighting a defensive war with better military training. Many of its leaders had been trained at West Point and served in the Mexican-American War.

- Smaller population—5.5 million whites and 3.5 million slaves (29 percent of total U.S. population) in 11 states.

- Less than one-third of railroad mileage.

- Less than 10 percent of industrial output.

- The few harbors in the South were susceptible to a Northern blockade.

- President Davis had extensive military training but clashed with Confederate Congress and governors over funding and war aims.

- Failed to get support from Great Britain and France.

Lesson 14-2: Years of Conflict

Many felt that the real issue at stake was the question of states' rights versus federal power—whether states could secede from the Union in protest against federal policy, regardless of whether that policy concerned slavery or another issue, such as tariffs. Slavery and the issue of nullification became the catalyst for the nation's split, but it was not until the **Emancipation Proclamation** by Lincoln in 1863 that slavery emerged as the central issue.

In the East, the Union army aimed to capture the Confederate capital of Richmond, Virginia, but failed. Most of the early battles ended in stalemates, with both sides suffering devastating losses. After assuming command of the Confederate troops in June 1862, Confederate General **Robert E. Lee** began to lead his forces on a powerful march northward from Virginia, attempting to break Union lines. What followed on September 17, 1862 was the bloodiest single-day battle in the Civil War: the **Battle of Antietam**, in which more than 8,000 men died on the field and 18,000 were wounded. Though strategically a draw, the battle proved to be a Union victory because it kept Lee from advancing into the North, and it dashed the Confederacy's hopes of gaining foreign support for the war.

Lincoln responded to the victory by issuing the Emancipation Proclamation. He also fired George McClellan, who had been in charge of the Northern troops, for not pursuing Lee in retreat at Antietam and replaced him with Ambrose Burnside. Lincoln had grown increasingly impatient with McClellan's reluctance to use military strategy and commit troops to battle, so he began taking the upper hand in commanding the war effort himself.

The aim of the war had now changed. Unconditional surrender by the South along with abolition of slavery became the focus of the war. The conflict was charged with reconquering the seceded states by making the war a full-scale struggle of people and resources aimed at defeating Confederate armies in pitched battles, destroying the Confederates' ability to make war.

General Lee struck northward into Pennsylvania in July 1863, but was again blocked by a strong Union defense. In the three-day **Battle of Gettysburg**, 90,000 Union soldiers fought 75,000 Confederates and secured a Union victory. The losses were ruinous to both sides: The Union dead and wounded numbered more than 23,000, and the Confederacy casualties totaled more than 25,000 dead and wounded. Overall, 7,000 soldiers died on the field and 40,000 were wounded in the bloodiest battle of the entire war. Although fighting would continue for nearly another year and a half after the Battle of Gettysburg, the battle was a decisive victory for the Union, and the war then tilted in favor of the Union.

By 1863, spiraling inflation had impacted the Southern economy, leaving it in shambles, and the continued battle losses further demoralized the Confederacy. On November 19th, Lincoln delivered his famed **Gettysburg Address**, in which he portrayed the war as a test of democracy's strength. His dedication speech at the military cemetery spoke of a resolve that it remained: "for us the living...[to] resolve that these dead shall not have died in vain—that this nation, under God, shall have a new birth of freedom—and that government of the people, by the people, and for the people, shall not perish from the earth."

In the West, the Union experienced successes much earlier on. In southwestern Tennessee, at the **Battle of Shiloh** in April 1862, Grant's troops were ambushed by a surprise attack by Confederate troops, but Grant won. Both sides suffered extremely heavy losses, with nearly 30 percent of 77,000 men killed. The war was now beginning to focus upon the total destruction of the enemies' forces.

As the war continued to spread further westward, Confederate troops occupied Santa Fe and Albuquerque in early 1862. The Union victory in New Mexico at the battle of **Glorietta Pass** in March 1862 helped to secure California and New Mexico as Union strongholds and prevent the spread of the Confederacy west of Texas.

Led by General Ulysses S. Grant, the Union fought in several skirmishes over nine months to gain control of the Mississippi River. The Union victory in July 1863 at **Vicksburg**, Mississippi, secured the entire river.

Prison camps such as those at **Andersonville**, Georgia, and **Rock Island**, Illinois, illustrated the harsh realities of war. Andersonville was the most notorious of all Civil War prison camps. The camp was built for 10,000 Union soldiers, but held more than 33,000 prisoners. As death and disease mounted and conditions deteriorated at the camp, more than 13,000 soldiers died. After the end of the war, the superintendent in charge of Andersonville was convicted and hanged for his actions in November 1865. At the Confederate prison camp at Rock Island, Illinois, more than 12,000 prisoners were held and more than 2,000 of them died. Poor sanitation, disease, and ration shortages were common. Out West, in retaliation for Indian raids on U.S. troops, Kit Carson invaded Navajo territory in 1863 and forced more than 8,000 Navajos to march from their homeland in Arizona to **Bosque Redondo** along the Pecos River in southeastern New Mexico, where they were held prisoner for nearly five grueling years.

Lesson 14-3: Union Victory

In early 1864, Lincoln appointed General **Ulysses S. Grant** commander of all Union armies. The string of Union victories that followed during the summer, especially General William T. Sherman's successes in Georgia, helped Lincoln win reelection in 1864. The election was a huge victory for Lincoln and the Republican party—all Northern governorships and 75 percent of Congress was now Republican—and they would be able to control the country's political agenda after the end of the Civil War.

Civil War 1861–1862 Battles Near Capitals

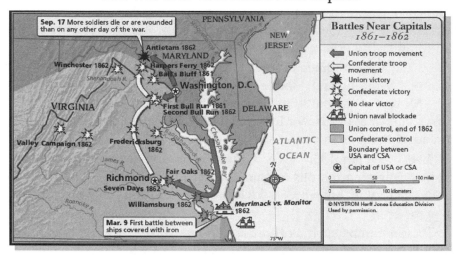

Civil War 1863–1865 Battles Near Capitals

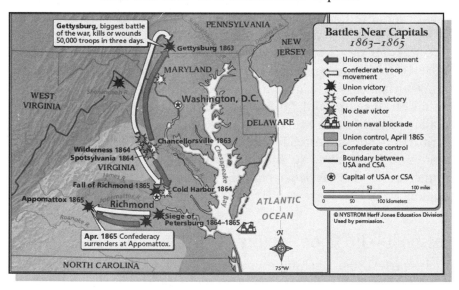

Union forces continued to rout the Confederate army after Lincoln's reelection, destroying much of Georgia and South Carolina in Sherman's infamous march to the sea. Sherman and his troops first burned Atlanta and then marched toward the coast at Savannah demolishing everything in their way by cutting a 40- to 60-mile-wide path of destruction that wiped out everything, including railroads and factories. Sherman's forces ruined an estimated $100 million worth of property. His goal was to utterly destroy the morale of the Confederacy.

One month after Sherman's forces conquered Charleston, South Carolina, April 1865 proved to be a pivotal time in the war's climax. Confederate president Jefferson Davis abandoned Richmond on April 2nd, and the following day Lincoln and Grant toured the capital, with Lincoln sitting at Davis's abandoned desk. The following week, Lee's forces surrendered to Grant at the **Appomattox Courthouse** on April 9th. As the Confederate soldiers laid down their weapons, the Union army gave them a salute of honor.

Two days later, in a White House speech on April 11th, Lincoln called for peace and reconciliation. An onlooker in the crowd, **John Wilkes Booth**, listened to Lincoln's speech and grew increasingly concerned about Lincoln's ideas. At Ford's Theater on April 14th, Booth shot the president. The bullet cut short not only Lincoln's life and his second term as president, but also his reconstruction plans for bringing the South back into the Union. Just six weeks earlier in his second inaugural address, Lincoln had spoken about binding up the nation's wounds with "charity for all and malice toward none" in order to achieve a lasting peace. The war was over, but now the plans for reconstruction and reconciliation were in doubt.

Lesson 14-4: The Impact of the War on American Society

Throughout the four long years of conflict, Northern and Southern societies were transformed. Families followed reports in newspapers and magazines. Photographers such as **Mathew Brady** gave many a firsthand glimpse of war's harsh reality. Although some businesses and their owners profited from war, for others it meant deprivation and hardship. Philanthropic organizations, such as the United States Sanitary Commission, helped in procuring supplies and medical care for the Union Army to provide care to wounded soldiers.

Republican Agenda

With the Republicans firmly in control of Congress during the war, Lincoln could pursue his Republican agenda to further stimulate the North's economy. The first pieces of legislation included the **Homestead Act** (1862), which provided 160 acres of public land virtually free to any citizen willing to occupy it for five years. An $18 filing fee was all that was needed to secure the land. It would be up to the settlers to make improvements to the property. The Homestead Act greatly impacted settlement of the West.

Next, the **Morrill Land Grant Act** (1862) provided 30,000 acres of land to each state for each congressional representative seat the state had. Proceeds of the land sales were to be used to establish public colleges in engineering, agriculture, and military science. More than 70 land grant colleges were established under the original bill. A second act in 1890 extended the land grant provisions to the sixteen Southern states.

With Southern opposition to the route of a transcontinental railroad no longer an issue, Northern congressmen were free to promote their version of a railroad bill, which would have a northern route (eventually making Chicago a major hub for railroad activity). The **Pacific Railroad Act** (1862) granted a contract to the Union Pacific to build west from Omaha and to the Central Pacific to build east from California. The bill included the creation of federally chartered corporations that would receive free public lands and generous loans to secure the building of the railroad. The railroad wasn't completed until May 10, 1869, when the two companies met at Promontory Point in Utah to drive the "golden stake" that finally united East and West.

Congress then passed a bill to raise tariffs to protect Northern industries. The **National Bank Act** (1863) created a national banking system. It stabilized the national currency and reduced conflicting state bank policies.

The Emancipation Proclamation

Early in the war, Union officials were uncertain how to treat Southern slaves who fled to the North or were captured by the army. Lincoln was cautious in his approach, because the Union still included four slave states and many proslavery Democrats. But Lincoln began to be attacked within his own party for not acting on emancipation sooner. He vaguely supported the policy of confiscation, in which slaves who had worked for the Confederate military were considered captives of war and put to work for the Union army. Each Union loss in the war, however, made emancipation a more attractive course, because slave labor drove the Southern economy and helped the Confederacy devote more white men to war. In reply to his critics for not previously taking action on the issue, Lincoln linked emancipation to the military necessity of saving the Union.

Lincoln eventually came to favor emancipation and looked for the right moment to announce his decision. Finally, after the Union victory at Antietam in September 1862, Lincoln issued the **Emancipation Proclamation**, declaring all slaves under rebel control free as of January 1, 1863. In practice, the proclamation freed very few slaves because it didn't affect the slave states within the Union or the parts of the Confederacy under Union control. As a political move, it proved to be decisive and brilliant. The proclamation continued to argue against French or British recognition of the Confederacy, and it appeased the Radical Republicans in Congress. Furthermore, blacks would now be recruited to enlist in the Union army, and they would provide 10 percent of the army troops by the end of the conflict. With this proclamation, the war was transformed from just preserving the Union to that of the abolition of slavery and of drastically altering the social, economic, and racial status quo in the South.

Following the proclamation, the president and the Republican party platform in the 1864 election continued to work for abolishing slavery. On January 31, 1865, the **13th Amendment**, abolishing slavery in the United States, was passed by Congress and sent to the states for ratification.

Black Soldiers

Lincoln finally acknowledged the use of blacks in the military with the **Militia Act of 1862**, authorizing the president to include blacks in military and naval service and giving Southern slaves freedom in return for service to Union. Initially designed to allow the use of blacks as laborers with military units, it was not long until black militia units were formed. Soon black soldiers would be engaged in the fight for equality on two fronts—equal treatment by the enemy and by their own government. By war's end, 16 black soldiers had been awarded the Medal of Honor for their valor.

The Emancipation Proclamation in 1863 significantly affected the war by bolstering the Union's forces. After the proclamation, the Union began to be flooded by a wave of black men wanting to enlist. These black soldiers in conquered areas of the South, provided yet another crucial turning point in the war for the Union. By the end of the war, black soldiers made up almost 10 percent of the Union army. In all, more than 180,000 blacks enlisted and 68,000 were killed or wounded in battle. They proved themselves in battles by demonstrating great courage and skill.

During the conflict, Southerners remained indignant at the sight of black soldiers in uniform, and even massacred captured black soldiers.

Although blacks were assigned to segregated units commanded by white officers, paid nearly half as much as white soldiers, and sent to less desirable posts, their military service was an important symbol of black citizenship and freedom. Black soldiers fought heroically in several major battles. One of the most memorable troops, the **54th Massachusetts Colored Infantry** regiment commanded by Colonel Robert Gould Shaw, fought valiantly, but more than half of the troops died when they attempted a frontal assault on Fort Wagner in South Carolina, in July of 1863. Not only did they fight well in battle, but they also refused pay until the government would agree to compensate black soldiers in the same manner as white soldiers. Their valor in this fight led other black soldiers and their white commanders to also fight for equal pay. By 1864, the federal government agreed to equal pay for both white and black soldiers.

Fort Pillow in southwestern Tennessee was the site of a distressing example of wartime abuse. In April 1864, Confederate soldiers shot to death several captured black Union soldiers. Confederate General Nathan Bedford Forrest witnessed this atrocity and did nothing to stop it. "Remember Fort Pillow" became a rallying cry for many black soldiers for the remainder of the war.

The Role of Women During the War

Women from both the North and the South played vital roles in the Civil War. Some, such as **Clara Barton** (the "Angel of the Battlefield") and Dorothea Dix, served as army nurses, despite strong objections that the work was unseemly for women. Lincoln helped establish the United States Sanitary Commission to aid in treatment of wounded soldiers on the battlefield. Women's service in this organization helped make nursing a respectable profession for women long after the end of the war. In 1881, Clara Barton founded the American branch of the Red Cross and became its first president in 1882.

Other women served the war effort by taking jobs in factories, sewing rooms, arsenals, and federal government offices. Some women served as spies during the war, and a few even disguised themselves as soldiers and fought with both Union and Confederate troops. Still hundreds of others accompanied both camps and served as laundresses, cooks, nurses, and camp followers. The war increased women's confidence in their abilities, but it also made thousands of widows and left many women devastated by the loss of fathers, husbands, and sons.

Lesson 14-5: North and South

At the outset of the conflict in 1861, both sides felt confident that skirmishes would be short-lived, but as time wore on, both sides sought to obtain soldiers, arms, munitions, and everything else that was needed to outfit an army. Maintaining a fresh supply of troops was a challenge for both sides during the war. The South passed the first wartime draft in April 1862, setting the age for service between 18 and 35 years of age for three years of service. Men could hire substitutes to take their place in the draft, and plantation owners with 20 or more slaves were given exemptions. This began to cause deep resentment among whites involved in the conflict in the South. The conflict became a "rich man's war and a poor man's fight." The North followed with its own conscription bill in 1863. Both sides dealt with dissension and draft dodgers. Draft riots in New York City broke out in July 1863, as a result of rising tensions between Democrats and Republicans, as well as problems with city merchants and conflicts between Irish immigrants and blacks.

The Northern economy grew throughout the war and quickly rebounded afterward. Postwar, it would grow so rapidly that the United States would become the leading economic power in the world. The increasing role of the federal government in this growth helped fuel this expansion as the government became more involved in facilitating economic development. The Southern economy, on the other hand, was ravaged by the war. With little food, worthless money, staggering inflation, an agricultural system in ruins, and devastation from war, Southerners would take decades to rebound from the war's effects.

Four long years of battle ended with the surrender of the Confederacy at Appomattox Courthouse. The end of the war marked a major turning point for the U.S. government because the Union victory resolved the question of secession and states' rights. The federal government would now be secure in its power over the states, although the issue of states' rights would still surface from time to time. The institution of slavery was finally abolished, but in its wake, fear, anger, and resentment fueled Southern apprehension about the future.

Review Exam

Multiple Choice

1. Lincoln's initial goal in the Civil War in 1861 was to:
   a) preserve the Union
   b) abolish slavery
   c) recognize the legitimacy of the Confederacy
   d) secure the border states

2. During the war, Lincoln strengthened his leadership by all of the following *EXCEPT*:
   a) declaring martial law and suspending the writ of habeas corpus (allowing Confederate sympathizers to be arrested and held without trial)
   b) having some Northern newspapers shut down for a brief time
   c) agreeing with Chief Justice Roger Taney on the need to preserve civil rights
   d) establishing a Republican agenda to stimulate the growth of the Northern economy during the war

3. Black soldiers played a key role in the Civil War as demonstrated by:
   a) 10 percent of the entire Union army being comprised of black soldiers by the end of the war
   b) black soldiers fighting in major battles
   c) black soldiers demonstrating great courage and skill in combat
   d) all of the choices on the list

4. The Emancipation Proclamation declared that:
   a) all slaves were to be freed as of January 1, 1863
   b) all slaves would be freed at the end of the Civil War
   c) all slaves under rebel control would be free as of January 1, 1863
   d) slaves would not be recruited for the Union Army

5. Lincoln's Gettysburg Address was significant because he:
   a) appealed to the South to surrender
   b) portrayed the war as a test of the strength of democracy
   c) promoted the hope of the country by having a "new birth of freedom"
   d) choices *b* and *c* only

6. With Lincoln's reelection in 1864, he assured the Republican party's ability to:
   a) control the country's political agenda after the end of the Civil War
   b) attempt control of rebuilding the country following the end of the war
   c) force the Southern Democrats to work towards a quick end to the war
   d) work on midterm elections in 1866

7. The significance of the 13th Amendment was that it:
   a) abolished slavery in the United States
   b) granted slaves citizenship
   c) gave black men the right to vote
   d) placed a 20-year limit on the future of slavery

8. Following the end of the Civil War, Ford's Theater on April 14, 1865, was the scene of a tragic event that:
   a) ended with the assassination of President Lincoln
   b) ended the hopes of a quick and lenient Reconstruction plan (according to Lincoln's goals)
   c) put in doubt the ability to achieve a lasting peace with the end of the war
   d) all of the choices on the list

9. Union advantages in the war included all of the following *EXCEPT*:
   a) having more than 60 percent of the railroad mileage in the country
   b) having 90 percent of the industrial output
   c) having a population that was slightly smaller than that of the South
   d) having 75 percent of the nation's wealth

10. One of the major war aims of the Confederacy over the Union (that was never realized) was to:
    a) secure a blockade of Northern ports
    b) gain the support of Britain
    c) use its large volunteer army to quickly defeat the North
    d) burn the capitol building in Washington, D.C.

Matching

a. Richmond, Virginia

b. Clara Barton

c. Robert E. Lee

d. Copperheads

e. Morrill Land Grant

f. Shiloh

g. Radical Republicans

h. Ulysses S. Grant

i. Gettysburg

j. Pacific Railroad Act

k. Colonel Robert Shaw

l. Rock Island

m. Bull Run

n. Antietam

o. Homestead Act

p. March to the Sea

q. Andersonville

r. Appomattox Courthouse

s. Fort Sumter

t. Fort Pillow

u. General Sherman

_____11. after heavy losses on both sides in this Union victory in April 1862, the war began to focus on the total destruction of the enemies forces in battles (by waging "total war")

_____12. where the opening battle of the Civil War was fought in April 1861

_____13. Northern Democrats who questioned Lincoln's approach to the war

_____14. the Union commander who stated, "War is hell" and who led brutal assaults on the Confederacy

_____15. the legislation that provided 160 acres of public land free to any citizen willing to occupy it for five years (this greatly impacted the settlement of the West after the war)

_____16. the capital of the Confederacy

_____17. the site of the surrender of the Confederacy to the Union ending the Civil War

_____18. the battle that was not only the bloodiest single-day battle of the Civil War, but proved to be a victory for the Union in keeping the Confederate Army from advancing into the North

_____19. the legislation that provided land for each state to sell in order to use the funds to establish public land-grant colleges (more than 70 colleges were established with the original bill)

_____20. a Confederate commander during the Civil War

_____21. the battle site where confederate soldiers shot to death several captured black soldiers

_____22. he accepted the surrender of the Confederacy on April 9, 1865

_____23. the extreme wing of the Republican party that openly challenged Lincoln's handling of the war (and later his plans for Reconstruction) and pushed for abolition of slavery

_____24. the turning point of the Civil War in the Union's favor

_____25. the Confederate prison camp that held more than 12,000 prisoners and resulted in the death of nearly 2,000 prisoners

_____26. the legislation that provided contracts to the Union Pacific and Central pacific railroad companies to construct a transcontinental railroad (that would be completed on May 10, 1869)

_____27. the "angel of the battlefield" who greatly aided in the care of wounded soldiers during the Civil War (and who went on to help found the American Red Cross after the war)

_____28. a Confederate prison camp that held more than 33,000 union prisoners; deplorable conditions at the camp led to the deaths of more than 13,000 soldiers

_____29. the commander of the 54th Massachusetts Colored infantry who died in battle at the assault on Fort Wagner

_____30. the plan to burn Atlanta and march to the coast, demolishing everything in the path to the coast

_____31. the first major battle of the war resulting in a Confederate victory

Short Response

32. What were the greatest problems facing both the Union and the Confederacy at the outset of the war?

33. What impact did the end of the war have on both the Union and the Confederacy?

34. Discuss the consequences of the war for the following groups:
   ▶ women   ▶ the Republican party
   ▶ blacks   ▶ the Democratic party

Answers begin on page 270.

Answer Key

Chapter 1 Answers

Multiple Choice

1. **C** is the correct answer. Ever since the exploration of the Orient by Marco Polo, Europeans were enamored with the exotic imports of gold, silk, and spices.

2. **D** is the correct answer. The three continental regions of Europe, Africa, and the Americas became intertwined with each other as exploration and trade occurred throughout the 1440s and 1500s.

3. **B** is the correct answer. Marco Polo's adventures in China sparked a great interest for trade with the region.

4. **A** is the correct answer. Portugal started the slave trade with Africa during its explorations in the 1400s. Spain got involved in the slave trade in the 1500s when the American Indians used for labor began dying of disease or harsh treatment.

5. **B** is the correct answer. Queen Isabella and King Ferdinand of Spain financed Columbus's trip to the New World in 1492.

6. **C** is the correct answer. Within a century of contact with the Native Americans by the Spanish (beginning in 1492) 90 percent of the American Indian population in North and South America was wiped out by 1600.

7. **A** is the correct answer. As Spain attempted to dominate the Native Americans in the New World, the Indians were subject to gruesome brutalities at the hands of Spanish conquistadores.

Matching

8. **I**	10. **K**	12. **C**	14. **D**	16. **A**	18. **G**
9. **B**	11. **H**	13. **F**	15. **E**	17. **L**	19. **J**

Short Response

20. As the Protestant Reformation raced across Europe, Spain sought to spread the Catholic faith by forcing those in the New World to convert or die. As Spain continued its explorations in the 1500s, several missions were established, ranging from present-day Florida to California.

21. As the Old and New Worlds collided in the 1500s, there was a great exchange of animals, crops, and diseases known as the "Columbian Exchange." Crops such as corn, pumpkin, squash, beans, chocolate, and vanilla were introduced to Europeans. Bananas, sugar cane, and coffee were introduced to the New World by Europeans. Smallpox and measles were brought over by the Europeans, and syphilis was brought back to Europe from the New World.

22. **Gold**—This concept of riches led Spain to deplete much of the gold and silver from the Americas and export it to Spain.

    Glory—This concept of land, wealth, and being first or taking the lead motivated explorers and countries to colonize the New World in an effort to boost their own exploits and make their country look great in the eyes of the world.

    God—This concept motivated several Spanish missionaries to establish missions in an effort to covert the American Indians to Catholicism.

Chapter 2 Answers

Multiple Choice

1. **C** is the correct answer. After the defeat of the Spanish Armada in 1588, Great Britain began to take the lead in colonization in the New World, especially with the colonization of Jamestown in 1607.

2. **B** is the correct answer. Tobacco is credited with saving the colony of Jamestown, as exports of the crop created increasing amounts of wealth for the colony. It also established the importance of agriculture for the colony's growth.

3. **A** is the correct answer. During the first winter at Jamestown, nearly half the settlers died. This caused John Smith to make the new rule of work for the colony to survive: "He who shall not work shall not eat."

4. **B** is the correct answer. When the first settlers arrived in Jamestown, their first and foremost goal was to "find gold and refine it." They did not care about food or anything else. This led to the deaths of many settlers during the first winter.

5. **D** is the correct answer. Slaves were imported to Jamestown in 1619 and auctioned as labor. As the time progressed, more slaves were brought to the colony and sold at auction. Slave labor began to be used as lifetime service, and by the end of the seventeenth century had replaced indentured servitude as the major labor source for agriculture in the southern colonies.

6. A is the correct answer. Nathaniel Bacon led a rebellion of frontier landowners against the wealthy elite farmers in the tidewater region. This rebellion illustrated several factors in the Virginia area: growing problems with the Indians in the frontier, and growing tensions between the wealthy landowners in the tidewater area and the new and less wealthy landowners in the frontier.

7. C is the correct answer. The pilgrims established their first colony in Plymouth in 1620. Over the next few years they would establish other colonies around the Plymouth area.

8. A is the correct answer. The pilgrims accepted help from the American Indians, which allowed them to survive and prosper in Plymouth. Other colonists, especially those in Jamestown, had hostile relations with the Native Americans.

9. B is the correct answer. John Winthrop delivered his sermon in which he proclaimed the new colony in the Massachusetts Bay area to be like "a city on a hill." His goal was for this colony to be a unique religious experiment in colonization and living. The church was to be the center of colony and the lives of the colonists.

10. C is the correct answer. Roger Williams proposed compensating American Indians for the land that was taken from them. The church leaders opposed Williams's views and banished him from the colony. He eventually fled to Rhode Island and started the colony of Providence with its founding goals of religious freedom and separation of church and state.

11. D is the correct answer. Anne Hutchinson challenged the male church authorities by her outspoken demeanor. She literally "stepped out of her role as a woman" by openly challenging church leaders and holding discussions of religious matters in mixed groups, and believed that the Holy Spirit enlightened the heart of every believer—male and female. After her trial, she was banished from the colony. She fled to Rhode Island, where she was later killed during a skirmish. Church leaders back in Massachusetts Bay felt that her death was God's justice.

12. A is the correct answer. The Puritan faith was the only accepted faith in Massachusetts Bay. In fact, a theocracy of sorts was created, combining religion and politics in the community. Church leaders controlled the colony, and no other faiths were allowed.

13. D is the correct answer. After the witchcraft hysteria in Salem in 1692, 20 people were put to death and several others were imprisoned. The power of the theocracy in Salem was broken in 1692 as the colony had strayed from Winthrop's original vision.

14. D is the correct answer. Because the Puritan church was the only accepted church in the colony, people were killed, children failed to follow in their parents' footsteps, and accusations of witchcraft broke out.

15. A is the correct answer. William Penn founded the colony of Pennsylvania as a safe haven for Quakers (and others) to freely practice their religious beliefs.

Matching

16. G	19. H	22. C	25. E	28. N	31. Q
17. J	20. A	23. B	26. L	29. P	32. F
18. D	21. K	24. I	27. M	30. O	

Short Response

33. **Role of religion in the colonies**:
   ▶ The Plymouth area was settled by Separatist pilgrims seeking freedom of worship in the colonies.
   ▶ The Massachusetts Bay colony was founded by Puritans seeking religious freedom in the colonies.
   ▶ Dissension was not tolerated in Massachusetts, as accusations of witchraft resulted in 20 deaths and hundreds jailed. Others who dissented were either killed or banished.
   ▶ Pennsylvania was founded as a safe haven for Quakers and other religious groups.
   ▶ Providence was established on the basis of religious freedom and separation of church and state.
   ▶ Jamestown, although British and religious, developed into a colony based on agriculture. Religion was not a dominate force in the colony.

34. **Difference in colonies by region**:
   ▶ Jamestown became a colony based on agriculture, especially the growth and export of tobacco. Indentured servants and slave labor were used in Virginia. The death rate remained high due to diseases and clashes with the Native Americans. Wealthy landowners had the majority of the best land in the tidewater region, forcing others to claim land in the frontier region. Relations with the Native American population remained tense. The House of Burgesses was established as a representative assembly for the colony.
   ▶ The Plymouth and Massachusetts Bay Colony in the New England area were founded on religious freedom. Families migrated to this region and prided themselves on a strong work ethic. Religion was a dominate feature of the colonies in the region. Church officials were also the political leaders in the colony. Relations with the American Indians were better in this region. Problems began occurring when the children of settlers did not strictly adhere to the religious practices of their parents. Dissension also broke out with the accusations of witchcraft.
   ▶ Pennsylvania became a haven for people of various religious backgrounds. They also had better relations with the Native Americans.
   ▶ Georgia was started with England's poorest people and prisoners. Eventually large landowners and slavery came to dominate this colony.

35. **Characteristics of settlement of North America in the 1600s:**

   ▶ **Land**—agriculture in Virginia and other southern colonies; headright system gave landowners land for paying the passage of indentured servants; clashes occurred between wealthy landowners and those in the frontier.

   ▶ **Opportunity**—economic opportunities in Virginia especially after the growth and export of tobacco; religious freedom to establish colonies as a "city on a hill" in the Massachusetts region; a "holy experiment" of religious tolerance established in Pennsylvania; families migrated to the Chesapeake region in large numbers.

   ▶ **Freedom**—economic and religious opportunities encouraged settlement; colonial governments began to reflect the values of the region, representative assembly in Virginia and the church dominated politics in the Chesapeake region; the lack of freedom was also obvious with the use of indentured servants and slaves as a labor supply in the colonies; some colonies were not tolerant of differing views.

Chapter 3 Answers

Multiple Choice

1. **D** is the correct answer. Britain attempted to keep control over the colonies by increasing exports, using the colonies for raw materials, and limiting manufacturing in the colonies.

2. **A** is the correct answer. The Navigation Acts sought to impose strict measures on the colonies by forcing all goods to be transported on British ships. All goods had to pass through British ports for taxation, and further restrictions were placed on colonial manufacturing.

3. **D** is the correct answer. Despite the regulations imposed on the colonies, they enjoyed nearly a century of economic growth due to salutary neglect (basically ignoring the colonies and not enforcing all laws and regulations). Britain was occupied by lingering problems in Europe that drew her attention away from the colonies.

4. **C** is the correct answer. Rice, indigo, and tobacco were major crops in the colonies during the 1700s. Cotton would not become a major crop until after the invention of the cotton gin in 1803.

5. **D** is the correct answer. The economy of the colonies flourished by the mid-1700s because of salutary neglect, a labor force in the colonies made up of indentured servants and slave labor, and by a tremendous population growth in the colonies (more than 2.5 million by 1750).

6. **B** is the correct answer. By 1750 the population in the colonies had swelled to more than 2.5 million people. This was due in part to a tremendous growth of the slave population (more than 20 percent of the total population) and by natural increase of colonial families.

7. A is the correct answer. The Middle Passage was the route used to transport between 10 and 12 million slaves to the New World by 1810, making this the largest forced migration of people in world history.

8. C is the correct answer. Slave labor began to be widely used in the colonies to replace indentured servants. Indentured servants were temporary workers, whereas slaves became lifetime property.

9. C is the correct answer. The Great Awakening in the 1730s and 1740s was a tremendous religious revival in the colonies, as evidenced in the large amount of religious converts and the growth of several protestant churches.

10. B is the correct answer. The middle colonies were known for their religious tolerance. The colonies accepting a wide range of religious beliefs (especially the Quakers).

11. D is the correct answer. The slave rebellions in New York City and in South Carolina raised fears of increased rebellions and led to the enactment of very strict slave codes to regulate slaves throughout the colonies. The rebellions in the two regions showed that slavery was not just limited to the southern colonies—all of the colonies had a certain degree of slave labor.

12. B is the correct answer. The small planter class in the southern colonies came to dominate the political and economic power base in the region.

Matching

13. E	16. A	19. C	22. M	25. K	28. N
14. R	17. J	20. F	23. P	26. G	29. D
15. L	18. I	21. Q	24. O	27. H	30. B

Short Response

31. Although indentured servants were comprised of both men and women, their term of service was generally limited to five to seven years. After they completed their term of service, they gained their freedom and were allowed to leave. Struggles over land ownership occurred between the wealthy landowners and the newly released indentured servants. By using indentured servants, the colonies created a problem of having to continually replenish the work force. Slave labor was different, in that once purchased they were treated as property and their term of service was lifelong. In addition, it became an inherited status, so that children born of slaves were also slaves. Slave labor greatly increased the profitability of plantation owners in the southern colonies and aided in other areas in the colonies (especially New York).

32. The table on page 243 shows the comparison of the colonial regions.

	New England Colonies	Middle Colonies	Southern Colonies
Economics	trade, commerce, fishing	"bread basket" of the colonies, abundant water power, shipping	dependent upon agriculture (tobacco, rice, and indigo were the major crops)
Geography	natural harbors, thin rocky soil	rich land, farming, fur trading	lack of natural harbors, abundant fertile soil
Climate	colder climate, longer winters	milder climate, shorter winters	warmer climate, longer growing seasons
Social/ Political	predominately Puritans, church dominated all aspects of life (including politics), non-Puritans often banished, used town hall meetings to discuss politics	ethnic and religious diversity, royal governors and local assemblies, religious tolerance	most ethnically diverse region of the colonies, large percentage of indentured servants and slave labor, land ownership became the symbol of political and economic power in the region

33. **Economics**—The economy of the colonies grew tremendously from the 1650s to the 1750s. Although Britain enacted certain legislative policies aimed at controlling the colonies, they enjoyed a great amount of freedom due to the lax enforcement of regulations. Shipbuilding, fishing, fur trading, and tobacco, rice, and indigo farming all helped the economy of the colonies to grow. Early on, the New England area around Massachusetts and New York became the hub of trade and commerce, whereas the middle and southern economies were largely agricultural.

   Growth—The population of the colonies grew to more than 2.5 million by 1750. Thirteen colonies had been established by the early 1700s. A significant portion of the growth in population was due to natural increase. Slave labor also became a fixture in the colonies with more than 500,000 slaves by the 1750s.

   Revival—The Great Awakening was a time of religious revival throughout the colonies in the 1730s to 1740s. Several preachers at this time included Jonathan Edwards, George Whitefield, and John and Charles Wesley. The revival was challenged by the scientific movement known as the Enlightenment that relied upon reason and natural laws for governing the daily lives of people. Several British and French philosophers and scientists (Locke, Rousseau, Copernicus, Galileo, and Newton) influenced people in the colonies (Benjamin Franklin and Thomas Jefferson).

Chapter 4 Answers

Multiple Choice

1. **C** is the correct answer. Washington surrendered in what became the first "skirmish" of the French and Indian War.

2. **C** is the correct answer. Franklin's unsuccessful attempt to unite the colonies was known as the Albany Plan of Union (and was depicted in the political cartoon that was printed throughout the colonies).

3. **D** is the correct answer. The colonists lacked a separate identity and unity as colonists and were not ready to break away from Britain.

4. **A** is the correct answer. Britain would not directly tax the colonists until after the war. All of the other selections were true about British actions during the war.

5. **A** is the correct answer. France lost all her claims to North America expect its control of New Orleans. All of the other selections were true about Britain after the war.

6. **B** is the correct answer. The policy of salutary neglect (basically ignoring the colonies) was changed after the French and Indian war when King George III began to focus more on the actions of the colonies. This was the starting point of actions that would lead to the Revolutionary War.

7. **A** is the correct answer. As Parliament continued to tax the colonists, the colonist resorted to even more measures of smuggling goods into the colonies to avoid paying British taxes.

8. **B** is the correct answer. The Proclamation Line of 1763 barred movement west of the Appalachian Mountains. The led to increased frustration with the colonists.

9. **A** is the correct answer. After the French and Indian War, King George began to look to the colonists to help pay for war expenses incurred by Britain during the French and Indian War.

10. **D** is the correct answer. The Stamp Act was a direct tax passed without colonial consent and meant to raise revenue for Britain.

11. **B** is the correct answer. Colonists began to be upset with taxation measures passed by Parliament because the colonists had no direct representation in Parliament.

12. **D** is the correct answer. Daughters of Liberty, Sons of Liberty, and acts at Boston and New York harbors were all measures of protests against British measures by colonists.

13. **A** is the correct answer. Resentment began to grow and protests become more overt and violent as Britain continued to enforce measures on the colonists.

14. **D** is the correct answer. Five colonists were killed in the Boston Massacre, and the events were depicted in a wood engraving and published in newspapers throughout the colonies.

15. **A** is the correct answer. King George began to realize that war would be inevitable as tensions increased between the colonies and Great Britain.

16. **D** is the correct answer. Thomas Paine's publication of *Common Sense* in January 1776 eventually led to the formal Declaration of Independence in July 1776, arguing that it made "common sense" for the colonies to break with Great Britain and declare themselves independent.

17. **C** is the correct answer. Thomas Jefferson borrowed from John Locke's theory of government by making the phrase "life, liberty, and the pursuit of happiness" the central theme of the Declaration of Independence.

Matching

18. **G**	22. **Q**	26. **I**	30. **D**	34. **J**
19. **H**	23. **K**	27. **P**	31. **B**	35. **S**
20. **N**	24. **O**	28. **A**	32. **E**	36. **R**
21. **L**	25. **C**	29. **F**	33. **M**	

Short Response

37. Although initially in support of the war as British subjects, the colonists began to see differences between themselves and Great Britain. Although an attempt was made by Benjamin Franklin for unity, they were not ready. During the conflict, colonial soldiers were under the direction of British commanders. The colonists also learned about British war tactics during the fighting. Parliament raised taxes in Great Britain to finance the war effort, but after the end of the war, King George began to look to the colonies for support for taxation measures to raise revenue to pay for war debts. Britain won the war and began to change is dealings with the colonies by directly interfering in the affairs of the colonies. The colonists began to resent these measures because they had enjoyed a measure of freedom from a lack of British intrusion into their affairs prior to the war.

38. Sense of **identity**:

   ‣ Franklin's proposal of the Albany Plan of Union in 1754 was rejected.

   ‣ The smuggling of goods to avoid paying British taxes increased.

   ‣ Anger and resentment over the Writs of Assistance grew.

   ‣ Local assemblies began protesting British measures.

   ‣ People were upset over the Proclamation Line of 1763 that limited colonial movement west of the Appalachian mountains.

▸ People such as Patrick Henry and others began speaking up in meetings and proclaiming themselves as "Americans" rather than colonists.

▸ Colonists began working together in boycotts and other forms of protests.

▸ Thomas Paine's pamphlet *Common Sense* argued the point of the colonists having an identity separate from that of Great Britain.

39. Sense of **unity**:

▸ Benjamin Franklin's Albany Plan of Union in 1754 began to promote the idea of colonial unity.

▸ Although mainly British in their makeup, unity was difficult because each of the 13 colonies was separate and each had its own identity.

▸ Boycotts and formation of groups such as the Sons of Liberty, the Daughters of Liberty, and the Committees or Correspondence began to demonstrate unity.

▸ The more Britain tightened its grip on the colonists the more that colonist began to see the need to unify themselves in protest against British measures.

▸ Thomas Paine's pamphlet *Common Sense* sparked a turning point in the colonists realizing that they all had a common foe and that declaring independence was necessary.

40. Role of the **media**:

▸ Franklin's Albany Plan of Union was depicted in the political cartoon "Join or Die."

▸ Newspapers carried accounts of British atrocities and increased British measures being imposed on the colonists.

▸ Paul Revere's description and engraving of the Boston Massacre was published in newspapers throughout the colonies.

▸ Committees of Correspondence published articles throughout the colonies. Accounts of the Boston Tea Party and British actions following that event were also published in newspapers.

▸ Thomas Paine's pamphlet *Common Sense* sold more than 120,000 copies in its first three months of publication.

▸ The Declaration of Independence marked the break of the colonists with Great Britain.

41. In light of *regulations, taxes, and protests*, could the Revolutionary War have been avoided?

▸ **Regulations**—King George and Parliament began to "micromanage" the affairs of the colonists by imposing taxes and interfering with local assemblies by passing taxes without their consent. Although British subjects, colonists began to resent interference. Britain countered this resentment with the idea of "virtual representation" that all of the affairs of the colonists were a concern of Parliament and because of their "virtue" of being British subjects that their concerns were being addressed in Parliament.

▶ **Taxes**—Taxation measures were being imposed on the colonists as an attempt by Parliament to raise revenue to pay for war debts incurred during the French and Indian War. Colonists resented direct taxation. As Britain continued to tax the colonists with a variety of measures, resentment began to grow. Discontent grew as appeals for direct colonial representation in Parliament were ignored. Colonists began to form groups such as the Sons of Liberty and Daughters of Liberty to protest taxation measures. Liberty poles were erected and tax collectors were tarred and feathered.

▶ **Protests**—Sons of Liberty, Daughters of Liberty, Committees of Correspondence, minutemen, and other protestors began to show their discontent with British measures. Tensions continued to escalate after crates of tea were thrown overboard in Boston and New York harbors. As protests grew more direct and violent, Britain responded by imposing harsher measures including closing the port of Boston and requiring colonists to quarter British troops. Newspapers throughout the colonies carried reports of protest and violence. The ultimate protest was the group of 56 men who signed the Declaration of Independence on July 4, 1776.

Chapter 5 Answers

Multiple Choice

1. **D** is the correct answer. Britain was not willing to make any concessions. The colonial militia were preparing for conflict, and the delegates at the Second Continental Congress signed the Declaration of Independence.

2. **B** is the correct answer. About 20 percent of the population of loyalists remained sympathetic to the British cause during the war.

3. **C** is the correct answer. Despite widespread resistance to Britain, fighting a war on their own terrain, and having France as a major ally, only 40 percent of the colonial population supported the war for independence.

4. **B** is the correct answer. A major turning point in the war occurred after the Battle of Saratoga, when France joined the Americans as a major ally.

5. **D** is the correct answer. The longer the colonial army could pursue the British army in battles, the better chance it had in wearing down the enemy. Britain began experiencing a lack of supplies and troops, and the colonial army began to use this to its advantage.

6. **C** is the correct answer. Florida remained under Spanish control after the war.

7. A is the correct answer. Because of currency and economic concerns during the war, inflation threatened the economic growth and stability of the new nation.

8. C is the correct answer. After the end of the war, women did not receive any rights, slavery was not abolished , and the Iroquois league had been broken up. The most significant outcome of the war was the spread of the ideal of liberty.

Matching

9. K	11. F	13. N	15. J	17. E	19. C	21. G
10. I	12. D	14. A	16. B	18. L	20. H	22. M

Short Response

23. The Loyalists were a large group (20 percent of colonial population) who sympathized with the British during the war. Although some fled during the war, several thousand served with the British. Places such as New York City, parts of the middle colonies, and regions in Georgia and South Carolina were loyalists strongholds. Loyalists supplied Britain with troops, spies, and supplies. Benedict Arnold was "recruited" by the British, and after his failed attempt to turn West Point over to the British, he joined the British army. After the war, the peace treaty encouraged the return of confiscated loyalist property. Many loyalists fled the country after the war, and others simply "faded away" as America began to focus on growth as a new country. Native American groups often sided with the British during the war and suffered great losses in the war and especially after the war. Britain attempted to lure slaves into combat by promising them freedom.

24. Although Britain had many advantages at the beginning of the war (including a large, well-trained army, Hessian soldiers, a large navy, and a strong centralized government), the longer the war lasted, the more difficult it became for Britain to fight the war. Britain greatly underestimated the amount of colonial resistance. The lack of supplies and soldiers and unfamiliarity with the terrain added to British disadvantages. American advantages included familiarity with the terrain, a cause for battle, leadership from Washington (and other leaders), an alliance with France, and widespread British resistance. Although only 40 percent of the population supported the war effort, they were able to prolong the war to wear down the enemy and emerge victorious. Their independence would serve as a model for other countries.

25. **Freedom**—This was the inspiring cause for the war. The desire for this can be best seen in the Declaration of Independence. Numerous accusations are directed toward King George III and the ultimate decision was made to sever bonds between the two countries. This was a great risk.

    Democracy—By severing ties with Great Britain, the colonies were now forming their own country and would be considered "free and independent states" and able to "have full power to levy War, conclude Peace, contract Alliances, establish Commerce, and to do all other Acts and Things which Independent States may of right do."

Independence—The colonists were taking a bold move to sever the ties. They were making a claim to "life, liberty, and the pursuit of happiness" and making the claim that the sole purpose of government was to secure those rights. Although not an easy decision to make, they ultimately decided that the time had come to claim their independence.

Chapter 6 Answers

Multiple Choice

1. **B** is the correct answer. The government under the Articles of Confederation was weak and had no power to regulate trade between the states.

2. **C** is the correct answer. The Northwest Ordinance of 1787 stated that from three to five new states could be created within the region and that they would all be equal with the original 13 states. Slavery would not be permitted north of the Ohio River.

3. **A** is the correct answer. The original intent of the Constitutional Convention was to attempt to amend the Articles of Confederation. This did not work so they decided to start from scratch and create a new government for the country.

4. **D** is the correct answer. The Articles of Confederation gave states more power than the weak central government, and it was a single-house government (unicameral) with no executive or judicial branches.

5. **C** is the correct answer. A two-house legislature was created. Each state would have equal representation in the senate, and representation in the House was proportional to each states population. The president would be elected by the electoral college.

6. **A** is the correct answer. The power structure of the new federal government would be divided between three branches: executive, legislative, and judicial.

7. **B** is the correct answer. The new federal government was given an unprecedented amount of power to not only do this expressly written in the Constitution, but it was given the power to create new laws that were deemed to be "necessary and proper" for the running of the government.

8. **D** is the correct answer. Slavery would soon become a hotly debated issue in the new country. By avoiding the mention of it directly in the Constitution and by only addressing the issue with the 3/5 Compromise and the ending of the slave trade in 1808, it was left up to individual states to decide upon the institution of slavery. This would become a huge "states rights" issue leading up to the Civil War in 1861.

9. **A** is the correct answer. All of the other selections were part of the original 10 amendments in the Bill of Rights. Women would not get the right to vote until the passage of the 19th Amendment in 1920.

10. **C** is the correct answer. Citizens in the new government under the Constitution would only be allowed to vote directly for representatives to the House. State legislatures appointed Senators (until the passage of the 17th Amendment in 1913) and the electoral college selected the president.

11. **D** is the correct answer. The United States began to be plagued by a series of problems and was powerless under the Articles of Confederation to make an adequate response. We were struggling to gain the respect of foreign nations.

Matching

12. **C**	14. **F**	16. **A**	18. **L**	20. **B**	22. **E**	24. **J**
13. **M**	15. **I**	17. **G**	19. **D**	21. **K**	23. **H**	

Short Response

25. **Weaknesses of the Articles of Confederation**:
    ▸ no authority to impose taxes to raise revenue for the central government
    ▸ no authority to regulate trade
    ▸ no executive branch
    ▸ no judicial branch
    ▸ fear of a strong centralized government
    ▸ lack of unity between all 13 states
    ▸ it only created "a firm league of friendship" between states and gave states more power than the central government
    ▸ amendment process required a unanimous vote of all 13 states
    ▸ each state had only one vote (no matter how large or small the population was within the states)

26. **The Constitution as a radical document**:
    ▸ delegated power to a centralized government
    ▸ divided the power of the central government into three branches: executive, legislative, and judicial
    ▸ allowed the citizens limited direct input into the government by having the representatives in the house elected by the general public (at the time, voting white males)
    ▸ Each branch of government had distinct powers that could be checked by the other branches of government.

- ▸ Even though the document empowered white males in the government, it virtually ignored blacks and women.

- ▸ For the sake of ratification it ignored the issue of slavery.

- ▸ It was based on the concept of federalism—dividing government power between the federal and state government.

- ▸ It also adopted a Bill of Rights in the form of 10 amendments that sought to protect the rights of citizens

27. Constitutional Convention compromises:

- ▸ Great compromise divided representation in the Congress between two houses: the Senate and House of Representatives.

- ▸ Each state would be allowed two senators (to keep each state even).

- ▸ Each state was allotted a number of representatives that was in proportion to its population—larger states with more, smaller sates with fewer representatives.

- ▸ Slavery was ignored.

- ▸ The slave trade would be abolished in 1808.

- ▸ A 3/5 Compromise was in place to count "all other persons" as 3/5 of a person for the purpose of representation.

Chapter 7 Answers

Multiple Choice

1. **A** is the correct answer. Because of the inflation that occurred under the Articles of Confederation, and the lack of our financial credibility with foreign nations, Hamilton proposed radical measures of assuming state debts to begin to deal with this crisis.

2. **C** is the correct answer. In order to secure passage of the Constitution, Madison had agreed to an addition of 10 amendments known as the Bill of Rights after the adoption of the Constitution.

3. **D** is the correct answer. Serious debate about the powers in the Constitution centered on matters of interpretation—loose and strict. Loose interpretation believed in the "elastic clause," the ability to add new laws that were "necessary and proper" to effectively run the county. The strict interpretation believed in the original wording in the Constitution that you could only do what was expressly written in the Constitution.

4. **D** is the correct answer. All of these men were appointed to Washington's first cabinet.

5. **A** is the correct answer. The vice president was NOT consulted for advice, but he did preside over the Senate and would be called upon to caste a deciding vote in the case of a tie in the Senate. It was assumed that the vice president would assume the office of the president in case of his death.

6. **B** is the correct answer. Disagreements between Hamilton and Jefferson about the Bank of the United States centered on northern industrial interests over that of farmers in the south and in the frontier. This led to heated debates about the loose and strict interpretations of the Constitution.

7. **D** is the correct answer. Fierce disagreements about the opposing viewpoints of a strong central government over that of the states and economic policies surrounding the Bank of the United States and tariffs eventually led to both Jefferson and Hamilton resigning their positions in Washington's cabinet.

8. **A** is the correct answer. The Kentucky and Virginia Resolutions argued a state's right of secession if it disagreed with a policy of the federal government. These were written to counter the policies enacted with the Alien and Sedition acts. It also represented a difference of opinion between the Federalist president (Adams) and anti-federalist vice president (Jefferson).

9. **D** is the correct answer. The Alien and Sedition Acts attempted to silence opposition from the opposing party (the anti-federalists), limiting the rights of individuals in a time of "crisis", and strengthening the power of the federal government.

10. **B** is the correct answer. Adams ran for re-election as a federalist in 1800 but lost the election to Jefferson, an anti-federalist (Democratic-Republican). Before leaving office in March 1801, and prior to Jefferson's inauguration, Adams made several appointments to the court system including the appointment of John Marshall, a federalist, to be the new chief justice of the Supreme Court.

11. **D** is the correct answer. Washington greatly influenced U.S. foreign policy by remaining neutral in the conflict in France, attempting to remove British troops from the frontier region, and by using his Farewell Address in 1796 to urge a continuance of not becoming entangled in conflicts with foreign nations.

12. **D** is the correct answer. Adams, a federalist was attempting to formulate policy and secure his legacy by signing the Alien and Sedition Acts into law (aimed at silencing opposition to his administration's policies) and by appointing a Federalist to serve as chief justice of the Supreme Court.

Matching

13. I	16. K	19. C	22. F	25. P	28. J
14. D	17. H	20. R	23. E	26. O	29. B
15. A	18. G	21. Q	24. L	27. M	30. N

Short Response

31.

Federalists	Anti-federalists
Belief in strong federal government	Belief in more power for the state governments
Belief in "elastic clause" for additional laws that are "necessary and proper"	Belief in limited federal government
Favored policies that benefited the industrial interests in the northeastern states	Favored polices that favored the farmers in the south and in the frontier region
Political strength in the northern states	Political strength in the southern states and with farmers in the western frontier region
Many in this party wanted to go to war against France (and this actually split the interests of the party and caused them to lose the election of 1800)	Opposed the policies in the Alien and Sedition Acts (and Thomas Jefferson voiced his opposition and promoted the idea of secession in the Virginia and Kentucky Resolutions)
Favored the Bank of the United States	Opposed the Bank of the United States
Supported appointments to the federal courts (including John Marshall to the Supreme Court)	Didn't favor the last-minute appointments

Even though Washington initially did not favor political parties, they were very much in place by the end of his second term in office in 1796. Political parties and their influence continue on to today in the realm of politics in this country.

32. **Washington:**

▶ Appointed men of opposing parties to his cabinet to get a broad range of ideas.

▶ These appointments led to the development of two political ideologies: federalists and anti-federalists.

▶ Attempted to stay out of foreign affairs (especially with the conflict in France).

▶ Ended the Whiskey Rebellion by sending in federal troops.

▶ Washington's actions in ending the Whiskey Rebellion caused many farmers in the frontier to shift their political loyalty to the anti-federalist party (Democratic-Republican) party.

▶ Negotiated Jay's Treaty and Pinckney's Treaty.

▶ Declared his goals for the future of foreign policy in his farewell address.

Adams:

▸ Ran for election as a Federalist in 1796.

▸ His vice president was Thomas Jefferson, an anti-federalist.

▸ Attempted to stay out of the conflict with France while at the same time increasing the size of the navy.

▸ Signed the Alien and Sedition Acts into law.

▸ Made an unsuccessful attempt for reelection in 1800 (losing to his opponent, Thomas Jefferson).

▸ Made last-minute appointments to the federal courts especially by appointing John Marshall (a Federalist) to be the new chief justice of the Supreme Court.

Therefore, both presidents attempted to deal with policies, conflicts, and opposition by using their power as the president to pursue policies in his best interest.

33. **Washington** attempted to greatly extend his policy/influence by being a strong president who helped end an armed uprising (Whiskey Rebellion), negotiated treaties favorable to the United States (Jay's and Pinckney's Treaties), used executive privilege, and urged neutrality for the United States when it came to becoming involved in foreign entanglements (Farewell Address), and by choosing not to run for re-election in 1796 and establishing the precedent of a president serving for two terms.

Adams attempted to extend his policy and influence by enacting the Alien and Sedition Acts (which silenced political opposition to him, the government, and its policies) and by making very strategic last-minute appointments to the federal courts (especially with John Marshall on the Supreme Court, and because this was a lifetime appointment, his influence would be long lasting).

Chapter 8 Answers

Multiple Choice

1. **B** is the correct answer. For the first time in the country's history, political power transferred from Adams (Federalist) to Jefferson (Democratic-Republican), and the country continued to function under the guidelines established by the Constitution.

2. **D** is the correct answer. The Louisiana Purchase increased the size of the United States, Jefferson sought approval for the purchase (although not specifically mentioned in the Constitution), and the United States had another opportunity to seek the Northwest Passage.

3. **A** is the correct answer. Aaron Burr was a very controversial figure. He was not an influential vice president for Jefferson. He served as vice president for one

term and was not even put on the ballot in 1804. Burr shot Hamilton in a duel, and in a controversial move, attempted to detach part of the recent Louisiana Purchase Territory into a separate country. Although tried for treason, he was found not guilty.

4. **D** is the correct answer. Fighting in Europe between France and Britain also led to the continued policy of impressment of U.S. sailors. The rights of the United States as a neutral country were blatantly being ignored by both France and Britain.

5. **D** is the correct answer. The Embargo Act of 1807 sought to reduce raw materials going to Britain, closed U.S. ports to trade, and sought to protect U.S. neutrality. Ultimately, the embargo dramatically crippled the U.S. economy.

6. **C** is the correct answer. Because Britain had grossly ignored U.S. neutrality, Madison urged Congress for a declaration of war.

7. **A** is the correct answer. The War Hawks in the South and West were in favor of the war. This group was also predominately Democratic-Republican. People in New England, who were still predominately Federalists, opposed the war.

8. **C** is the correct answer. Most of the War of 1812 went badly for the United States, and, as a result, scored very few significant victories. A low point of the war occurred when the British attacked Washington, D.C., in the summer of 1814 and burned the U.S. capitol. A major victory occurred after the official end of the war when in January 1815 Jackson scored a major defeat over the British in the Battle of New Orleans.

9. **A** is the correct answer. The Treaty of Ghent in 1814 officially ended the war by ending the fighting and mainly returning to the status quo of 1812. There was no formal winner declared in the conflict.

10. **D** is the correct answer. The Hartford Convention in late 1814 brought about a serious sectional challenge by threatening secession over disagreements about the war. The Federalists eventually were labeled as traitors for the actions they were pursuing at the convention when the Treaty of Ghent ended the war and the final battle was fought at New Orleans, scoring a major victory for the U.S. troops. The War Hawks would use this victory to their advantage in their continued opposition to the federalists.

Matching

11. **G**	14. **C**	17. **L**	20. **M**	23. **I**
12. **E**	15. **A**	18. **B**	21. **H**	24. **F**
13. **D**	16. **O**	19. **J**	22. **N**	25. **K**

Short Response

26. **Transition:**
    ▶ Switching from one major political party to another in the election of 1800 with Jefferson being elected president.

    ▶ Attempting to stay out of European conflicts by maintaining neutrality.

    ▶ Military cuts in spending led to a reduction in U.S. troops.

    ▶ Sectional interests became evident in politics (Federalists in New England and Democratic-Republican strength in the South and West).

    ▶ Sectional interests became evident with economics—South and West agricultural, and New England manufacturing and trade.

    Discovery:
    ▶ Sending the Corps of Discovery to explore the Louisiana Purchase Territory from 1804 to 1806.

    Challenge:
    ▶ Maintaining neutrality in the face of ongoing conflicts in Europe.

    ▶ Encouraging economic growth and trade with Europe.

    ▶ Britain and France both ignored the U.S. neutrality with the policy of impressments (kidnapping sailors).

    ▶ How to secure economic stability during an embargo (the disastrous embargo of 1807).

    ▶ Gaining support throughout the county for war in 1812.

27. Although Jefferson held a belief about strict interpretation of the constitution, meaning he only had powers that were expressly written in the constitution, his purchase of the Louisiana Territory and the Embargo of 1807 demonstrated that a president sometimes needs to use broad powers implied in the constitution to govern in the best interests of the people.

28. The War of 1812 served to highlight the serious sectionalism beginning to develop in the country. War Hawks in the South and the West, led by Calhoun and Clay, favored the country going to war because economic policies were threatening their livelihood as farmers. People in New England, the stronghold of the Federalist party and the manufacturing and industrial section of the country, opposed the war and refused to cooperate with the War Hawks. When the Hartford Convention was held in 1814 and the threat of secession surfaced, it illustrated a deep rift in the country. Although it was overlooked by the American victory at the Battle of New Orleans, sectional differences brought about by the Hartford Convention illustrated the growing political tension in the country.

Chapter 9 Answers

Multiple Choice

1. **C** is the correct answer. Andrew Jackson became an instant war hero after the Battle of New Orleans, the Democratic-Republic party came to dominate politics in the next decade, and the economy began to grow. The only thing that did not change was slavery—the debate about slavery would begin to heat up during this decade.

2. **D** is the correct answer. Advancements and improvements in transportation, and technological and industrial advancements helped to shape the "Era of Good Feelings."

3. **A** is the correct answer. The Lowell Girls in Lowell, Massachusetts, helped provide a cheap source of labor for the textile mills in the region by becoming part of the factory-working class.

4. **D** is the correct answer. King Cotton came to symbolize the importance of the cotton crop and the slave labor that allowed for its growth in the South.

5. **D** is the correct answer. Transportation improvements with roads, canals, and steamboats allowed goods to be shipped to market in a timely manner and at lower costs.

6. **B** is the correct answer. In the panic of 1819, the price of cotton fell, credit policies were tightened, and loan payments were recalled. Activity in the market began to dwindle causing a panic that would last for several years.

7. **B** is the correct answer. In addition to the states of Missouri (slave) and Maine (free), the Missouri Compromise stipulated that slavery would be barred north of the 36° 30' line.

8. **A** is the correct answer. The Monroe Doctrine closed the Western Hemisphere to European influence. The United States was sending a message to Europe that if Europe stayed out of United State affairs in the Western Hemisphere, then the United States would stay out of European affairs.

9. **B** is the correct answer. John Marshall's influence as chief justice of the Supreme Court can best be seen in his service on the Court for 35 years, and in authoring more than half of the rulings handed down by the Supreme Court during his tenure.

10. **C** is the correct answer. Madison ran unopposed as the Democratic-Republican candidate in his 1820 re-election bid for the presidency. The Federalist party was virtually dead as a political party at this time.

Matching

11. G	14. O	17. M	20. L	23. N	26. Q
12. C	15. P	18. K	21. E	24. A	27. H
13. B	16. I	19. D	22. J	25. F	

Short Response

28. **Idealism**:
    ▶ national pride
    ▶ the name of the period—Era of Good Feelings
    ▶ the Monroe Doctrine—keeping European influence out of the western hemisphere and keeping the United States out of European affairs
    ▶ both North and South are affected by the panic of 1819

    Improvements:
    ▶ canal building (especially the Erie Canal)
    ▶ the national road
    ▶ steamboat travel up and down the Mississippi River
    ▶ interchangeable parts
    ▶ cotton gin (helped revolutionize agriculture and cotton in the South)

    Industry:
    ▶ factory system (Lowell Girls)
    ▶ factory growth due to water power
    ▶ increase in manufacturing
    ▶ sectionalism concerns—the North becomes the industrial leader while the South becomes heavily agricultural
    ▶ all three regions (North, South, and West) dependent upon each other for agriculture, trade, and commerce

29. The Monroe Doctrine sought to keep the United States out of European affairs (as did Washington in 1796 in his Farwell address). Europe would not interfere in the Western Hemisphere and the United States would not interfere in European conflicts. The Farewell Address and the Monroe Doctrine would basically guide America's foreign policy until WWI (and the addition of the Roosevelt Corollary to the Monroe doctrine in 1905, making the United States the "policemen" of the Western Hemisphere).

30. In the rulings in the cases that went before the Supreme Court, Marshall extended the power and influence of the Supreme Court and the federal government by ruling in favor of the federal government when there was an apparent conflict between states and the federal government. Marshall was also appointed to the court in 1801 by the outgoing Federalist president John Adams. Therefore, Marshall was able to extend Adams's legacy on the court by adhering to Federalist beliefs.

31. The Adams-Onis Treaty allowed the United States to acquire Florida from Spain. This would eventually become another slave state in the South. Maine

was admitted as a free state and Missouri was admitted as a slave state. Slavery would not be allowed above the 36° 30′ line. Slavery could continue to spread below this line. The Adams-Onis Treaty also recognized claims to Oregon.

Chapter 10 Answers
Multiple Choice

1. **A** is the correct answer. In addition to the federal government's regulation of the economy, slavery and issues between slave and free states dominated party politics in the decades of 1820–1860 leading up to the Civil War.

2. **C** is the correct answer. The Jacksonian Democrats typically did not support the federal government's role in regulating the economy. He felt that the country would best be served by addressing the needs of the common man (especially farmers).

3. **D** is the correct answer. During his term in office, John Quincy Adams faced increasing opposition from the newly formed Democrat party and was forced to answer to claims that a "corrupt bargain" had been arranged after the outcome of the election allowing the House to select Adams as the president. While president, he proposed a broad agenda of proposals, but Congress failed to act upon any of them.

4. **B** is the correct answer. All four candidates in the presidential election in 1824 were from the same political party. Although Jackson emerged from the race with the highest number of votes (both in the electoral college and popular vote) he failed to secure the majority of votes needed in the electoral college. This threw the race to the House of Representatives to select the winner. It was clear that during the race and its outcome that sectional interests were clearly at work.

5. **C** is the correct answer. Andrew Jackson is best known for his emphasis upon the "common man," which illustrates his support for farmers in the West and South during his presidency.

6. **D** is the correct answer. The Nullification Crisis over the Tariff of 1828 brought about the issue of states rights giving states the right to nullify a law/regulation of the federal government. In theory, this would give the states authority over the federal government.

7. **A** is the correct answer. The Indian Removal Act gave the president the authority to remove Indians from their native lands to lands in the Oklahoma territory.

8. **D** is the correct answer. The two Supreme Court cases, *Cherokee Nation v. Georgia* and *Worcester v. Georgia*, ruled that the Indian nations were "independent nations" and that the federal government, not the state governments, would be responsible to govern Indian affairs.

9. **B** is the correct answer. The Whig party capitalized on the mistakes of the Democrats and blamed the panic of 1837 on the Democrats, thereby helping the Whigs win the election of 1840.

10. **A** is the correct answer. Clay, Calhoun, Webster, and Jackson all represented sectional interests that would dominate politics until the Civil War.

11. **C** is the correct answer. The Second Bank of the United States was denounced by Jackson and denied a recharter because he felt the bank policies favored the business elite over that of the "common man" or farmer. He removed federal deposits to "pet banks" (state banks). This policy crippled the economy of the United States and became one of the factors of the panic of 1837.

Matching

12. **R**	15. **B**	18. **D**	21. **G**	24. **J**	27. **M**	30. **T**
13. **U**	16. **L**	19. **E**	22. **P**	25. **S**	28. **O**	31. **Q**
14. **F**	17. **H**	20. **C**	23. **I**	26. **K**	29. **N**	32. **A**

Short Response

33. Jackson's overall policies helped further define the office of the president by making it a powerful office.

   ▸ He used the veto power 12 times.

   ▸ He openly defied the chief justice of the Supreme Court by ignoring two key rulings in cases involving Native Americans.

   ▸ He helped destroy the Second Bank of the United States by removing federal deposits to state banks.

   ▸ He not only appointed people to his regular presidential cabinet, but he used an informal group of advisors that became known as the "kitchen cabinet."

   ▸ He appointed political friends and supporters to government jobs after the election of 1828.

   ▸ He supported Peggy Eaton during the Eaton Affair.

   ▸ He openly defied Calhoun, his vice president, over the issue of the Tariff of 1828.

   ▸ He supported the cause of the "common man."

   ▸ He also supported the final authority of the federal government over that of a state when the two were in conflict.

34. After the election of 1824, the Republican party split and the Democrats and Whigs emerged. All of this was due to differing sectional interests in the North, South, and West. Southern Republicans, northern Democrats, and southern Republicans agreed upon one thing: their dislike of Andrew Jackson (who they dubbed "King Andrew I" in a political cartoon). The Whig party was in place by the 1836 election but was unable to beat Jackson's Democrat successor,

Martin Van Buren. Because of the panic of 1837, the Democrats would be blamed for this economic crisis and lose the election of 1840, allowing the Whig candidate, William Henry Harrison, to win. This victory would be short-lived, because Harrison died one month into his term of office, and his vice president, Tyler, assumed the presidency and turned his back on the Whig supporters. All of this sectional political squabbling would continue over the remaining two decades leading up to the Civil War.

35. **Corruption**:
   ‣ The flawed election of 1824.
   ‣ Political favors being made to benefit Adams over Jackson in the 1824 election.
   ‣ South Carolina threatened secession over the Tariff of Abominations in 1828 claiming that states had the right to nullify a law of the federal government.
   ‣ Andrew Jackson openly defying the Supreme Court over rulings favorable to Native Americans.
   ‣ Andrew Jackson's cabinet resigned over the Peggy Eaton affair.

   Bargains:
   ‣ Political favors being made to benefit Adams over Jackson in the 1824 election.
   ‣ "Pet banks" (state banks) used to deposit federal funds aimed at destroying the Second Bank of the United States.
   ‣ Adams agreed to make Calhoun his vice president in return for securing enough votes for the House to elect him president in 1824.

   Spoils:
   ‣ Jackson looses the 1824 election and sets his sights on the 1828 campaign (and in 1826 the Democrats gain control of Congress, setting the stage for the Democratic candidate to win in 1828).
   ‣ Jackson wins the 1828 election an appoints several friends and political supporters to government positions.
   ‣ The split in the Democrat party in 1840 allowed Harrison, the Whig candidate, to win the election.

Chapter 11 Answers

Multiple Choice

1. **D** is the correct answer. The Abolitionist movement gained increasing momentum with the publication of Garrisons *The Liberator*, Douglass's *North Star* and speeches, and the Grimke sisters speaking out against slavery. It showed that the movement contained a cross-section of society: Northerners, Southerners, blacks, and women.

2. **B** is the correct answer. At the Seneca Falls Convention in 1848, women began to speak out for equality and the right to vote.

3. **C** is the correct answer. The "cult of domesticity" promoted the proper role of a woman and defined the "woman's sphere of influence"—that of being a wife and mother and maintaining a proper home. It also stressed the values of piety, purity, submissiveness, and domesticity for women.

4. **B** is the correct answer. The temperance movement began to stress the need for total abstinence from alcohol, due to the damaging effects liquor had on families.

5. **D** is the correct answer. The Supreme Court case involving Cinque and the slaves from the *Amistad* was important because it became the most significant court case involving the issue of slavery before the Dred Scott case in 1857. The *Amistad* case was also argued by former president John Quincy Adams. The ruling was in favor of Cinque and the other slaves and allowed them to return to Africa.

6. **C** is the correct answer. Lucretia Mott and Susan B. Anthony argued in the Declaration of Sentiments that women should be treated equally as men, be allowed the right to vote and be allowed to own property. They modeled the document closely after the *Declaration of Independence*.

7. **A** is the correct answer. Transcendentalism was an American literary movement that dealt with knowledge coming through the intellect and insight that came through the senses and intuition. It denied that there was an absolute truth and also sought to rely on emotion and not just logic and analysis.

8. **B** is the correct answer. Women from the North made up a large segment of reformers. They were not only advocating women's rights, but were also advocating for abolition and other reform areas.

9. **A** is the correct answer. Horace Mann advocated education as an "equalizer for the conditions of men" and promoted wide access for education. Books such as McGuffey's *Reader* were used to teach reading, writing, and morals.

10. **D** is the correct answer. During the Second Great Awakening, the messages of revivalist preachers appealed to women, blacks, and young men. Several protestant groups increased their membership. Revival messages also included hymns, prayers, and sermons of repentance.

11. **D** is the correct answer. Utopian movements were characteristic of alternative lifestyles of simplicity and the pursuit of human perfection.

Matching

12. K	15. G	18. D	21. R	24. P	27. O
13. I	16. B	19. A	22. H	25. L	28. M
14. E	17. J	20. F	23. N	26. C	29. Q

Short Response

30. **Goals**:

▸ The abolition of slavery

▸ Women's right to vote

▸ Temperance

▸ Mental health reform

▸ Women's right to own property

▸ Education reform

▸ Religious revival

▸ Utopian movements

Accomplishments:

▸ *Amistad* court case.

▸ Publication of two abolitionist newspapers

▸ Speeches given to crowds to inform them about the evils of slavery

▸ Publication of the Declaration of Sentiments advocating women's rights

▸ Mental health reforms

▸ Conversions during religious revivals

▸ Establishment of several utopian communities (Brook Farm, New Harmony, Shaker communities, and the Mormons in Utah)

▸ Several women were key figures in the reform movement

▸ Laid the foundation for future reforms (the abolition of slavery, women gaining the right to vote, prohibition of alcohol, and so on)

Setbacks:

▸ Women denied the right to vote

▸ The continuance and expansion of slavery

▸ Temperance movement faced obstacles in banning alcohol

▸ Education reform was slow to catch on

▸ Women continued to be denied the right to vote and were still limited in roles they could play in society.

▸ As the debate about slavery heated up especially after 1850, reform movements were largely ignored

31. **Political characteristics of slavery**:

▶ The gag rule in Congress limited the discussion of slavery in Congress.

▶ Southern women such as the Grimke sisters spoke out against slavery.

▶ Northerners became involved in the abolition movement (especially William Lloyd Garrison and the publication of his newspaper, *The Liberator*, and the formation of the Anti-Slavery Society).

▶ Former slaves becoming involved in the abolitionist movement (such as Frederick Douglass, Harriet Tubman, and Sojourner Truth).

▶ The publication of Douglass's newspaper, *The North Star*, and public speeches advocating abolition.

32. **Women in the reform movement**:

▶ Many of the women involved in this movement were very well educated.

▶ Women began to advocate openly for rights—the right to vote, the right of equality, the right to own property, and so on.

▶ Areas of reform appealed to a broad range of women attempting to make a difference in society (education, temperance, crime, mental health, and so on).

▶ Although mainly Northern women were involved in the movement, there were also former female slaves and Southern women who became involved in the movement.

33. **Foundation for future reforms**:

▶ Abolition—finally occurred at the end of the Civil War in 1865 with the 13th Amendment to the Constitution.

▶ Women gained the right to vote in the 19th Amendment to the constitution in 1920.

▶ The temperance movement succeeded in gaining a constitutional amendment (18th) in 1920 banning the manufacturing, transportation, and sale of alcohol (but was repealed by the 21st Amendment in 1933).

▶ Education reform would continue to be an area of focus (especially in the early twentieth century).

▶ Women would continue to pursue their equal rights in society in future reform attempts.

▶ Religious movements and developments in literature would once again be components of reform movements.

▶ Reform movements in the future would not only appeal to and involve large numbers of women, but also men and blacks would become involved.

Chapter 12 Answers

Multiple Choice

1. **B** is the correct answer. Manifest Destiny promoted the idea that "God had ordained" the spread of the United States from the Atlantic to the Pacific. This was used to justify expansion westward in the decades leading up to the Civil War.

2. **D** is the correct answer. Texas was a focal point for nearly two decades due to the lost battle at the Alamo (and the battle cry "Remember the Alamo"), the independence of the Lone Star Republic for nine years, and the desire of the United States to acquire Texas for land for cotton and the expansion of slavery.

3. **D** is the correct answer. The 1844 campaign with Polk became focused on the annexation of Texas. Tyler, the outgoing president, urged Congress to pass a joint resolution to admit Texas to the Union as a slave state just days prior to Polk's inauguration.

4. **C** is the correct answer. The flash point of the Mexican War occurred when Mexico crossed the Rio Grande River (a disputed area between Mexico and Texas) resulting in the deaths of 11 American soldiers. This caused Polk to ask Congress for a declaration of war on May 11, 1846, on account of "American blood being shed on American soil."

5. **D** is the correct answer. Journalists played a huge role in the Mexican War by fueling the public's appetite for current war news. Reporters would use the telegraph to report news of the war that the penny press published.

6. **A** is the correct answer. The failed Wilmot Proviso tried to ban slavery in territory acquired from Mexico in the Mexican War. Although the measure went down in defeat, the new Free-Soil party would adopt its provisions in its party platform.

7. **D** is the correct answer. With the victory in the war with Mexico, the United States acquired new territory and the debate about the expansion of slavery excalated.

8. **C** is the correct answer. The Santa Fe, Oregon, and California trails all were significant in providing routes for settlers traveling westward.

9. **B** is the correct answer. In an effort to prevent a military clash between the United States and Britain over the Oregon Territory, both countries agreed to a new common border at the 49th parallel. Polk was bold to claim 54° 40 or fight, but with war looming with Mexico, this northern conflict was resolved without bloodshed.

10. **D** is the correct answer. Southerners vigorously defended their "peculiar institution" of slavery by using historic, biblical, scientific, and moral justifications.

11. **A** is the correct answer. Southerners began to fear the outbreak of slave rebellion on account of the large slave population in the South. Many states, especially those in the Deep South, had percentages of slave population near or

more than 50 percent, and this fact frightened the white Southerners. They imposed harsh measures to prevent outbreaks of slave rebellions.

12. **B** is the correct answer. Popular sovereignty was the concept that was developed to allow new territories to vote for themselves to determine what the status of slavery would be in their territory. This was also an attempt to keep the federal government from regulating slavery and to allow the concept of "states rights" to prevail in the debate about slavery.

Matching

13. **J**

14. **C**	17. **A**	20. **F**	23. **Q**	26. **M**	29. **I**
15. **E**	18. **D**	21. **K**	24. **N**	27. **R**	30. **B**
16. **P**	19. **L**	22. **G**	25. **O**	28. **H**	

Short Response

31. **Destiny**:

▶ Manifest Destiny was the concept that God had ordained, that it was the destiny of the United States to expand westward.

▶ Journalist John L. O'Sullivan used the concept of Manifest Destiny to proclaim that America was destined to "become the great nation of futurity" and that it would be an era of "American greatness."

Riches:

▶ When gold was discovered at Sutter's Mill in 1848 it sparked a flurry of people traveling west in 1849 (the forty-niners) in search of gold.

▶ A boom and bust cycle began occurring in the West: Towns would spring up when minerals (gold and silver) were discovered, but as soon as the mines played out, the town would dry up into a ghost town.

▶ By 1850 more than 100,000 settlers were in California, resulting in the pressure in California to apply for statehood as a free state.

Expansion:

▶ Polk was an expansionist bent on war, if necessary, to acquire land for the expansion of slavery.

▶ Polk declared war on Mexico by stating that American blood had been shed on American soil (albeit in a disputed region between Texas and Mexico along the Rio Grande River).

▶ The United States emerged victorious from the Mexican war and acquired more territory in the Treaty of Guadalupe Hidalgo (ending the war in 1848).

▶ The United States acquired additional territory in the southern Arizona-New Mexico region with the Gadsden Purchase for a possible southern route for a transcontinental railroad.

32. **Political implications of the Mexican-American War included**:

  ▸ A war being fought for political aspirations of one political party (Democrats).

  ▸ A war being challenged by the opposing political party (Whigs).

  ▸ New territorial acquisitions would bring up the debate about the expansion of slavery.

  ▸ Popular sovereignty became a way to allow territories to decide upon the status of slavery within their borders.

33. **Expansion and the debate on slavery**:

  ▸ The Wilmot Proviso raised the question of the status of slavery in new territory acquired from Mexico by trying to prevent the expansion of slavery into new territories.

  ▸ Polk's desire for expansion with the acquisition of Texas included land for cotton and the expansion of slavery.

  ▸ The possibility of slave rebellions frightened many Southerners, and harsh measures were enacted to prevent further outbreaks.

  ▸ A new political party, the Free-Soil party, was formed with its platform of not allowing the expansion of slavery into new territories.

  ▸ Popular sovereignty became a way to allow territories to decide upon the status of slavery within their borders.

  ▸ Texas was admitted as a slave state in 1845.

  ▸ California was admitted as a free state in 1850.

  ▸ Oregon was admitted as a free state in 1859.

  ▸ Manifest Destiny was the concept that God had ordained, that it was the destiny of the United States to expand westward.

Chapter 13 Answers

Multiple Choice

1. **C** is the correct answer. The Compromise of 1850 allowed California to be admitted as a free state, allowed New Mexico and Utah to use popular sovereignty to decide upon the issue of slavery themselves, and appealed to Southerners with the inclusion of a strict Fugitive Slave Act to return runaway slaves. With the admission of California as a free state, the balance of free and slave states (which began with the Missouri Compromise in 1820) was broken.

2. **D** is the correct answer. The Underground Railroad and Fugitive Slave Act not only helped to fuel antislavery sentiment in the North, but it also caused many Southerners to begin thinking about secession over the issue of slavery.

3. **B** is the correct answer. Harriet Beecher Stowe's novel, *Uncle Tom's Cabin*, enraged Northerners because of is cruel depiction of slavery in the South. Southerners were appalled by the work and condemned it as a collection of "falsehoods" about slavery.

4. **B** is the correct answer. The violence over the issue of slavery extended to the Senate floor with the beating of Senator Charles Sumner from Massachusetts, citizens from Missouri crossing over to Kansas to attempt to tilt a vote in Kansas, and the attack at Lawrence, Kansas, that became known as "Bleeding Kansas." The Underground Railroad was still operating and Harriet Tubman was never captured.

5. **D** is the correct answer. Slavery and property rights became hotly debated issues in the 1850s with Justice Taney ruling in the Dred Scott case that stated popular sovereignty violated the 5th Amendment protection of property. Northerners continued to be outraged by the Fugitive Slave Act, which allowed for the return of runaway slaves.

6. **B** is the correct answer. Fierce opposition to the Kansas-Nebraska Act focused upon the concept of popular sovereignty—allowing the territories of Kansas and Nebraska to decide upon the issue of slavery within their own borders. It was widely believed that Nebraska would be free and Kansas would be slave. This would also add another state north of the 36° 30 line of the Missouri Compromise (which angered many Northerners).

7. **C** is the correct answer. During the Lincoln-Douglas Debates, Lincoln favored the "free soil" theory of keeping slavery out of all new territories. He believed that slavery should remain where it already existed and not be allowed to spread any further.

8. **A** is the correct answer. South Carolina became the first southern state to leave the Union as a direct result of the outcome of the election of 1860 in which Lincoln was elected president.

9. **C** is the correct answer. The Republican party was able to capitalize on anti-slavery sentiment around the country by selecting Abraham Lincoln as their presidential candidate in 1860. Lincoln won the majority of Electoral College votes, but only gained 40 percent of the popular vote. Lincoln did not appear on any ballots in the South.

10. **D** is the correct answer. The Crittenden Compromise was a final effort to avoid secession by the Southern states. It proposed a variety of measures all aimed at appeasing Southerners. It was rejected in both the Senate and the House of Representatives.

11. **A** is the correct answer. The Confederate States of America was formed with its new president, Jefferson Davis, in response to the belief that secession was a legal and peaceful response to resolve the dilemma of states rights and slavery.

Matching

12. G	15. A	18. D	21. M	24. H
13. F	16. I	19. N	22. O	25. J
14. B	17. L	20. K	23. C	26. E

Short Response

27. **Challenges**:

   ▸ California was admitted as a slave state in 1850.

   ▸ New Mexico and Utah territories decided the issue of slavery with popular sovereignty.

   ▸ Kansas and Nebraska debate on the issue of slavery in 1854 with the Kansas-Nebraska Act allowing again for popular sovereignty to decide on the issue of slavery.

   ▸ The Republican party platform of antislavery.

   ▸ The Know-Nothing and Free Soil platforms of antislavery.

   ▸ The *Dred Scott* court case ruling denied slaves the right to sue on the basis that slaves were not citizens.

   Threats:

   ▸ John Brown and his sons at the Pottawatomie massacre in Kansas, where 200 people lost their lives in a battle over slavery in 1854.

   ▸ South Carolina threatened secession once before over the Tariff of 1828.

   ▸ *Uncle Tom's Cabin* fueled the debate over slavery in both North and South.

   ▸ The Lincoln-Douglas Debates in Illinois in 1858 focused on the slavery debate.

   Secession:

   ▸ The election outcome of 1860 with the victory of Lincoln the Republican candidate led South Carolina to secede on December 20, 1860.

   ▸ Ten other states left the Union to form the Confederate States of America by March 1861.

   ▸ Jefferson Davis was chosen to be the president of the Confederacy.

28. Southerners always held to the position that slavery was solely a states' rights issue—that the states, not the federal government, could regulate the institution of slavery. Southerners believed it was their right to continue the institution of slavery as it spread into new territories and states. Their entire economic base depended upon slave labor. As Northerners began learning more about slavery in the South through newspapers, the Fugitive Slave Act in the Compromise of 1850, the failed attempt of the Ostend Manifesto, and Harriet Beecher Stowe's novel, *Uncle Tom's Cabin*, many came to believe that the federal government had the authority to regulate slavery. Many citizens began pushing for total

abolition of slavery whereas others sought a compromise to allow slavery where it already existed but not allow it to spread. Violence in Kansas, on the floor of the Senate, and at Harpers Ferry in Virginia enraged many Northerners.

29. Compromises were a temporary fix to the problem of slavery but offered no long-term solutions. The Compromise of 1820 lasted 30 years until the Compromise of 1850. The Compromise of 1820 attempted to prevent the spread of slave states north of Missouri and keep the balance of slave and free states equal for representation in the Senate. When California was admitted as a free state in 1850, this upset that delicate balance. A new compromise in 1850 and the Kansas-Nebraska Act of 1854 began to promote the concept of popular sovereignty—let the territories decide upon the issue of slavery themselves. As debates centered on the issue of states rights and federal regulation of slavery, compromises were no longer feasible.

30. The Republicans placed Abraham Lincoln on the presidential ballot in 1860. The Republican party platform was one opposed to slavery. Southerners felt threatened by this and refused to allow Lincoln's name on the ballot in the Southern states. The election had four names of candidates running for the presidency: Douglas, Breckenridge, Bell, and Lincoln. When Lincoln won the election, the Southerners felt they had no other recourse than to secede. The Crittenden Compromise was proposed as a final effort to preserve the Union, but it failed. South Carolina was the first state to secede on December 20, 1860, and by April 1861, 11 Southern states left the Union to form the Confederate States of America. The Confederate attack on Fort Sumter on April 12, 1861, was the beginning of a fierce struggle that would last for four years.

Chapter 14 Answers

Multiple Choice

1. A is the correct answer. Lincoln's initial goal at the outset of the Civil War in 1861 was to preserve the Union. It was not until after Gettysburg that the goal of the war also included freeing the slaves.

2. C is the correct answer. Lincoln used the war to strengthen his leadership by declaring martial law, suspending the writ of habeas corpus, shutting down newspapers, and establishing the Republican agenda in Congress to strengthen the Northern economy. Lincoln's heavy-handed approach in dealing with the war caused him to be in conflict with Roger Taney, chief justice of the Supreme Court, over the issue of civil rights.

3. D is the correct answer. During the Civil War, black soldiers played a key role by making up 10 percent of the Union army, and by their courage, skill, and valor in battle.

4. **B** is the correct answer. The Emancipation Proclamation declared that as of January 1, 1863, all slaves in rebel states would be free. This also changed the focus of the war to one of not only restoring the union but also freeing all slaves.

5. **D** is the correct answer. Lincoln's Gettysburg Address portrayed the war as a test of the strength of democracy, and that he hoped the country would soon have a "new birth of freedom." His focus on restoring the Union was evident.

6. **A** is the correct answer. When Lincoln won reelection in 1864 it assured the Republican party the ability to control the agenda following the end of the war. They would be able to dictate the terms of peace and restoration.

7. **A** is the correct answer. The 13th Amendment was proposed in January 1865 (and ratified by December 1865), abolishing slavery in the country.

8. **D** is the correct answer. The assassination of Lincoln by John Wilkes Booth at Ford's Theater created a series of tragic events: the death of Lincoln, the end of his Reconstruction plan, and the ability to achieve a lasting peace between the Union and Confederacy.

9. **C** is the correct answer. The Union had several advantages over the Confederacy: a larger population (with more men to fight in the war), a stronger economy (to finance the war effort), more railroad mileage (to move troops and supplies), and the major amount of industrial output (to produce goods for the war effort). Throughout the war, the Confederacy would be at severe disadvantages with a smaller population (and suffering a high amount of casualties in war that were not easily replaced), a lack of industry, the loss of their major export crop (cotton), and a lack of finances and infrastructure to finance the war.

10. **B** is the correct answer. At the outset of the war, the Confederacy hoped to gain the support of Britain (its major trade partner for cotton). As the war continued, this hope for support was never realized, and Britain and France did not become involved with the war. The North was able to successfully blockade the South. As the war lingered, casualties mounted, forcing the Confederacy to draft even more men into service for longer periods of time.

Matching

11. F	14. U	17. R	20. C	23. G	26. J	29. K
12. S	15. O	18. N	21. T	24. I	27. B	30. P
13. D	16. A	19. E	22. H	25. L	28. Q	31. M

Short Response

32. **Union:**
    ▸ Belief that the war would be won quickly.
    ▸ They lost the first skirmishes of the war (Fort Sumter and Bull Run) and had to face a Confederate army that was bent on winning the war.

▶ Had strong leadership in Lincoln, but he faced opposition from the Copperheads and Radical Republicans.

Confederacy:

▶ Smaller population.

▶ Lack of infrastructure to fight a prolonged war.

▶ The North was able to blockade ports in the South.

▶ As the war progressed into 1862, Confederate soldiers were forced to be drafted for the duration of the war.

▶ Suffered loss of morale when the Union troops began winning battles and preventing an invasion of the North.

33. By 1865, the war had lasted four long years. More than 620,000 Union and Confederate soldiers were dead, and thousands more were wounded. The economy in the South was in shambles. Because the war was fought in their territory, they suffered the greatest losses. Agriculture in the South was at a standstill, and cotton was no longer king. Sherman's march to the sea also devastated parts of the South. Not only did the South lose the war, but it would take several years for the economy to rebound from the devastating effects of the war. On the other hand, the Union emerged victorious from four years of battle. Their economy was strong. In fact, it grew during the war. Following the end of the conflict, the Northern economy was poised for unprecedented growth. The North was able to dictate the terms of peace in the reconstruction efforts. Lincoln sought for a quick and lenient restoration of the Confederate states to the Union. However, his assassination and the goals of the Radical Republicans would change the focus during the Reconstruction Era.

34. Consequences of the war upon:

Women:

▶ Active participants in the war as nurses, spies, cooks, and so on.

▶ Proved to be a valuable asset to the war effort.

▶ Took jobs as factory workers, sewing rooms, and federal government offices.

▶ Thousands became widows during the war.

Blacks:

▶ After the Emancipation Proclamation they joined the union Army.

▶ Comprised 10 percent of the Union army by the end of the war.

▶ Proved their strength and valor in war at battles that included Fort Wagner and Fort Pillow.

▶ Became dedicated to seeing the war end with a Union victory.

▶ Slavery was abolished with the passage of the 13th Amendment.

The Republican party:

▶ Controlled the presidency.

▶ Was divided within the party with the moderate and radical wings of the party.

▶ Sought to control certain aspects of the war and the plans for Reconstruction following the end of the War.

▶ At the outset of the war Lincoln's goal was that of preserving the Union.

▶ Pushed Lincoln for the war to be one of also "freeing the slaves."

▶ Was able to pass their economic agenda in 1862 to stimulate economic growth in the North.

The Democratic party:

▶ Because the Southern states left the Union to form the Confederacy, the remaining Democrats in the North and the border states were the minority in Congress.

▶ Northern democrats (the Copperheads) were able to challenge Lincoln early in the war.

▶ They were at a disadvantage when it came to planning Reconstruction because they were the minority party and the 11 Confederate states would be forced to abide by the terms of the Republicans for readmission to the Union.

Glossary

A

Adams, Abigail—In 1776, she wrote a letter to her husband John Adams and encouraged him and other men working on the new frame of government for the country to "Remember the Ladies!" John Adams felt that women and poor landless males should be excluded from extended participation in the new government on the grounds that they were "too little acquainted with public affairs to form a right judgment."

Adams, John—He was the husband of Abigail Adams, who also worked on the Declaration of Independence and served as the second president of the United States as a Federalist.

Adams, Samuel—Along with some his close friends, he encouraged the hostile feelings against the British by publishing newspaper accounts of supposed confrontations and threats from British soldiers in and around Boston. In 1772, Adams also helped form the Boston Committee of Correspondence to continue the protest efforts against Britain.

Adams-Onis Treaty—In 1818, Andrew Jackson rushed into Florida to capture a Spanish fort, alarming Spain. In 1819, the matter was settled when Spain agreed to this treaty, also known as the Transcontinental Treaty. The United States assumed $5 million of debt owed to Spain. Spain also ceded eastern Florida to the United States, and renounced all claims to western Florida. Spain agreed to a southern border west of the Mississippi River that extended all the way to the Pacific Ocean, recognizing U.S. claims to the Oregon Territory. The treaty also gave the United States its first legitimate claim to the west coast.

Age of the Common Man—By the end of the 1820s, most states had eliminated property ownership as the basis for voting requirements, resulting in universal white male suffrage. Voter participation rose dramatically from 1824 to 1840, nearly tripling to 78 percent. A democratic and egalitarian spirit filled the nation, prompting many historians to call the 1820s and 1830s the age of the common man. Women, Native Americans, and blacks, however, were still barred from political involvement.

Alamo—The Spanish mission that was attacked by Santa Ana and his forces on March 6, 1836, in which 186 Americans were killed (including Davy Crockett, Jim Bowie, and William Travis). Sam Houston, commander of the Texan troops, met Santa Ana at the San Jacinto River in April with the battle cry of "Remember the Alamo!"

Albany Congress—An inter-colonial meeting in New York that met to discuss matters with the Iroquois Indian tribe. Representatives of seven colonies gathered with 150 Iroquois chiefs. At the meeting, Benjamin Franklin submitted the Albany Plan of Union.

Albany Plan of Union—A plan that called for the colonies to unify in the face of French and Native American threats. They would have the power to coordinate a colonial defense, levy taxes, and regulate Native American affairs. It attempted to establish a unified colonial government. The plan won the support of the delegates, but was rejected by the separate colonies because they weren't yet ready for union.

Alien and Sedition Acts—In 1798, this legislation asserted the power of the central government over the liberty of individuals in an unprecedented way by not allowing any dissenting opinion about the government to be spoken or written. It could also deport anyone suspected of being an "enemy alien" in the Untied States. The acts were enacted by the Federalists and signed into law by John Adams. They were also seen as a political move to squash mounting Republican opposition.

American Anti-Slavery Society—To spread the abolition fervor, Garrison founded this group in 1833, vowing to end the immoral practice of the "peculiar institution" of slavery in the United States. By 1840, abolitionist organizations had more than 1,500 local chapters and were distributing literature throughout the North. Garrison's newspaper spoke for the most extreme abolitionists.

American System—Madison proposed plans for the nation that would be carried out by Monroe's administration. In Congress, Henry Clay fleshed out these nationalist economic policies in programs that aimed at economic self-sufficiency. The major goal was to unite the country's economic interests, with the North producing manufactured goods, the South and West buying the manufactured goods, and the South and West raising grain, meat, and cotton needed by the North. The program included enacting a bill in 1816 to charter the Second Bank of the United States, pushing through a moderate tariff bill to protect America's growing industries, and urging federal funding for internal improvements, including a national system of roads and canals. Support was proposed for federal funding of internal improvements, though there was hesitation about authorizing direct federal involvement.

Annapolis Convention—Here delegates were originally concerned with interstate commerce, but they turned their focus to the shortcomings of the national government. They proposed a convention to consider amending the Articles of Confederation, and asked the states to appoint delegates to meet in Philadelphia in May 1787. George Washington was elected to preside over the closed-door meeting for the next four months.

Anthony, Susan B.—A women's rights activist who argued that men and women were created equal and should be treated equally under the law. In 1848, Lucretia Mott and Stanton organized a women's rights convention in Seneca Falls, New York. The Seneca Falls Convention issued a Declaration of Sentiments, modeled on the Declaration of Independence, stating that all men and women were created equal. She also worked with Elizabeth Cady Stanton.

anti-federalists—People who opposed ratification of the Constitution, claiming that it granted too much power to the national government. They argued that under the Constitution, the states could be dominated by a potentially tyrannical central government. They pushed for the addition of a bill of rights in order to secure ratification of the Constitution in 1789. They also advocated states' rights over that of a central power (or federal government) and drew their greatest support from the agrarian interests in the South and West.

Appomattox Courthouse—The site on April 9, 1865, where General Lee's forces surrendered to General Grant. As the Confederate soldiers laid down their weapons, the Union army gave them a salute of honor.

Arnold, Benedict—The commander of West Point who attempted to turn the outpost over to the British. Arnold (an American traitor) escaped in September 1780 and received a commission as a brigadier general in the British army.

Articles of Confederation—The articles became law in 1781 and provided for a "loose confederation" in which "each state retains its sovereignty, freedom and independence" and "powers not delegated to the United States." The "firm league of friendship" of the 13 states would soon see its loose bonds severely challenged.

Austin, Stephen F.—After Mexico gained its independence from Spain in 1821, Mexico country lured people to Texas for settlement and economic gain. Austin brought 300 families into the region and established a colony along the Brazos River.

B

Bacon, Nathaniel—A wealthy newcomer who soon clashed with Berkeley and other elite landowners over their economic and political control over the colony. Bacon finally challenged Berkeley's leadership, and violence erupted along the frontier with the Native Americans.

Bacon's Rebellion—Nathaniel Bacon and his men led an uprising in Virginia against the Colonial government in 1676. High taxes, low prices for tobacco, and resentment against special privileges given those close to the governor, William Berkeley, provided the impetus for the uprising. Berkeley claimed that Bacon and his fellow conspirators were "rebels and traitors." The ongoing conflict resulted in Bacon's forces capturing Jamestown and Berkeley's estate. By the end of September, Jamestown was burned to the ground. A month later, after Bacon's sudden death from dysentery, the rebellion collapsed.

Bank of the United States—The bank was Hamilton's proposal to establish a national bank to promote the fledgling commercial interests of the United States. It would provide a secure depository for federal revenue, issue currency and federal loans, regulate the activities of smaller banks, and extend credit to U.S. citizens. Hamilton wanted people to invest in U.S. commercial ventures, believing that a sound economy would be beneficial to all. Opposing the proposal, anti-federalists (such as Thomas Jefferson) feared that the bank would tie private individuals too closely to government institutions.

Barton, Clara—The "Angel of the Battlefield," who worked as a nurse in the Civil War and who would go on to found the American Red Cross in 1881.

Battle of Bunker Hill (June 17, 1775)—The English redcoats successfully dislodged the colonials from this hillside stronghold, but suffered a 40-percent casualty rate.

Battle of Fallen Timbers—In 1794, U.S. troops under the command of "Mad Anthony" Wayne routed a group of Native American warriors at this battle, and afterwards 12 Native American tribes signed the Treaty of Greenville, clearing the Ohio territory of Indian tribes and opening it up to further European settlement.

Battle of Lexington and Concord (April 19, 1775)—The attack of the British persuaded many colonists to take up arms and fight back in the first skirmish of the Revolutionary War.

Battle of New Orleans (January 8, 1815)—General Andrew Jackson's troops defended the city of New Orleans in a surprise attack that resulted in Jackson's troops killing more than 2,000 British troops while losing only 13 men. The timing of the Battle of New Orleans inspired the popular misconception that the United States had won the war and forced the British to surrender and sign the treaty. Even without officially winning the war, the United States succeeded in protecting itself against one of the world's premier powers.

Battle of Saratoga (June to October 1777)—Led by Benedict Arnold (who would later become a traitor at West Point) the Americans pushed back the British at Saratoga. During this battle in New York, American forces under General Horatio Gates surrounded the British troops, forcing General Burgoyne to surrender his entire army. The British surrender not only raised the American army's morale, but also persuaded France to recognize American independence and to join the battle against Britain.

Battle of Tippecanoe—A Shawnee chief, Tecumseh, and his brother, "The Prophet," attempted to unite a number of tribes in Ohio and Indiana under an anti-white government. In response, future president William Henry Harrison (then governor of the Indiana Territory) crushed the Shawnees in the 1811 at the Battle of Tippecanoe by burning The Prophet's town to the ground, though his own forces also suffered heavy losses. Almost 30 years later, Harrison would run for president on his popularity as an Indian fighter, using the campaign slogan, "Tippecanoe and Tyler too!"

Bear Flag Revolt—A revolt staged by John Fremont to gain California's independence from Mexico in the summer of 1846.

Berlin Decree—This French policy in 1803 issued by Napoleon tried to diminish trade with Britain by subjecting to seizure any ship that first stopped in a British port.

Berkeley, William—The leader of the Virginia colony in the 1670s. Tensions mounted between the elite planter class and those along the frontier. Overproduction and price fluctuations led to a bust in the tobacco market. In addition, social unrest began to swell under his leadership. Taxes were being raised, and those who didn't own land saw their voting rights revoked.

Biddle, Nicholas—President of the Second Bank of the United States who opposed Jackson's financial policy regarding the Second Bank of the United States in 1832.

Bill of Rights—The first 10 Amendments to the Constitution that were proposed as a concession to demonstrate that a strong government could still guard the rights of individuals and states. It listed certain liberties that the federal government would protect. James Madison led the group who drafted the first 10 amendments to the Constitution, seeking to safeguard personal and states' rights. The state legislatures ratified the amendments in December 1791, and they became an enduring part of the Constitution.

Black Death—The bubonic plague that killed nearly 30 percent of the population of Europe in the mid-1300s.

boom-and-bust—In the West, this cycle was evident as minerals were discovered and mining towns were established, but when those mines played out, the towns were abandoned, becoming ghost towns.

Booth, John Wilkes—At Ford's Theater on April 14, 1865, Booth assassinated President Abraham Lincoln. He was caught several weeks later and killed by an armed soldier in Port Royal, Virginia.

Boston Massacre—Tensions flared with the this event in March 1770, when an unruly mob, ready for a fight, bombarded British troops with rocks, snowballs, and insults. In the ensuing chaos, five colonists were killed. A later report claimed that former slave Crispus Attucks, along with four other men, had been "killed on the spot" by British redcoats. The account of British cruelty and brutality helped to inflame anger toward the British and became a turning point in relations with Britain.

Boston Tea Party—A well-organized and aggressive attack by rebel colonists on British tea. Samuel Adams was among those who helped plan and coordinate Boston's resistance to the Tea Act that culminated in the infamous Tea Party. In December 1773, with several thousand onlookers, a group of colonists dressed as Native Americans dumped nearly 700,000 pounds of tea into Boston Harbor.

boycott—A ban on goods from a particular county. This is often used in retaliation for unfair economic measures by the other nation. This was one method of protest the colonists used to protest British taxation measures leading up to the Revolutionary War.

Braddock, General—Leader of an expedition to expel the French from Fort Duquesne during the French and Indian War, but instead he was ambushed and killed by the French.

Brady, Mathew—A famous Civil War photographer whose work greatly illustrated the horrors of the Civil War.

British East India Company—Suffered from the American boycott of British tea. By the 1770s, 90 percent of American tea was contraband to escape British taxes. In an effort to save the company, in 1773 Parliament passed the Tea Act, which eliminated import tariffs on tea entering England. The act allowed the company to sell directly to consumers rather than through merchants, giving it a monopoly on the tea trade.

Brook Farm—Founded by George Ripley near Boston in 1841. It was an economic community that became famous with its connection to the transcendentalist movement.

Burgoyne, General—The British commander who was forced to surrender to General Horatio Gates at the Battle of Saratoga.

Burr, Aaron—Became vice president after the House broke the tie vote in the 1800 election, making Jefferson president in 1801. In 1804, while making a bid for governorship of New York, Alexander Hamilton accused Burr of being a "dangerous man...one not to be trusted with the reins of government." After losing the election, Burr challenged Hamilton to a duel for his damaging remarks during the campaign. After Burr shot Hamilton at the dueling grounds of Weehawken, New Jersey, he faced murder charges in New York and New Jersey. While fleeing from those charges, Burr began a conspiracy to detach Louisiana from the United States and join it with Texas and Mexico to create a new nation.

C

cabinet—A group of advisors to the president that originally included three executive positions (secretaries of state, war, and treasury), and the office of Attorney General.

Calhoun, John C.—A Southerner and one of the War Hawks in Congress in 1810 who began asserting his power during Madison's administration. He resented the recession that had plagued southern and western regions from 1808 to 1810 and advocated war rather than disgraceful terms of peace. Calhoun would later serve as vice president for two presidents (John Quincy Adams and Andrew Jackson). He later became a states rights advocate.

Cherokee Nation v. Georgia (1831) and *Worcester v. Georgia* (1832)—These two court rulings by the Supreme Court stated that the Indian self-governing bodies were "domestic independent nations" under the authority of the United States government rather than under the authority of the states. Because of that status, the states had to defer to the federal government in regards to the welfare and governance of Indian affairs. This meant the Indians couldn't be forced to give up their lands by the state of Georgia. Jackson opposed the ruling and proceeded with removal, purportedly commenting in defiance, "John Marshall has made his decision; now let him enforce it."

Chesapeake-Leopard Affair—Occurred in 1807 when in 1807, when the British frigate *HMS Leopard* opened fire on the American frigate *USS Chesapeake* off the Chesapeake Bay, after its request to board had been denied. The British killed three men, wounded 18, and took four men aboard the *Leopard*. Although he was outraged, Jefferson wanted to avoid war because of the downsizing of the U.S. army and navy, so he banned all British warships from American waters.

Cinque—Along with 52 other slaves, he commandeered the slave ship *Amistad* off the coast of Cuba in 1839. The ship eventually ended up off Long Island. President Van Buren wanted Cinque and the slaves returned to Spain. The judge in the original case announced his decision in January 1840 and ruled that because the *Amistad* captives were born free and kidnapped in violation of international law, they should be allowed to return to Africa. This ruling was appealed to the Supreme Court, where former president John Quincy Adams argued for the slaves and won their case.

Civil Disobedience—One of Thoreau's most important works, written in 1849. It was inspired by his conscientious refusal to pay a poll tax that supported the Mexican War. After an overnight stay in prison to protest paying a tax that he felt also represented an effort to extend slavery, Thoreau published his thoughts on civil disobedience as a means for an individual to protest unjust government actions.

Clay, Henry—A War Hawk from Kentucky who advocated war in 1810. He also served as Speaker of the House, promoted his agenda to strengthen and unify the nation, the American System, during the Era of Good Feelings, and worked on the Missouri Compromise of 1820. Clay would also be one of the contested candidates in the hotly debated election of 1824 in which the House selected John Quincy Adams as president and Clay was appointed secretary of Sstate. Clay would later work on the Compromise of 1850 as his final achievement.

Columbian Exchange—Brought together the Old and New Worlds. Crops, animals, and diseases were exchanged and had a dramatic impact on the world stage. Crops and animals including corn, pumpkin, squash, chocolate, vanilla, turkey, sunflower, peanuts, and beans were introduced to Europeans, and bananas, oranges, lemons, sugar cane, coffee bean, grains, horses, and honey bees were brought over to the Americas. The Europeans introduced smallpox and measles, along with other diseases, and the Europeans brought back syphilis from the new World. Because of a lack of resistance to these new diseases, millions of people died.

Columbus, Christopher—Made four trips to the New world. His original trip with three ships marked Spain's entrance on the world stage of exploration. Although he failed to find the shortcut to Asia (the fabled Northwest Passage) during his four voyages to the Americas, Columbus did discover a new part of the world for exploration.

Committees of Correspondence—Nearly 250 "committees" not only linked political leaders of almost every colony in resistance to the British, but they became the method by which the colonies coordinated their efforts to preserve their rights.

Common Sense—This book was published and widely distributed. Its author, Thomas Paine, called for economic and political independence, and he proposed that America become a new kind of nation founded on the principles of liberty. "We have it in our power to begin the world over again." In the first three months, more than 120,000 copies were sold. Paine's greatest contribution was persuading the common man to sever ties with Great Britain.

Compromise of 1850—A series of bills in 1850 that included the admission of California as a free state and enacted a tough Fugitive Slave Act to return runaway slaves to their masters. The Mexican cession would be divided into two new territories, New Mexico and Utah, and use popular sovereignty to decide upon the status of slavery in the territories.

Confederate States of America (1861-1865)—Formed when South Carolina and the states of Mississippi, Florida, Alabama, Georgia, Louisiana, and Texas formed a confederacy and swore in Jefferson Davis as president on February 18, 1861. Four more states (Virginia, North Carolina, Tennessee, and Arkansas) joined the confederacy prior to the attack on Fort Sumter in April of 1861.

conquistadores—Spanish soldiers or conquerors who enslaved and killed many American Indians in their quest for riches in the New World in the 1500s.

Constitutional Convention—In May 1787, this meeting included George Washington, John Dickinson, John Jay, Benjamin Franklin, Alexander Hamilton, and James Madison. The delegates were convinced of the need for a stronger national government and decided to create a new framework, embodied by a new constitution.

Convention of 1800—Was reached with Napoleon whereby France canceled U.S. debt and didn't pay for any attacks on American ships. In some respects, the Federalists were upset because war was avoided. Hamilton and others had favored a war, and this caused a split in the Federalist party in 1800.

Corps of Discovery—In 1804, Lewis and Clark set off from St. Louis with 45 soldiers to explore the region of the Louisiana Purchase. While they were in the Dakotas, they met Canadian fur trader Toussaint Charbonneau and his wife, a Shoshone woman named Sacajawea, who proved indispensable as a guide. Their route followed the Missouri River and, after a winter at Fort Mandan, they continued through the Rocky Mountains to the Columbia River. During the winter of 1805–1806, they stayed near present-day Astoria, Oregon, and then returned to St. Louis in the spring after traveling nearly 3,000 miles in two and a half years. They brought back a large botanical collection, maps of the region, sketches and journals, and information about the valuable fur trade, and they laid the foundation for the American claim to Oregon.

D

Dartmouth College v. Woodward (1819)—Marshall ruled that New Hampshire couldn't convert Dartmouth College into a state university because the college's charter, issued by Britain before the American Revolution, qualified as a contract; the Constitution doesn't allow states to interfere with contracts. The grant of the college charter was a private matter and not subject to public regulation.

Daughters of Liberty—Colonists appealed to women to help boycott British goods. One example of their activities (in an effort to avoid buying material spun in Britain) was to meet in large spinning bees to spin wool into yarn and to weave it into a rough fabric known as homespun.

Davis, Jefferson—The president of the Confederacy from 1861 to 1865.

Declaration of Independence—Crafted by Thomas Jefferson, Benjamin Franklin, John Adams, Roger Sherman, and Robert Livingston in 1776. Jefferson borrowed several ideas from John Locke's writings when he crafted this document. This document outlined the grievances of the 13 colonies with the King of England, King George. The colonies used this document to declare their independence from Britain on July 4, 1776.

Declaration of Sentiments—Issued at the Seneca Falls Convention in 1848. the document was modeled on the Declaration of Independence and stated that all men and women were created equal. The activists argued that women should be given the right to vote and should be freed from unjust laws that gave their husbands control of their property, persons, and children.

Declaratory Act—Parliament repealed the Stamp Act in March 1766 and at the same time passed the this measure to strengthen British rule in the colonies. It stated the absolute right of Parliament to pass legislation and raise taxes "in all cases whatsoever."

Democratic party—Following the contested election of 1824, Jackson's supporters, led by Martin Van Buren and John C. Calhoun, rallied and formed this new political party. In 1828 they nominated Andrew Jackson to run as their first presidential candidate.

Democratic-Republican party—The strict constructionists made up the core of this party also known as anti-federalists or Republicans (not to be confused with the modern Republicans, who formed their party in 1854).

Dix, Dorothea—In 1843, as a Massachusetts schoolteacher, described to the state legislature the conditions of the insane in prison and encouraged the construction of insane asylums to better treat the mentally ill. In the following years, asylums opened throughout the United States.

Donner-Reed party—Became trapped in the Sierra Nevada Mountains on their trek to California in 1846. The survivors were rescued in the spring of 1847.

Douglass, Frederick—Soon became outspoken in his opposition to slavery. His 1845 autobiography, *The Narrative of the Life of Frederick Douglass*, and his speeches were compelling firsthand accounts of slavery. He also began publishing an antislavery paper called *The North Star* in Rochester, New York, in 1847. Douglass decided that political reforms should be used to end slavery. He realized that blacks would have to pay a heavy price to win their freedom, and that they "must do this by labor, by suffering, by sacrifice, and if needs be, by our lives and the lives of others."

Dred Scott v. Sanford—In the 7–2 supreme Court ruling, the five Southern justices concurred with Taney's decision that Scott, as a slave, had no right to sue in federal court, and furthermore claimed that no black, slave or free, could become a citizen of the United States. Slaves were property only, according to Taney, and would remain so even if they resided in free territory. In addition, Taney ruled that Congress couldn't forbid slavery in any U.S. territory because doing so would violate the 5th Amendment's protection of property, including slaves, from being taken away without due process.

Dyer, Mary—A one-time disciple of Anne Hutchinson, she suffered for her religious beliefs after becoming a Quaker. Mary Dyer and her husband, William Dyer, were excommunicated from the Boston Puritan Church and banished from the colony. Mary became a follower of the Society of Friends (Quakers) and returned to Boston where she was twice imprisoned due to her defiance of a new law passed in 1658 banishing Quakers under pain of death. Eventually, she was expelled, but defied the court and returned several times. Defiant to the end and refusing to repent, she was hanged for her beliefs on June 1, 1660.

E

Eaton, Peggy—Grew up as a tavern-keeper's daughter in the Washington area. The "affair" involved the refusal of the cabinet members' wives to receive Peggy at formal socials. Peggy O'Neale Timberlake's 1829 marriage to Secretary of War John Eaton raised eyebrows because of her previous marriage to John Timberlake, a naval officer who recently died at sea. Rumors of John Eaton marrying Peggy included references to him marrying "his mistress" who had also been the "mistress of nearly a dozen others." Vice President John Calhoun's wife, Floride, led the anti-Peggy crusade because Eaton was considered to be a "fallen woman" and "unfit for polite society."

election of 1800—The presidential election in which Jefferson, an anti-federalist, defeated the federalist candidate, Adams. It represented a "changing of the guard"—that of transferring political power from one party to another. It proved that the Constitution was still intact and that the government would keep on running.

electoral college—A proposal of the Great Compromise at the Constitutional Convention in 1787 that established a group of competent leaders who would meet and choose the president. Members of the Senate would be appointed by state legislatures. The House of Representatives would be the only segment of the government in which the members were elected by popular vote. This compromise would allow the people some say in the new government.

Emancipation Proclamation—Issued by Lincoln in September 1862, it declared all slaves under rebel control free as of January 1, 1863. As a political move, it proved to be decisive and brilliant. The proclamation continued to argue against French or British recognition of the Confederacy, and it appeased the radical Republicans in Congress. Furthermore, blacks would now be recruited to enlist in the Union army, and they would provide 10 percent of the army troops by the end of the conflict. With this proclamation, the war was transformed from just preserving the union to that of the abolition of slavery and of drastically altering the social, economic, and racial status quo in the South.

Embargo Act of 1807—Legislation that prohibited any ship from leaving a U.S. port for a foreign port, targeting all imports and exports. Jefferson and Congress hoped that such a measure would so damage the British and French economies that the countries would be forced to honor U.S. neutrality. The goal was to reduce raw materials going to Great Britain, but the results were disastrous to the U.S. economy as commerce came to a virtual standstill. The United States was driven into a deep depression, and illegal trade began as merchants attempted to make profits.

Enlightenment—In eighteenth-century Europe during the Age of Reason, this intellectual movement embodied the principles of rationalism and logic, and the Scientific Revolution worked to demystify the natural world. The Enlightenment movement questioned how the world was viewed and sought to apply reason and the scientific method to obtain knowledge.

Era of Good Feelings—The decade immediately following the end of the War of 1812. America was fast becoming a great nation, spurred on by the economy's growth. The new market economy was quickly shaping the nation. Transportation advances helped spur economic growth, and a revolution in manufacturing was taking off. Despite the good feelings, there were serious problems also forming during this time: the panic of 1819, party strife with the anti-federalist (Republican) party, and sectionalism due to the spread of slavery.

Erie Canal—The first major canal project in the United States. When it was completed in 1825, the canal stretched 363 miles from Albany to Buffalo, much farther than any other American or European canal.

excise tax—A tax on domestically manufactured goods used to raise revenue for the federal government.

F

factions—Self-serving political parties.

The Federalist Papers—A series of 85 essays written by James Madison along with Alexander Hamilton and John Jay. The essays argued in favor of ratifying the Constitution and cited a strong link between American prosperity and a powerful central government. Various essays dealt with the need for such a government and the separation of powers into three branches of government.

federalists—Defended the necessity of a strong national government and supported the Constitution as the best possible framework. They advocated for a strong central government and drew their greatest support from the mercantile interests of the New England and mid-Atlantic regions.

54° 40' or fight—Expansionists pressured Congress to annex the entire Oregon Territory in 1844 with their motto, "54° 40' or fight," along the border of Russian Alaska and British Canada. Northerners also pushed for acquisition, because the admission of Oregon, a free state, would balance the admission of slave-holding Texas.

First Continental Congress—In September 1774, the Committees of Correspondence of every colony except Georgia sent delegates to this meeting. The congress endorsed Massachusetts' Suffolk Resolves, declaring that the colonies didn't have to obey the Coercive Acts because they infringed upon basic liberties. The delegates also voted for an organized boycott of all British goods. In preparation for possible British retaliation, the delegates called upon all colonies to raise and train local militias. By the spring of 1775, colonists had established provincial congresses to enforce the decrees of the Continental Congress. The final business agenda was an agreement to meet again in May 1775 for a second congressional gathering.

First Great Awakening—In response to the waning of religion and the spread of skepticism bolstered by the Enlightenment, the 1730s and 1740s, this movement ushered in a broad movement of religious commitment. During this time, revival ministers John and Charles Wesley, George Whitefield, Jonathan Edwards, and others stressed the emptiness of material comfort, the corruption of human nature, and the need for immediate repentance to avoid incurring the divine wrath.

Force Bill—Part of a compromise bill over the Tariff of 1828. Senator Henry Clay brokered a compromise bill that Jackson signed into law. The Tariff of 1833 provided for a gradual lowering of duties over the next decade. The second measure, the Force Bill, authorized the president to use the army and navy, if necessary, to force the collection of customs duties in South Carolina. South Carolina at first nullified the Force Bill, but under threat of force, reconsidered and rescinded its previous nullifications. This would be the most serious threat to the Union until South Carolina led the secession movement in December of 1860.

Fort Necessity—French troops repulsed the Virginia force and captured Washington and his garrison here in what became the first "official" skirmish of the French and Indian War. With 30 percent of his men lost in the conflict, Washington surrendered on July 4, 1754.

Fort Pillow—This site in southwestern Tennessee became the place of a distressing example of wartime abuse when, in April 1864, Confederate soldiers shot to death several captured black Union soldiers. Confederate General Nathan Bedford Forrest witnessed this atrocity and did nothing to stop it.

Fort Sumter—On April 12, 1861, General Beauregard, under orders from Confederate president Jefferson Davis, led the attack on this federal military installation at the entrance to Charleston Harbor. The Civil War had begun.

Franklin, Benjamin—Devoted his life to the intellectual pursuit of social, political, and economic improvements. He conducted experiments with electricity and developed several inventions, including spectacles, a wood stove for heating, and the lightning rod. Franklin also founded a library in Philadelphia, and in 1769 he created a scientific organization known as the American Philosophical Society. His published work in *Poor Richard's Almanac* in 1732 contained a collection of proverbs and information about colonial life. Franklin, along with his close friends John Adams and Thomas Jefferson, played a pivotal role in the independence movement that swept across the colonies.

Free-Soil party—This new party was formed in 1848 and vowed to keep the territories free with its platform of "free soil, free speech, free labor, free men." This new party tried to shift the focus away from the morality of slavery to the question expansion. They supported allowing slavery to exist where it was established, but preventing the extension of slavery into any new territory. Many Free-Soilers meant "anti-black" when they said "anti-slavery" and proposed banning all black people from the new territories. The Free-Soil party was denounced by some as a racist effort to make the territories all white.

French and Indian War—France and Britain vied for position in both Europe and the New World, resulting in occasional wars on both continents. This series of wars, which ranged through the first half of the eighteenth century, culminated in the Seven Years War in Europe, and its counterpart the French and Indian War in the colonies.

Fugitive Slave Act—Passed in 1850, this law denied alleged fugitives the right to a trial and didn't allow them to testify in their own defense. It also granted court-appointed commissioners higher payments for every slave returned. Fines and jail time could be imposed on those who failed to cooperate with the commissioners. In addition, the law authorized federal marshals and Southern men to enter the North and search for runaway slaves who had escaped decades earlier. All of these actions gave slave owners increased power to capture escaped slaves, while reminding Northerners of their longstanding complicity with the institution of slavery.

Fulton, Robert—Inventor of the Clermont steamboat that made its maiden voyage on the Hudson river in New York in 1807.

G

Gadsden Purchase—To facilitate a Southern railroad, the United States acquired parts of present-day southern Arizona and New Mexico for $10 million from Mexico in 1853.

gag rule—In 1836, this rule tabled all abolitionist petitions in Congress, serving as a preemptive strike against all antislavery discussions. The gag rule wasn't repealed until 1844, when it came under increased pressure from Northern abolitionists and others concerned about restricting the right to petition granted by the Constitution.

Garrison, William Lloyd—In 1831, he launched an abolitionist newspaper called *The Liberator*, earning himself a reputation as the most radical white abolitionist. Past abolitionists had suggested blacks be shipped back to Africa, but Garrison worked with prominent black abolitionists, including Frederick Douglass, to demand equal civil rights for blacks.

Gates, General Horatio—Surrounded the British troops forcing Burgoyne to surrender his entire army at the Battle of Saratoga.

Genet, Edmund—A French Ambassador who came to the United States and began soliciting contributions for the French Revolution. Crowds of supporters greeted him, and he tried to get the United States to raid British ships. Genet wanted Washington to call Congress into a special session to debate neutrality, but Washington wanted Genet recalled. Meanwhile, as France called for his arrest, Genet opted to quietly settle in the United States rather than face the guillotine back home.

Gibbons v. Ogden (1824)—A ruling that concerned interstate commerce. It involved a New York state steamboat franchise that had been granted a monopoly by the state legislature to run passenger ships between New York and New Jersey. The state license conflicted with a federal license, granted to another boat operator, to run the same steamboat route. Marshall ruled in favor of the federal license, arguing that a state can't interfere with Congress's right to regulate interstate commerce. Marshall interpreted "commerce" broadly to include all forms of business, not just the exchange of goods.

Great Compromise—In June 1787 a committee was assigned to resolve the conflict approved the Connecticut Compromise, or Great Compromise, which created a bicameral legislature where each state received an equal vote in the upper house (Senate), and representation in the lower house (House of Representatives) was proportional to population. The compromise also proposed an electoral process in which an electoral college, a group of competent leaders, would meet and choose the president.

Grenville, George—Prime Minister of Britain after the French and Indian War. Together with King George III, he reasoned that because the colonies benefited most from the war they should be taxed to pay for England's war debt. England was ending its century-long policy of salutary neglect. This dramatic change in policy sparked escalating tensions between England and its colonists that eventually led to the American Revolution.

Grimke, Sarah and Angelina—Sisters from South Carolina who had moved north to Philadelphia. In 1837 they were the first women in the United States to publicly argue for the abolition of slavery. They traveled throughout the North and lectured extensively about their firsthand experiences about slavery on their family plantation.

H

halfway covenant—This allowed for more lenient membership rules in the Puritan church due to declining membership. To resolve this dilemma, adult church members (who had been baptized themselves as full members of the church) were allowed to have their unconverted children baptized, thus allowing them to become "halfway" members. While people were awaiting conversion, they could also participate in church affairs with the exception of communion.

Harpers Ferry—In October 1859, John Brown followed "a leading by God" to instigate a slave rebellion in Virginia, attempting to seize the federal arsenal. After Brown and 22 men seized the arsenal and armory, they took several local citizens hostage and issued a call through the countryside for other slaves to join the rebellion. However, slaves failed to answer the call to rebel, and Brown and his survivors were taken prisoner after two days of battle. Brown was indicted for treason and criminal conspiracy to incite a slave insurrection. His trial ended with a conviction, and he was hanged along with four of his band on December 2nd. Many Northerners mourned his death as a martyr, and Southerners reacted with fear to the possibility of further slave rebellions.

Hartford Convention—A group of disillusioned Federalists met and enumerated their complaints against the ruling Republican party. Some Federalists threatened New England's secession. Others called for a resolution summarizing New England's grievances, both general ones and those specifically relating to the War of 1812. The group at the Hartford Convention also drafted seven constitutional amendments intended to politically strengthen the Northeast and restrict federal power. The Federalists had hoped to deliver their resolution to Madison, but they arrived in Washington, D.C., just as news spread of the victory at New Orleans and the signing of the Treaty of Ghent. Their central complaints and the threat of secession made them look to be traitors. Many Republicans accused the Federalists of treason, weakening their power and influence as a party. The embarrassment of the Hartford Convention marked the end of the Federalist party, leading to its demise as a prominent influence in national politics by 1820.

Harvard University—The first Puritan institution of higher learning in the colonies. It was founded in 1638 to train ministers.

headright system—The Virginia Company instituted this system of land grants by dispatching money and supplies and awarding land grants of 50 acres to anyone able to pay for his own passage to Virginia, and an additional 50 acres was distributed for each person or laborer brought to the colony.

Homestead Act (1862)—Provided 160 acres of public land virtually free to any citizen willing to occupy it for five years. An $18 filing fee was all that was needed to secure the land. It would be up to the settlers to make improvements to the property. This act greatly impacted settlement of the West.

House of Burgesses—In 1619 the colonists of Jamestown formed a general assembly. This became the first representative government in the New World, though its power was limited because the Virginia Company could still overrule its actions. Landowners elected representatives to make laws for Virginia.

Houston, Sam—As the commander of the Texan troops, he met Santa Ana at the San Jacinto River in April with the battle cry of "Remember the Alamo!" The Texans defeated nearly half of Santa Ana's army in 15 minutes. While Santa Ana's army was resting, Houston's troops made a surprise attack. A treaty was signed on May 14, 1836, declaring Texan independence and creating the Lone Star Republic.

Huguenots—French Protestant followers of John Calvin who tried to challenge Spain's authority in Florida by establishing a colony at Port Royal Sound in South Carolina in 1562.

Hutchinson, Anne—Her religious teachings were taken by some as attacks on Puritan religious codes. She hosted religious discussions in her home, but the weekly meetings troubled the local authorities. Her religious beliefs put her at odds with the religious leaders. In 1637, Hutchinson and her followers were banished; most of them settled in Rhode Island. After her husband's death in 1642, Hutchinson took most of her children to the Dutch colony in New York. A few months later, 15 Dutchmen were killed in a Native American raid, and in August 1643, Mohicans Indians raided the Hutchinson house and slaughtered Anne and five of her youngest children.

I

impressment—Britain and France seized U.S. naval crews at sea and "kidnapped" them by forcing their crews into service.

indentured servants—In exchange for payment for their trip to the colonies and for their labor for five to seven years, these servants, often the lowest class of British society, received their freedom. When they gained their freedom and sought land, they often clashed with established landowners along the tidewater. They were forced to live in the unsettled frontier area in the western region of the colony.

Indian Removal Act—This act granted Jackson the funds and the authority to move Native Americans to assigned lands in the West, using as much force as necessary. U.S. officials began aggressively clearing out the Cherokee tribe from the Southwest, and Georgia took control of the formerly Cherokee territory.

Intolerable Acts—Parliament responded swiftly and angrily to the actions in Boston with a string of legislation that included closing the Port of Boston until the tea dumped in the harbor by rebel colonists had been paid for.

Iroquois League—Comprised of five Indian nations (the Cayuga, Mohawk, Oneida, Onondaga and Seneca) and lived in the central and western regions of the New York colony.

J

Jamestown—In 1607, a group of ships from the Virginia Company set out to claim for the British crown the "great and ample country of Virginia" from modern-day Maine to North Carolina. The employees of the Virginia Company of London were successful in their colonization attempt near the Chesapeake Bay.

Jay's Treaty—John Jay negotiated this treaty in 1795 with Britain, securing the removal of British troops from American land and reopening limited trade with the British West Indies, but he didn't address British seizure of American ships or the impressment of American sailors.

Jefferson, Thomas—Author of the Declaration of Independence in 1776. He served as an ambassador to France and later became the third president in 1801.

joint stock company—Stock was sold to investors, who provided capital for the venture. In return for the investment, the stockholders gained wealth only if the colony prospered. The leaders in the colonization ventures were often landless, second-born English sons eagerly searching for wealth (in the form of gold) in the New World.

Judiciary Act of 1789—Created a federal court system by establishing a Supreme Court with five justices and a chief justice, three circuit courts, and 13 federal district courts.

K

Kansas-Nebraska Act—According to the concept of popular sovereignty, a territory or state would be able to decide for itself on the issue of slavery. Douglas wrote an additional clause in a bill before Congress explicitly withdrawing the antislavery provision in the Missouri Compromise, and he added an adjustment, creating two territories in the region (Nebraska and Kansas) so that the new Kansas Territory might become a slave state. In its final form, the measure gained the support of President Pierce. After a lengthy debate, it became law in May 1854, with the unanimous support of the South and the partial support of Northern Democrats.

Key, Francis Scott—After the burning of the White House in 1814, he was inspired to write *The Star Spangled Banner* as he watched the battle over Fort McHenry.

King George III—Became the ruler in Britain following the French and Indian War. It was his close scrutiny and management of the American colonies (especially with taxation policies) after the French and Indian War that led to the outbreak of the Revolutionary War.

Kitchen Cabinet—This was an unofficial group of advisors used by Andrew Jackson. This group of advisors, which didn't include the vice president, was made up of newspaper editors, the treasury department head, and the secretary of state. They offered advice on setting national and party policies.

Know-Nothing party—The members of this party met secretly and refused to identify themselves. The party was a nativist organization that spread anti-German, anti-Irish, and anti-Catholic propaganda. Many members also favored temperance and opposed slavery. The party remained divided on the issue of slavery, and in 1855 the Know-Nothing party found itself weakened and near ruin. Despite dissension about slavery, the party managed to gain a sizeable percentage of the popular vote with presidential candidate Millard Fillmore in 1856.

L

Land Ordinance of 1785—outlined the protocol for the sale of land and settlement. Land was to be plotted into townships of 36 square miles. Each square mile comprised 640 acres that could be divided into various section configurations for sale. Income from the sale of the section 16 was reserved for public school support.

de Las Casas, Bartholome—A former Spanish soldier turned priest, he condemned the Spaniards' treatment of the natives. The Black Legend soon developed, intended to make Roman Catholic Spain look evil in the eyes of the Protestant world.

Letters from the Federal Farmer—Written by Richard Henry Lee, and became the most widely read anti-federalist publication during the debate over ratification of the Constitution. It argued for a Bill of Rights to protect certain freedoms. Samuel Adams and John Hancock objected to the Constitution without a Bill of Rights. After the Constitution was ratified in 1791, Madison kept his promise and a Bill of Rights (the first 10 amendments to the Constitution) was soon adopted.

Liberty party—Founded in 1840 by abolitionists who wanted to draw attention to the increasingly important issue of slavery. Even though their candidate, James Birney, didn't win the 1840 presidential election, the party helped draw attention to the issue of ending slavery. Third-party politics had a significant influence in the 1844 election when the Liberty party candidate received 62,000 votes, allowing James Polk, the Democratic candidate, to narrowly defeat Henry Clay, the Whig candidate.

Lincoln-Douglas Debates—In a series of seven debates in 1858, Douglas advocated popular sovereignty while Lincoln promoted the Free-Soil argument. Lincoln was attacked as being a "black Republican." He stated that a "house divided against itself cannot stand." Lincoln pledged the Republican party to the ultimate extinction of slavery, but also stated, "I am not nor ever have been in favor of bringing about the social and political equality of the white man and the black man." Lincoln condemned slavery as a moral, social, and political wrong. In attacking his opponent, Lincoln contended that Douglas's belief in popular sovereignty, in particular his Freeport Doctrine, was incompatible with the *Dred Scott* decision. In the Freeport Doctrine, Douglas stated that territorial governments could effectively forbid slavery by refusing to enact slave codes, even though the *Dred Scott* decision had explicitly deprived Congress of the authority to restrict slavery in the territories.

Locke, John—An English philosopher who developed the concept of the contract theory of government and the need for that government to protect a person's "life, health, liberty, and possessions."

Louisiana Purchase—Napoleon agreed to sell all of the Louisiana Territory to the United States to finance French efforts in the war in Europe. After some negotiations in 1803, the price was set at $15 million (roughly 13 and a half cents per acre). With the Louisiana Purchase, Jefferson and the United States gained an enormous, uncharted piece of land, almost doubling the country's size, and eliminating French (and remnant Spanish) control of New Orleans and the Mississippi River.

Lowell Girls—In 1822, Appleton and Johnson built a manufacturing operation in Lowell, Massachusetts, that employed hundreds of young women. This textile mill would eventually employ hundreds of young women known as "Lowell girls." By 1839, Lowell would become the leading textile producer in the world. The rise of mills and industries in the North led to the development of a factory-working class of people: children, young single women, poor whites, and immigrants.

loyalists—Tories who were British loyalists and sympathizers during the Revolutionary War.

M

Macon's Bill No. 2—In 1810, Congress substituted this legislation for the Non-Intercourse Act, as a ploy for either Britain or France to lift trade restrictions. It resumed open trade with both Britain and France and stated that, if either nation repealed its restrictions on neutral shipping, the United States would start an embargo against the other nation. Napoleon seized the opportunity and repealed French restrictions, provoking an American declaration of non-intercourse with Britain. Despite Napoleon's promise, however, the French continued to seize American ships.

Madison, James—He was the "father of the constitution." At the constitutional convention he presented the Virginia Plan, a framework of government that contained a potential solution to the problem of representation in the new government. The plan called for a bicameral legislature with representation in both houses proportional to population.

Manifest Destiny—Coined by John L. O'Sullivan, a New York journalist who, in 1939, wrote that America "is destined to be the great nation of futurity...the far-reaching, the boundless future will be an era of American greatness." It came to embody the belief that the United States was "destined by God" to spread over the entire continent of the Untied States. It fueled a great movement to the West in the mid 1800s.

Mann, Horace—An educator in Massachusetts who became secretary of that state's board of education. He reformed the school system by increasing state spending on schools, lengthening the school year, dividing the students into grades, instilling strict discipline, using standardized textbooks, and introducing professional teacher training. Mann stated that education was "the great equalizer of the conditions of men" and that it promoted the acquisition of basic knowledge and skills necessary for success.

Marbury v. Madison (1803)—Supreme Court ruling in which it marked the first time the Supreme Court declared an act of Congress (the Judiciary Act of 1796) to be unconstitutional. It established the concept of judicial review.

Marshall, John—A Federalist who was appointed by Adams as Chief Justice of the Supreme Court in 1801. He would serve on the court for 35 years, and during his tenure, he authored more than half of the nearly 900 decisions handed down by the Court, securing the Federalist influence on policy long after Adams left office.

Massachusetts Bay—A Puritan colony established by John Winthrop in 1630 as a religious experiment.

Mayflower Compact—Signed by the Pilgrims in 1620 and established the colony of Plymouth Plantation as a "civil body politic" under the sovereignty of King James I of England. The Mayflower Compact is often described as the first example of true self-government in the New World—a government based on the consent of the governed.

McCulloch v. Maryland (1819)—A ruling that questioned whether Maryland could tax the Second Bank of the United States. Marshall argued that the federal government's power must be considered supreme within its sphere, and that states couldn't have the power to interfere with the exercise of federal powers. That made the Maryland tax unconstitutional.

mercantilism—A theory of trade said that a nation could build economic strength only by exporting more than it imported. This policy also kept the colonies in a subservient role, providing raw materials and trade outlets for the mother country.

Mexican-American War—Fought from 1846 to 1848 when the United States insisted that the southern Texas border lay along the Rio Grande River; Mexico claimed that the border lay much further north at the Nueces River. The Mexican-American War ranged throughout Texas, New Mexico, and California, and into the Mexican interior. It ended in 1848 with an American victory.

Middle Passage—An estimated 10 to 12 million Africans were transported from Africa to the New World by 1810 along this route (76 percent of them arrived from 1701 to 1810). This was the largest forced migration in world history. By the time the slave trade ended, more than 520,000 slaves had been transported to America.

midnight judges—Judicial appointments made by Adams during his final few hours in office. The most influential appointment Adams made was naming Federalist John Marshall to the Supreme Court as chief justice. Marshall would serve on the court for 35 years. During his tenure, he authored more than half of the nearly 900 decisions handed down by the Court, securing the federalist influence on policy long after Adams left office.

Militia Act of 1862—Authorized the president to include blacks in military and naval service and giving Southern slaves freedom in return for service to Union. Initially designed to allow the use of blacks as laborers with military units, it was not long until black militia units were formed. Soon black soldiers would be engaged in the fight for equality on two fronts—equal treatment by the enemy and by their own government.

minutemen—Farmer-soldiers in Massachusetts who formed a colonial militia and who pledged to be ready to fight "at a minute's notice."

Missouri Compromise—This legislative compromise in 1820 stated that Maine was to be admitted as a free state and Missouri as a slave state. In the remainder of the Louisiana Territory, slavery would be prohibited north of 36° 30' latitude (the southern border of Missouri). With this statement, Congress asserted its right to restrict slavery. The compromise temporarily cooled tensions between the North and South.

Molasses Act (1733)—Taxes on molasses, rum, and sugar imported from non-British territories. This was an attempt of Britain to regulate prices and trade in the colonies.

Monroe Doctrine—In 1823 this doctrine declared American dominance in the Western Hemisphere and warned against European interference in the Americas: "God and nature had ordained the U.S." Although the United States had little military power to back up its claims, the declaration had immense symbolic importance because the country was declaring itself a world power equal to the great European nations. It served as a warning to Europe and demonstrated the growing strength and spirit of the United States.

Mormonism—The Church of Jesus Christ of Latter-Day Saints, also known as Mormonism, was the most controversial challenge to traditional religion. Its founder, Joseph Smith, claimed that God and Jesus Christ appeared to him and directed him to a buried book of revelation in 1830.

Mott, Lucretia—women's rights activist who argued that men and women were created equal and should be treated equally under the law. In 1848, Lucretia Mott and Elizabeth Cady Stanton organized a women's rights convention in Seneca Falls, New York. The Seneca Falls Convention issued a Declaration of Sentiments, modeled on the Declaration of Independence, stating that all men and women were created equal.

N

National Bank Act (1863)—Created a national banking system. It stabilized the national currency and reduced conflicting state bank policies.

National Republican party—after the contested election of 1824, the remnants of the old anti-federalist (Republican) party formed a new Republican party and called themselves the **National Republican party**. They supported Adams for reelection in 1828.

national road—By 1818 this road system stretched from Cumberland, Maryland, to Wheeling, Virginia.

Navigation Acts—Between 1651 and 1673, the English Parliament passed four types of legislation that were intended to ensure the proper mercantilist trade balance between the colonies and England and restrict trade between the colonies and Britain.

necessary and proper clause—This clause of the Constitution is also known as the "elastic clause." Article I, Section VIII of the Constitution states that Congress shall have the power "to make all laws which shall be necessary and proper for carrying into execution...powers vested by this Constitution in the government of the United States." For loose constructionists such as Hamilton, this elastic clause gave Congress the power to establish policy not expressly forbidden by the Constitution, including founding a national bank.

New Harmony—A town founded by a Welsh social reformer, Robert Owen, in 1814 in Indiana. It became a village of cooperation that ultimately disbanded because of disharmony. Nearly one hundred such communities with about 100,000 members were established in the United States between 1820 and 1860.

New Jersey Plan—The proposal at the constitutional convention that had the support of William Paterson's idea which called for a unicameral Congress in which each state would have an equal number of seats.

New Orleans—A port city at the mouth of the Mississippi controlled at times by the French and the Spanish.

Non-Intercourse Act—Madison urged Congress to replace the Embargo Act with this legislation in 1808 to prevent trade only with Britain and France, opening up all other foreign markets for trade with the United States. The act did little to stimulate the struggling U.S. economy because the British and French were the largest and most powerful traders in the world.

Northwest Ordinance of 1787—Provided for the territory above the Ohio River to be organized into three to five states and outlined the process for statehood. When a region had 5,000 adult males, it could organize a government in the territory by electing a legislature. Once a region had 60,000 inhabitants, it could draft a constitution and apply for statehood on equal footing with the original 13 states. This would solve land claims by various states in the region. In addition, it also forbade slavery in the territory above the Ohio River and included a settlers' bill of rights.

Northwest Passage—A shortcut from Europe to the Orient.

Nullification Crisis—Southern politicians grew so angry at the trade imbalance that they named the 1828 tariff the Tariff of Abominations. South Carolina reacted particularly strongly, flying its flags at half-mast when the 1828 bill was passed, and the state threatened to boycott New England's manufactured goods. Led by John C. Calhoun the state denounced the tariff as unconstitutional, arguing that Congress could levy only tariffs that raised revenue for common purposes, not tariffs that protected regional interests. Calhoun contended that federal laws must benefit all equally in order to be constitutional, and urged southern states to nullify, or void, the tariffs within their own borders.

O

Olive Branch Petition—An effort to reconcile with King George in May 1775. It attempted to offer peace under the conditions that included a cease-fire in Boston, the repeal of the Coercive Acts, and negotiations between the colonists and Britain to begin immediately. The attempted reconciliation was rejected by King George, who declared New England to be in a state of rebellion in August 1775.

Oneida community—This utopian society in New York survived from 1848 to 1881. Its leader, John Humphrey Noyes, believed that the Second Coming had already occurred and promoted "free love," denouncing traditional marriages in favor of a practice called complex marriage. The community stressed two basic values: self-perfection and communalism. They translated their values into everyday life through shared property and work benefiting the community at large.

Orders in Council—In 1803 a series of countermeasures issued by Britain tried to counteract the Berlin Decree by blockading French-controlled ports in Europe. The British also began searching American ships for goods from the French West Indies and threatening continued impressment of American crews into the Royal Navy. More than 200 American ships were seized in 1805 alone.

Oregon Trail—From 1842 through the 1850s, this route began at Independence, Missouri, and then turned northward at the South Platte River. It extended through Wyoming, down to the Colorado River, across the Salt Lake Basin, over the mountains, and finally on to the Columbia River and the Willamette Valley. More than 150,000 people made the arduous trek westward, hoping to shape a new future for themselves despite the possibility of hardship, disease, and death.

O'Sullivan, John L.—Coined the phrase "Manifest Destiny" in 1839 while working as a New York journalist by writing about "our Manifest Destiny is to overspread and to possess the whole of our continent which Providence has given us for the development of the great experiment of liberty." This notion of Manifest Destiny appealed to America's nationalist spirit, which had been growing since the War of 1812, and echoed Protestant beliefs that America was a "called nation" chosen by God as a haven from which Protestants could spread their faith. Manifest Destiny supporters believed that free development allowed democracy to grow, and that more land was needed for the booming population.

P

Pacific Railroad Act (1862)—Granted a contract to the Union Pacific to build west from Omaha and to the Central Pacific to build east from California. The bill included the creation of federally chartered corporations that would receive free public lands and generous loans to secure the building of the railroad. The railroad wasn't completed until May 10, 1869, when the two companies met at Promontory Point in Utah to drive the "golden stake" that finally united East and West.

Paine, Thomas—Author of the pamphlet *Common Sense* in January 1776 that argued that it made "common sense" for the colonists to make a break with Britain.

Panic of 1819—When the government and the Second Bank of the United States tightened up credit policies demanding immediate repayment of loans with hard currency, state banks followed their lead, and the tight credit and loan recalls drove the economy over the edge. Land values fell 50 to 75 percent, rich land speculators lost fortunes, and homesteaders became mired in debt. This led to a panic, or depression, that lasted for nearly six years.

Penn, William—Founded a colony in Pennsylvania and planned the city of Philadelphia as a "holy experiment in living" by basing the colony on religious tolerance.

Perry, Commodore Oliver—He cornered the British fleet at the Battle of Lake Erie on September 10, 1813 and captured a British squadron of warships. This victory allowed the United States to gain control of Lake Erie. Oliver Perry's victory over the British on Lake Erie in September 1813 came at a steep price.

Pike, Zebulon—Was sent to find the source of the Mississippi River, and in 1806, he went to Colorado, where he explored the region, as well as naming Pike's Peak near Colorado Springs. He then traveled in the Rio Grande region, where he found the headwaters of the Rio Grande River. Soon thereafter in 1807, Spanish authorities intercepted his party's small fort near Alamosa, Colorado, and took him captive to Santa Fe, New Mexico, for a time. Although Spain thought Pike to be a spy, he was escorted back to U.S. territory in July 1807. His later description of the Southwest as "desert-like and inhospitable" endured for many years.

Pinckney's Treaty—This treaty was negotiated with Spain in 1795 and recognized the 31st parallel as the southern U.S. boundary. It granted the United States free navigation of the Mississippi River with the right of deposit at New Orleans. Spain adopted a conciliatory note toward the United States in negotiating the treaty, attempting to protect its possessions in America and to secure recognition of its borders from foreign powers.

Pitt, William—British commander during the French and Indian War. His goal was to expel France from the New World colonies.

Pontiac, Chief—Led an unsuccessful effort in 1763 to resist the British in Ohio Valley regions formerly claimed by France.

popular sovereignty—the concept of leaving the decision about slavery to the citizens of each territory. This would prove to be a very controversial move in the 1850s when violence erupted Kansas in 1854 over the issue.

Pottawatomie Massacre—In 1854, in opposition to the new legislature in Kansas, abolitionist John Brown, together with his four sons and two helpers, went to Lawrence armed with broad swords, murdering and mutilating five proslavery settlers. This massacre provoked reprisals and initiated a guerrilla war that cost about 200 lives, earning the territory the nickname Bleeding Kansas.

predestination—The belief that God had chosen a person for salvation.

Proclamation Line (1763)—Barred colonial settlement west of the Appalachian Mountains. Britain claimed the line was needed to protect the colonists from attacks in the frontier. The terms of the Proclamation Line stated that colonists already settled in the region must leave, negating their claims and limiting colonial expansion

Prosser, Gabriel—A black slave and blacksmith who in 1800 carefully recruited several hundred slaves in hopes of marching on Richmond, Virginia. Bad weather postponed the plot, and after its discovery Prosser and 25 others were executed.

Protestant Reformation—A religious movement led by Martin Luther and John Calvin. Luther's message in 1517 that faith alone, not good works, would save Christians sparked upheaval in Roman Catholic communities throughout Europe.

Puritans—In 1629, this mainly middle-class group of people received a royal charter for a joint-stock enterprise from the English government. They left England and settle north of the Plymouth Plantation in the Massachusetts Bay area on the condition that they would have political control of their colony.

Q

Quakers—A religious group that had long been discriminated against in both the Americas and England for their religious beliefs, including the idea that God's inner light burned inside everyone, and pacifism, a refusal to bear arms. Seeking religious freedom, many Quakers flocked to Pennsylvania, along with Mennonites, the Amish, Moravians, and Baptists.

Quartering Act—Forced civilians to provide room and board in Boston to support British soldiers.

R

Republican party—Formed in 1854 as a party with antislavery as its main platform. Their first presidential candidate, Abraham Lincoln, was elected in 1860. The Whig party, an alliance between Southern Republicans and Northern Democrats, disintegrated in the 1850s over the increasingly contentious issue of slavery and out of this fallout developed the Republican party.

Revere, Paul—Depicted the horrors of the "Massacre in Boston" giving a vivid account of the five "martyrs" and 11 wounded, along with a wood engraving. The image of British cruelty and brutality helped to inflame anger toward the British and became a turning point in relations with Britain. Revere along with William Dawes warned of the impending arrival of the redcoats in April 1775.

Roanoke Island—In 1585, Sir Walter Raleigh helped plant a British colony just south of the Chesapeake Bay region. A year later, Drake took the disheartened settlers back to England. It was later abandoned. A second effort two years later also proved a failure.

Rolfe, John—An Englishman who married the Powhatan leader's daughter, Pocahontas, and introduced West Indian tobacco to the colony of Jamestown. Instead of gold or precious metals, tobacco proved to be the perfect crop for the colony.

royal colony—A colony under the direct control of the king.

S

Sacajawea—A Shoshone woman who proved indispensable as a guide for Lewis and Clark in their exploration of the Louisiana Purchase Territory from 1804 to 1806.

Salem Witchcraft Trials—In 1692, these trials resulted in the hanging of 19 people and one man being pressed to death on account of accusations of witchcraft. By the end of the conflict, 175 men and women had been arrested in Salem.

salutary neglect—The British policy of lax governance of the colonies. During this time from the mid-1600s to the mid-1700s, the colonists saw their economy grow nearly twice as fast as that of England because, in general, Britain didn't enforce the trade laws that most hurt the colonial economy.

Santa Fe Trail—This 900-mile trail opened up the New Mexico region in 1822 for lucrative trade with the United States. It extended from Independence, Missouri, to Bent's Fort, where the trail turned to the southwest and on to Taos and Santa Fe. The trail served as a profitable trade route until the Santa Fe Railroad opened in 1880.

Scott, Dred—A Missouri slave who, in the 1850s, sued for his freedom on the basis that his owner had taken him to live in a free state (Illinois), and later a free territory (Wisconsin). He lost the case, and the court's decision sparked a wave of controversy around the country.

secession—The belief that a state had the right to leave the Union if it disagreed with an action of the federal government. It also believed that the states had endowed he federal government with power, therefore it gave the states the right to overrule any action of the federal government.

Second Bank of the United States—This was the recharter of the First bank of the United States in 1816. Andrew Jackson would fight renewal for the recharter for this bank in 1832.

Second Great Awakening—Emerged during the early 1800s, partly as a backlash against the spread of rationalism, and partly in response to calls for an organized religion more accessible to the common man. As in the First Great Awakening, revivalist ministers urged followers to reach a personal, emotional understanding of God. Women, blacks, and young men participated in the revival meetings.

sectionalism—Differences of opinions by different regions of the country.

separatists—Families who wanted to separate from the Anglican Church (the Church of England).

Seven Years War—France and Britain vied for position in both Europe and the New World, resulting in occasional wars on both continents. This series of wars, which ranged through the first half of the eighteenth century, culminated in the Seven Years War in Europe and its counterpart, the French and Indian War in the colonies.

Shaker community—This utopian society was under the leadership of Mother Ann Lee. In 1774 she believed that she was the female incarnation of Christ, and her new religion was based on sexual equality. The group believed in universal salvation and practiced celibacy while living apart from the rest of the world. Followers were dubbed "shakers" because of their movements in the ritualized dances at their meetings. They promoted a simple lifestyle and had minimal contact with the outside world while awaiting the Second Coming of Christ. By the late 1840s, 6,000 Shakers lived in more than a dozen northern communities.

Shays's Rebellion—The first armed uprising in the new nation occurred in August 1786 when Daniel Shays, a Revolutionary War veteran who was angered by high taxes and debt he couldn't repay, led about 2,000 men to close the courts in three western Massachusetts counties, to prevent farm foreclosures. The Massachusetts government had increased taxes to pay off war debts, and creditors and sheriffs were hauling delinquent farmers into court, imposing high legal fees, and threatening them with imprisonment for failure to pay debts. Shays and his men dared to take control of the weapons arsenal at Springfield, Massachusetts, exposing the central government's inability to enforce order. The Massachusetts militia put down the rebellion.

Sherman, General—Commander of the Union troops in the West. He also planned the march to the sea in 1864 from Atlanta to Savannah. His goal was to end the enemy's ability to wage war and to utterly destroy the morale of the Confederacy.

slave codes—Laws that were established governing slavery and reducing the enslaved people to property, deprived of basic civil rights. These laws developed out of fear that the increasing black population needed to be kept under control. Slaves became the chattel or property of their masters, making slave ownership a profitable long-term investment.

slave trade—The forced migration of 10 to 12 million blacks from Africa to the New World from the mid 1400s to the early 1800s.

Smith, John—Emerged as a prominent leader of the community at Jamestown and organized work gangs to ensure that the colony had food and shelter. He made rules to control sanitation and hygiene. "He who shall not work shall not eat!"

Smith, Joseph—Claimed that God and Jesus Christ appeared to him and directed him to a buried book of revelation in 1830. He founded the Mormon Church that year and it grew to over 1,000 members within a short time. He moved a group of believers to Missouri in 1838, and after they were expelled from there moved to Illinois. Smith became unpopular in Illinois due to church teachings, which included his belief in polygamy. He was killed in 1844.

South Carolina Exposition and Protest—Calhoun's justification for nullification, published in 1828, was largely derived from Jefferson's and Madison's arguments in the Virginia and Kentucky Resolutions (1798). Calhoun, as had Jefferson and Madison, argued that the states were sovereign over the central government, and the states should have the final authority to judge the constitutionality of laws affecting their regions. Calhoun saw the Constitution as a compact of states, with the states independent and sovereign even before the Constitution was approved. States had created the federal government and endowed it with strictly limited powers, so a state had the right to nullify a federal law.

Spanish Armada—The British defeated this Spanish fleet in 1588, which signaled the end of Spanish dominance in the exploration and settlement of the New World.

specie circular—Jackson's financial policy after the 1832 election included distributing federal government surpluses to states, which stimulated spending and inflation. To check the inflationary spiral, Jackson issued the specie circular, which required gold and silver for land purchases. Before the panic of 1837, English bankers called in loans to states and investors, which depleted gold supplies, prevented banks from making payments, and forced failures. Many of the policies Jackson used to destroy the bank created major economic problems for the next president.

Stamp Act Congress—Representatives of nine colonial assemblies met in New York City, where they prepared a petition in which Parliament was asked to repeal the Stamp Act because it violated the principle of "no taxation without representation." The congress argued that Parliament couldn't tax anyone outside of Great Britain and couldn't deny anyone a fair trial.

Stanton, Elizabeth Cady—A women's rights activist who argued that men and women were created equal and should be treated equally under the law. She worked with Lucretia Mott and Susan B. Anthony.

Stono Rebellion—Occurred when 20 slaves broke into a store for weapons and ammunition. As they marched toward freedom in St. Augustine, Florida, they gathered more black recruits, attacked and burned houses, and killed twenty white men, women, and children. At each plantation, they recruited other slaves, and as they moved south, their numbers grew. Several planters caught up with the large band of rebel slaves; more than 20 whites and 40 slaves were killed before the suppression of the rebellion. They were captured and put to death.

Stowe, Harriet Beecher—No event did more to encourage Northern abolitionism and sympathy for runaway slaves than the 1852 publication of *Uncle Tom's Cabin*. Stowe's book became a runaway bestseller, selling 300,000 copies within the first year of publication and more than two million in the next decade. Its depictions of the corruption of slavery was turned into a play, and along with the book, it was praised by large audiences in the North, who saw it as a graphic depiction of the horrors of slavery. The work was condemned in the South for its "falsehoods" of slavery.

strict constructionists—Led by anti-federalists who held to a strict interpretation of the Constitution by arguing that it didn't explicitly give the federal government the power to grant a charter such as the Bank of the United States. According to this concept, the new federal government only had powers that were expressly written in the constitution. Because the Constitution did not mention a bank, they opposed it.

Sugar Act—(1765) This was the first direct tax on the colonies to raise money by taxing vital goods and services. The act, passed over the authority of local colonial assemblies, required Americans to buy special watermarked paper for 15 classes of documents. It met with fierce resistance. In the colonies, legal pamphlets condemned the acts on the grounds of "taxation without representation."

Sumner, Senator Charles—A staunch abolitionist, he insulted South Carolina and its senator, Andrew Butler, while calling for the admission of Kansas to the Union as a free state. Butler's cousin, Preston Brooks, a member of the House, used a cane to attack Sumner in the head and then kept beating him after he fell to the floor. Attempts to expel or censure Brooks in the House failed. Brooks became a Southern hero and was invited to dinners and receptions and given souvenir canes, one of which was engraved with the phrase, "Hit him again!" Sumner was reelected in 1857, but he was out recovering from the inflicted wounds until 1860. His empty seat became a symbol of southern brutality and further inflamed the slavery debate.

Sutter's Mill—Gold was discovered at this mill near present-day San Francisco in 1848. this discovery led to the infamous forty-niner gold rush that saw thousands of people flock to the region in search of gold.

T

Taney, Chief Justice Roger B.—Delivered the majority opinion in *Dred Scott v. Sanford*. In the 7–2 ruling, the five Southern justices concurred with Taney's decision that Scott, as a slave, had no right to sue in federal court, and furthermore claimed that no black, slave or free, could become a citizen of the United States. Slaves were property only, according to Taney, and would remain so even if they resided in free territory. In addition, Taney ruled that Congress couldn't forbid slavery in any U.S. territory because doing so would violate the 5th Amendment's protection of property, including slaves, from being taken away without due process. The decision rendered the Missouri Compromise unconstitutional. Taney further suggested that the Compromise of 1850 and the Kansas-Nebraska Act were unconstitutional, since they enforced popular sovereignty, which allowed territorial governments to prohibit slavery and therefore violated the 5th Amendment as interpreted by the Court. Taney's arguments supported the states' rights position favored by John Calhoun years earlier.

tariff—A tax on imports.

Tariff of 1789—A high protective tariff of 5 to 50 percent was proposed to generate revenue for the national government and to foster industrial development in the United States. Northerners generally favored the tariff as a means of protection against foreign competition. Both Jefferson and Madison, however, opposed this protectionist economic policy, fearing that industries would become too dependent on government aid. Many congressmen also opposed the tariff because it favored industrial and merchant interests of the North over the more rural and agrarian South.

temperance movement—Emerged as a backlash against the rising popularity of drink. Founded in 1826, the American Temperance Society advocated total abstinence from alcohol. Many advocates considered drinking immoral or sinful and thought that it caused poverty or mental instability. Others saw it as a male indulgence that harmed women and children, who often suffered abuse at drunkards' hands. During the 1830s, an increasing number of workingmen joined the movement, concerned about alcohol's effects on job performance. By 1835, about 5,000 temperance societies were affiliated with the American Temperance Society.

tidewater—The region from the coastline to the furthest upstream river.

Tories—British loyalists and sympathizers during the Revolutionary War.

town meetings—The New England colonies quickly established a tradition of self-government where male landowners were granted the right to vote and were encouraged to participate in the political process in local meetings.

Trail of Tears—Between 1835 and 1838, the U.S. Army forced Cherokee Indians to move westward on a journey known as the Trail of Tears. General Winfield Scott, with an army of 7,000, was sent to enforce the treaty. The Indians were rounded up and relocated to government camps in Oklahoma. Along the 1,200-mile journey, nearly 25 percent of the 16,000 migrating Cherokees died.

transcendentalism—A literary movement that emerged during the 1830s and argued that knowledge didn't come exclusively through the intellect but also through the senses, intuition, and sudden insight. It promoted the belief that concepts such as God, freedom, and absolute truth were inborn and could be accessed through inner experience and emotional openness. Ralph Waldo Emerson and Henry David Thoreau were prominent in this movement.

Treaty of Greenville—Cleared the Ohio territory of tribes and opened it up to further settlement after "Mad Anthony" Wayne routed a group of Native American warriors at the Battle of Fallen Timbers in 1794.

Treaty of Guadalupe Hidalgo—Signed in February 1848 ending the Mexican-American War. Mexico ceded Texas, New Mexico, and California to the United States for $15 million. The ceded territory encompassed present-day Arizona, Nevada, California, Utah, and parts of present-day New Mexico, Colorado, and Wyoming. The treaty secured the West for American settlement, and American land stretched continuously from the Atlantic Ocean to the Pacific Ocean.

Treaty of Paris (1763)—This ended the French and Indian War between the British and French. The treaty stipulated that Britain gained all of the land in North America east of the Mississippi, and France lost all of its claims in North America except the city of New Orleans.

Treaty of Ghent—In December of 1814, this treaty ended the War of 1812 and restored the status quo. The treaty resolved almost nothing because no mention was made of impressment, blockades, or neutral rights. The treaty simply stopped the conflict and set up commissions to deal with lingering disputes after the war's end.

Treaty of Paris of 1783—Signed in September 1783, this agreement with Britain recognized American independence and defined the new borders of the United States: the northern border along Canada, the western border along the Mississippi, and the southern border along Spanish Florida (a line disputed by Spain). The treaty recommended that the United States return Loyalist property seized during the war.

Treaty of Tordesillas—This treaty in 1494 split the New World between Spain and Portugal. The line gave Portugal only a small claim in the New World by granting it Brazil and everything east of the line; everything west of Brazil was assigned to Spain.

Trenton and Princeton—Washington's Christmas victories in 1776 in New Jersey helped revive the lagging spirits of the American troops. Washington's Christmas night crossing of the Delaware River ended up surprising the British and the Hessian brigades and brought about a much-needed American victory in the war at Trenton. This would be followed a few days latter with another crossing and victory at Princeton.

triangular trade—A trade network that linked the American colonies, the West Indies, Africa, and England. New England rum was shipped to Africa and traded for slaves, who were brought to the West Indies and traded for sugar and molasses, which went back to New England. Other raw goods were shipped from the colonies to England, where they were swapped for a cargo of manufactured goods.

Truth, Sojourner—A former slave, outspoken abolitionist speaker and advocate of women's rights.

Tubman, Harriet—Gained her freedom in 1849 when she escaped to Philadelphia and began working as a domestic servant in order to save money and make plans to rescue several family members. In 1850, she began the first of 19 trips back into the South to guide more than 300 slaves to freedom in the North and Canada. This former slave had become a "conductor" on the secret, shifting routes of the Underground Railroad.

Turner, Nat—A Virginia slave preacher who could read and write, and began planning a slave rebellion in 1831 in Southampton County. Turner claimed he was an instrument of God's wrath while he and several others were lynched after killing 55 white men, women, and children.

U

Underground Railroad—A network of shifting routes from the South across the Ohio river in the North that allowed slaves to escape to their freedom. Outraged slaveowners in Maryland placed a $40,000 bounty for the capture of Harriet Tubman for her activism in leading more than 300 slaves to their freedom. Another significant purpose of the Underground Railroad was that it provided an opportunity for abolitionists, including Quakers such as Levi and Catharine Coffin, to play an active role in openly resisting slavery by providing assistance to escaped slaves as they traveled from one destination to another in their pursuit of freedom.

V

Valley Forge—In early December 1777, 11,000 troops under George Washington's command marched through the snow to spend a long, cold winter here in Pennsylvania, where they regrouped and trained.

Vesey, Denmark—A slave who, in 1822, planned to take over Charleston and then flee to Haiti. After two domestic servants disclosed the plan, Vesey and more than 35 conspirators were hung.

veto power—Any president can exercise this authority over bill that the House and Senate send to him to sign into law. By exercising this power he declares the bill "null and void." This is one of the areas of checks and balances included in the Constitution.

Virginia and Kentucky Resolutions—Written anonymously by Thomas Jefferson and James Madison in 1798 and declared that state legislatures could deem acts of Congress unconstitutional, on the theory that the rights of the states superseded federal rights. They argued that the federal government was merely a representative of the compact of states, not an overriding power, and therefore states had the final say on federal laws. In 1799, Kentucky passed a further resolution that declared states could nullify objectionable federal laws. This doctrine of states' rights and nullification would emerge again in later political crises between the North and South about congressional authority on issues of tariffs and slavery.

virtual representation—This meant that Parliament members not only represented their specific geographical constituencies, but that they also considered the welfare of all British subjects.

W

War Hawks—Southerners and Westerners, led by South Carolina's John C. Calhoun and Kentucky's Henry Clay, began asserting their power during Madison's administration. They resented the recession that had plagued Southern and Western regions from 1808 to 1810. They advocated war rather than disgraceful terms of peace.

Washington's Farewell Address—In 1796, Washington implored future generations to concentrate on the creation of "efficient government" at home—"The great rule of conduct for us in regard to foreign nations is, in extending our commercial relations to have with them as little political connection as possible. Why entangle our peace and prosperity in the toils of European ambition, rivalship, and interest." This would keep the United States out of European interests until World War I.

Washington, George—Commander of the colonial army in the Revolutionary War. Also presided over the Constitutional Convention in Philadelphia in 1787 and became the first president of the United States in 1789.

Whig party—Leaders of the National Republican party and other opponents of Jackson teamed up to form this new party in 1834. Led by Henry Clay, Daniel Webster, and John C. Calhoun (who had split from Jackson and the Democratic party over tariffs and nullification), the Whigs encompassed all different factions. Southern Republicans, northern Democrats, and social reformers united in their hatred of Jackson, whom many considered so tyrannical that they referred to him as "King Andrew I."

Whiskey Rebellion—Occurred in 1794 when farmers resented the excise tax on whiskey tax because it lowered the profits they could make from selling whiskey. This conflict was the first major test of the federal government's ability to enforce its laws within the states. Farmers were further angered when local officials ordered the arrest of the leaders of the whiskey tax resistors. A month later, the commander of the local militia was shot and killed by federal troops defending a tax official. This enraged the local anti-tax settlers, who set fire to some outlying buildings. In reaction, the president recruited a militia force in August 1794 from Pennsylvania, Maryland, New Jersey, and Virginia. After negotiations failed between federal commissioners and the rebels, Washington led the army of more than 12,000 troops into western Pennsylvania. The farmers quickly dispersed, and resistance faded.

Whitney, Eli—Invented the cotton gin in 1803 and made it possible for Southern farmers to grow short-staple cotton for a profit. It relied heavily on slave labor.

Williams, Roger—A dissenter in the Massachusetts Bay area who argued that total separation of church and state was the only way to maintain the purity of the church. Williams feared that without separation, the state would corrupt the church: "Forced religion stinks in the nostrils of God." He also proposed that the Native Americans be compensated for their land. Unable to be silenced, Williams was banished from Massachusetts in 1635. He eventually established the colony of Rhode Island in 1647.

Wilmot Proviso—Sectional debate heated up again in 1846 when David Wilmot, a Northern Democrat, proposed an amendment to a war appropriation that banned slavery in all territories acquired from Mexico. Slavery would be allowed to remain where it already existed, but it couldn't expand into territorial regions. Sectional interests triumphed over party loyalty when Northerners and Southerners voted along sectional lines, reopening the national debate about the place of slavery in the country. The final vote was delayed until the end of the Mexican-American War. Threats were made and fistfights broke out on the floor of the House of Representatives. The amendment was defeated, but a newly formed political party, the Free-Soil Party, eventually adopted its provisions.

Winthrop, John—Leader a fleet of 17 ships that migrated to the Massachusetts Bay region by transporting a thousand people across the Atlantic to set up a colony at the site of modern-day Boston and in 10 other towns across the area. He sought to make his colony a biblical "city on a hill" to serve as a role model for the rest of the world.

Worcester v. Georgia (1832)—see *Cherokee Nation v. Georgia*

writs of assistance—General search warrants, allowing British customs officials to enter and investigate any ship or building suspected of holding smuggled goods.

X

XYZ affair—In 1797, Adams attempted to defuse growing tensions with France by sending three diplomats to Paris to meet with the foreign minister Charles de Tallyrand. The French minister refused to meet with the commissioners and instead sent three anonymous agents to deliver a bribe. Tallyrand wouldn't negotiate with the United States until he received $250,000 for himself and a $12 million loan for France. In his report to Congress about the event, Adams labeled the three agents X, Y, and Z. This extortion attempt aroused public outrage among the American people, some of whom rallied for war. The XYZ affair actually boosted Adams's popularity when the American delegates refused the bribe.

Y

Yorktown—On September 28, 1781, Washington, along with Lafayette's troops and 3,000 of de Grasse's men, arrived here, and in October these troops besieged the British base until the British troops forced Cornwallis to surrender. The British defeat crushed their troops' fighting spirit and forced them to concede to the Americans.

Young, Brigham—Led the Mormons to Utah to the Great Salt Lake Basin in 1847 (present-day Provo and Salt Lake City), where they prospered.

Z

Zenger, John Peter—A New York printer who, in 1735, went to trial for libel for his printed attacks on the royal governor. His acquittal helped expand freedom of the press and encouraged the growth of more newspapers to express diverse colonial opinions.

Resources

Primary Documents

Primary documents provide a valuable resource for any history student. Although primary documents are not included in this Homework Helpers review text, I am including information about where to locate a valuable collection of documents.

"Our Documents: 100 Milestone Documents from the National Archives" is located at *www.ourdocuments.gov* and has a list of 100 documents that provide a valuable resource of primary documents for any student in a U.S. History course. It would benefit you as you review the content of your U.S. History course and review material presented in the *Homework Helpers: U.S. History* series, to visit the government Website and review several of the primary documents listed here.

Although the documents on this list begin in 1776 and go to 1965, there are other websites that contain primary source material from 1607 to 1776 and 1966 to the present. Depending on material covered in your class or material anticipated on your exams, you may want to conduct a web search for additional primary documents. You can access more primary documents at the National Archives at *www.archives.gov/historical-docs*.

The following is a list of the documents that can be found at the National Archive site and that apply to *Homework Helpers U.S. History (1492–1865)*.

1. Lee Resolution (1776)
2. Declaration of Independence (1776)
3. Articles of Confederation (1777)
4. Treaty of Alliance with France (1778)

5. Original Design of the Great Seal of the United States (1782)

6. Treaty of Paris (1783)

7. Virginia Plan (1787)

8. Northwest Ordinance (1787)

9. Constitution of the United States (1787)

10. Federalist Papers, No. 10 & No. 51 (1787–1788)

11. President George Washington's First Inaugural Speech (1789)

12. Federal Judiciary Act (1789)

13. Bill of Rights (1791)

14. Patent for Cotton Gin (1794)

15. President George Washington's Farewell Address (1796)

16. Alien and Sedition Acts (1798)

17. Jefferson's Secret Message to Congress Regarding the Lewis & Clark Expedition (1803)

18. Louisiana Purchase Treaty (1803)

19. *Marbury v. Madison* (1803)

20. Treaty of Ghent (1814)

21. *McCulloch v. Maryland* (1819)

22. Missouri Compromise (1820)

23. Monroe Doctrine (1823)

24. *Gibbons v. Ogden* (1824)

25. President Andrew Jackson's Message to Congress "On Indian Removal" (1830)

26. Treaty of Guadalupe Hidalgo (1848)

27. Compromise of 1850 (1850)

28. Kansas-Nebraska Act (1854)

29. *Dred Scott v. Sanford* (1857)

30. Telegram Announcing the Surrender of Fort Sumter (1861)

31. Homestead Act (1862)

32. Pacific Railway Act (1862)

33. Morrill Act (1862)

34. Emancipation Proclamation (1863)

35. War Department General Order 143: Creation of the U.S. Colored Troops (1863)

36. Gettysburg Address (1863)

37. Wade-Davis Bill (1864)

38. President Abraham Lincoln's Second Inaugural Address (1865)

39. Articles of Agreement Relating to the Surrender of the Army of Northern Virginia (1865)

40. 13th Amendment to the U.S. Constitution: The Abolition of Slavery (1865)

Index

A

Abolitionist movement, 172-174
Adams, Abigail, 89
Adams, John Quincy, 140-146, 157-158, 173
Adams, John, 49, 81, 88-89, 108, 109,
    116-117, 118, 119
Adams, Samuel, 67, 68, 73, 102
Adams-Onis Treaty, 144
Alamo, the, 187-188
Albany Congress, 60
Albany Plan of Union, 60
Alien and Sedition Acts, 117-118
Alien Enemies Act, 117
Alien Friends Act, 117
American
    Anti-Slavery Society, 172
    Bible Society, 178
    Red Cross, the, 230
    System, 140-141
    Temperance Society, 178
Amistad, 173
Annapolis Convention, 98
Anthony, Susan B., 174
Anti-federalists, 102, 110-112
Appleton, Nathan, 143
Appomattox Courthouse, 227, 231
Arnold, Benedict, 85, 87
Articles of Confederation, 94-98
Attucks, Crispus, 69
Austin, Stephen F., 187

B

Bacon, Nathaniel, 26-27
Bacon's Rebellion, 27
Bank of the United States, the, 111
Barton, Clara, 230
Battle of
    Antietam, 223-224
    Bunker Hill, 74
    Fallen Timbers, 114
    Gettysburg, 224
    Lexington and Concord, 73-74
    New Orleans, 134
    Saratoga, 85
    Shiloh, 224-225
    Tippecanoe, 131, 165
Bear Flag Revolt, 189-190
Bell, John C., 212
Berkeley, William, 26
Berlin Decree, 129
Bible, slavery and the, 195
Biddle, Nicholas, 163
Bill of Rights, 102, 109
Black Death, 16
Black soldiers, the Civil War and, 229
Blacks, the Revolutionary War and, 88-89
Bleeding Kansas, 205-207
Booth, John Wilkes, 227
Bosque Redondo, 225

Boston, 44
  Massacre, 69
  Tea Party, 70
Bowie, Jim, 187
Braddock, General, 61
Brady, Matthew, 227
Breckenridge, John, 212
Britain, 129-131, 131-135
  the Civil War and, 221
British East India Company, 70
Brooks, Preston, 207
Brown, John, 207, 212
Buchanan, James, 209
Burgoyne, General, 85
Burnside, Ambrose, 224
Burr, Aaron, 118, 129

C

Cabinet, 109
Calhoun, John C., 131, 154, 155, 157,
  158, 159-160, 202, 211
Calvin, John, 16-17
Carolina region, 34
Cass, Lewis, 196
Charbonneau, Toussaint, 128
Charleston, 86
Checks and balances, 101
Cherokee Nation v, Georgia, 162-163
Chesapeake-Leopard Affair, 129-130
Chief Pontiac, 64
China, 16
Church of England, 27
"Civil Disobedience," 175-176
Civil War, 135, 194, 219-231
  the road to, 201-214
Clay, Henry, 131, 140, 146, 155, 157, 158,
  161, 196, 202, 203
Coercive Acts of 1773, 71, 73, 74
Colonial America, 39-53
Colonial period, 23-24
Columbian Exchange, 18
Columbus, Christopher, 17
Committees of Correspondence, 69
Common Sense, 75

Compromise of 1850, the, 202-203
Confederate States of America, 213-214,
  219-231
Congregationalism, 29
Congress, 108
Connecticut Compromise, 99
Conque, 173
Constitution, 100-102, 108-110, 111, 160
  slavery and the, 194-195
Constitutional Convention, 98-103
Convention of 1800. 117
Cornwallis, 87
Corps of Discovery, 128
Cotton, 143, 194
Court system, 110
Crawford, William, 155, 157, 158
Crime, 177-178
Crittendon Compromise, 213-214
Crittendon, John J., 213
Crockett, Davy, 187
Cuba, 205
Cult of Domesticity, 175

D

Dartmouth College v. Woodward, 147
Daughters of Liberty, 68
Davis, Jefferson, 213-214, 220, 222
Dawes, William, 73
De Grasse, Admiral, 87
De Las Casas, Bartholome, 19
De Tallyrand, Charles, 116
Declaration of Independence, 49, 75
Declaration of Sentiments, 174-175
Declatory Act, 66
Democratic party, 155
Democratic-Republican party, 112-113, 126
Dickinson, John, 67, 95, 98
Dix, Dorothea, 177-178
Donner, George, 193
Douglas, Stephen A., 203, 205-206, 211, 212
Douglass, Frederick, 172-173, 204
Drake, Sir Francis, 19
Dred Scott v. Sanford, 209, 211
Dyer, Mary, 30-31

E

Eaton, John, 159
Eaton, Peggy, 159-160
Education, 176-177
Edwards, Jonathan, 50
Elastic clause, 111
Electoral college, 99
Emancipation Proclamation, 223, 228-229
Embargo Act of 1807, 130
Emerson, Ralph Waldo, 175
Enlightenment, 48-49
Era of Good Feelings, the, 139-149
Erie Canal, 142
Excise tax, 113
Exploration, the age of, 15-20

F

Federalist Party, 140
    the end of the, 135
Federalists, 102, 110-112
Fillmore, Millard, 203, 209
Finney, Charles, 179
First Continental Congress, 71-73
First Great Awakening, 49-50, 178
Florida, 144-145
Force Bill, 161
Fort Necessity, 60
Fort Sumter, 214, 221
France, 129-131
France, U.S. neutrality and, 114-115
Franklin, Benjamin, 49, 60, 64, 88, 98, 191
Free-Soil party, 196
Fremont, John, 189
French and Indian War, 61-62
French Huguenots, 19
French Revolution, 114
Fugitive Slave Act, 204
Fuller, Margaret, 176
Fulton, Robert, 141

G

Gadsden Purchase, 190
Gag rule, 174

Gage, General Thomas, 73-74
Gallaudet, Thomas Hopkins, 177
Garrison, William Lloyd, 172, 174
Gates, General Horatio, 85
Genet, Edmund, 114
Gerry, Elbridge, 100
Gettysburg Address, 224
Gibbons v. Ogden, 148-149
Glorietta Pass, 225
Gold, 24-25, 193
Grant, Ulysses, 225-227
Great Compromise, 99
Great Debate, 202, 204
Great Migration, 29
Greene, Catherine, 89
Greenville, George, 62, 65
Grimke
    Angelina, 173
    Sarah, 173
Gutenberg, Johann, 16

H

Halfway covenant, 32
Hamilton, Alexander, 98, 109, 110-112,
    113, 114, 129
Hammond, James Henry, 194
Hancock, John, 67, 73, 102
Harpers Ferry, 212
Harrison, William Henry, 131, 132,
    156, 165
Hartford Convention, 134-135
Harvard University, 44
Hawthorne, Nathaniel, 176
Hays, Mary, 89
Headright system, 25, 34
Henry, Patrick, 60, 66
Homestead Act, 227-228
House of Burgesses, 26
House of Representatives, 99
Houston, Sam, 188
Howe, Samuel Gridley, 177
Hutchinson, Anne, 30

I

Indentured servants, 25, 48, 51
Independent Treasury Bill, 164-165
Indian Removal Act, 161-163
Indigo, 48
Industrial Revolution, 142-143
Intolerable Acts, 71
Iroquois Confederacy, 86
Iroquois, 60

J

Jackson, Andrew, 134, 153-164
Jamestown, 20, 24-27, 46
Jay, John, 88, 98, 115
Jay's Treaty, 115, 116
Jefferson, Thomas, 49, 75, 109, 110, 112, 116, 118, 119, 125-135
Johnson, Patrick, 143
Joint stock company, 2
Judicial review, 147
Judiciary Act of 1789, 110

K

Kansas-Nebraska Act, 206, 209
Kearney, Stephen, 189
Key, Francis Scott, 133
King George III, 62, 66, 73, 74, 88
Kitchen Cabinet, 159
Know-Nothing Party, 209
Knox, Henry, 109

L

L'Ouverture, Toussaint, 127
Land Ordinance of 1785, 96
Lee
    Mother Ann, 180
    Richard Henry, 102
    Robert E., 223-227
Lewis and Clark, 128
Liberty Party, 196
Lincoln, Abraham, 189, 205, 207, 211, 212, 219-231

Lincoln-Douglas Debates, 211-212
Literature, 175
Livingston, Robert, 49, 127
Locke, John, 49, 75
Louisiana. 62
    Purchase, 127-128
Lowell
    Girls, 143
    Francis, 143
Loyalists, 83-84
Luther, Martin, 16

M

Macon's Bill No. 2, 130
Madison, James, 98-99, 100, 112-113, 118, 130
Manifest Destiny, 186-196
Mann, Horace, 176-177
Marbury v. Madison, 119, 147
Marbury, William, 119
Market economy, 141-143
Marshall, John, 119, 129, 147-149, 162
Massachusetts Bay, 29
Mayflower Compact, 27-28
Mayflower, 27
McClellan, George, 224
McCulloch v. Maryland, 148
McGuffey, William, 177
Melville, Herman, 176
Mercantilism, 19, 40-42
Mexican-American War, 188-191
Mexico, 187-191
Middle colonies, 32-34, 45-46
Middle Passage, 50
Midnight judges, 119
Militia Act of 1862, 229-230
Minutemen, 71, 73
Mississippi River, 186
Missouri Compromise, 145-146, 202, 206, 211
Molasses Act, 63
Monroe Doctrine, 146-147
Monroe, James, 127, 140, 146
Morrill Land Grant Act, 228
Mott, Lucretia, 174

N

Napoleon Bonaparte, 127, 129, 130
National Bank Act, 228
National Gazette, The, 112
National Republican Party, 155
National Road, 142
Native Americans, 31, 34, 161-163
    the Revolutionary War and, 89
Naturalization Act, 117
Navigation Acts, 40-41
Necessary and proper clause, 111
Neutrality, 129-131
New England colonies, 43-45
New Harmony, 180
New Jersey Plan, 99
Non-Intercourse Act, 130
North, Lord Frederick, 69
Northwest Ordinance of 1787, 97
Nott, Josiah, 195
Noyes, John Humphrey, 180
Nullification Crisis, 160-161

O

O'Sullivan, John L., 186
Oglethorpe, James, 34
Olive Branch Petition, 74
Oneida community, 180
Orders in Council, 129
Ordinance of Nullification, 161
Oregon Territory, 145, 192
Oregon Trail, 192
Orient, 16, 17
Ostend Manifesto, 205
Owen, Robert, 180

P

Pacific Railway Act, 207, 228
Paine, Thomas, 75, 84
Panic of 1819, 144
Paterson, William, 99
Penn, William, 34, 46
Perry, Commodore Oliver, 132

Pet banks, 163
Pierce, President, 206
Pike, Zebulon, 128
Pinckney, Charles, 118
Pinckney's Treaty, 115
Pitt, William, 61
Plantations, 48
Plymouth Plantation, 28
Poe, Edgar Allen, 176
Political parties, 109-119
Polk, James K., 186, 188-191, 192
Polo, Marco, 16
Popular sovereignty, 196, 202, 206
Pottawatomie Massacre, 207
Predestination, 29
Prison camps, 225
Prison reform, 177
Proclamation Line, 64
Proclamation of American Neutrality, 114
Prosser, Gabriel, 195
Protective tariffs, 111-112
Protestant Reformation, 16-17
Puritan New England, 27-32
Puritans, 28, 44

Q

Quakers, 31, 34
Quartering Act, 71
Quasi-War, 117
Quebec Act, 71

R

Radical Republicans, 222
Railroads, 207
Raleigh, Sir Walter, 19
Randolph, Edmund, 109
Reed, James, 193
Religion, 178-179
Renaissance, 16
Republican party, 206-207, 208-209
Republican Womanhood, 89
Revenue Act of 1767, 67

Revere, Paul, 69, 73
Revolutionary War, 44-45, 81-89
Rice, 34, 48
Ripley, George, 180
Roanoke Island, 19
Rolfe, John, 25
Royal colony, 26

S

Sacajawea, 128
Salem Witchcraft Trials, 32
Salter, Samuel, 143
Salutary neglect, 41
Sampson, Deborah, 89
Santa Fe Trail, 191-192
Scientific Revolution, 48
Scott
    Dred, 209
    General Winfield, 163
    Winfield, 189-190
Secession, 213-214, 220
Second Bank of the United States, 141,
    144, 148, 163-165
Second Coming of Christ, 180
Second Continental Congress, 74
Second Great Awakening, 178
Sectionalism, 135
Sedition Act, 117
"Self-Reliance," 175
Senate, 99
Seven Years War, 61
Shaker community, 180
Shawnee Indians, 131
Shays, Daniel, 97-98
Shays's Rebellion, 97-98
Sherman, General, 222, 226-227
Sherman, Roger, 49
Slave
    codes, 51
    rebellion, 51
    trade, 17, 50-54
Slavery, 26, 154, 194-195, 219-231

Smith
    John, 25
    Joseph, 179
Sons of Liberty, 66
South Carolina Exposition and Protest, 160
Southern colonies, 32-34, 46-48
Spain, 115, 128, 144, 205
Spanish
    Armada, 19
    Florida, 88
Specie circular, 164
Spoils system, 159
St. Augustine, 19
Stamp Act, 65-66
Stanton, Elizabeth Cady, 174
"Star Spangled Banner, The," 133
State banks, 163
Steamboats, 141-142, 207
Stono Rebellion, 53
Stowe, Harriet Beecher, 205
Sugar Act, 65
Sumner, Charles, 207
Supreme Court, 110, 119, 173, 211
Sutter's Mill, 193

T

Tallmadge, Jr., James, 145
Taney, Roger B., 209, 211, 221
Tariff and Abominations, 160, 161
Tariff of 1789, 111-112
Tariff of 1833, 161
Tariffs, 41
Taylor, Zachary, 189, 196, 202, 203
Tea Act, 70
Tecumseh, 131
Temperance movement, 178
Texas, 187-188
Thoreau, Henry David, 175-176
3/5 Compromise, 100
Timberlake, John, 159
Tobacco, 25, 48
Tories, 83-84

Town meetings, 44
Townshend
    Duties, 67-69
    Charles, 67
Trade, 141-142
Trail of Tears, 163
Transcendentalism, 175
Transportation, 141-142
Travis, William, 187
Treaty of
    Paris of 1783, 88
    Ghent, 134
    Greenville, 114
    Guadalupe Hidalgo, 190
    Paris (1763), 62
    Tordesillas, 17
Triangular trade, 41-42
Tubman, Harriet, 173
Turner, Nat, 195
Two-party system, 154-156
Tyler, John, 165
Types of Mankind, 195
Tyranny, 84

U

Uncle Tom's Cabin, 205
Underground Railroad, 173, 204
Utopian communities, 179-180

V

Vailey Forge, 85
Van Buren, Martin, 156, 159-160,
    164-165, 196
Vesey, Denmark, 195
Veto power, 158
Virginia and Kentucky Resolutions,
    118, 160
Virginia Company, 24, 25
Virginia Plan, 99

Virginia Resolves, 66
Virtual representation, 65
Voting, 94, 100

W

Walden, 175
War debt, 95-96
War Hawks, 130-131
War of 1812, 131-135, 141, 143, 186
Washington, D.C., 110, 111
Washington, George, 64, 74, 84, 87, 98,
    108-109, 112, 114, 115-116
Webster, Daniel, 155, 158, 202
Webster, Noah, 177
Whig Party, 155-156, 208
Whigs, 83-84
Whiskey Rebellion, 112, 113
White, John, 20
Whitney, Eli, 143
Williams, Roger, 30
Wilmot Proviso, 191
Winthrop, John, 29, 31
Women
    the Civil War and, 230
    the Revolutionary War and, 89
Women's issues, 174
Worcester v. Georgia, 162
Writs of assistance, 63-64

X

XYZ affair, 116

Y

Yorktown, 87
Young, Brigham, 180

Z

Zenger, John Peter, 45

About the Author

RON OLSON, co-teacher, leader, and faculty member of the Achiever School at Clover Park High School in Lakewood, Washington, has more than 23 years of teaching experience, including extensive experience with AP U.S. history, American literature, AP government, and humanities courses. Ron earned his BA in history and English from New Mexico State University in 1981 and earned his MA in secondary education from Adams State College in 1983. In addition, he serves as a faculty consultant for the College Board and is currently pursuing his National Board Teacher Certification. He currently resides in Bonney Lake, Washington.

The Essential Help You Need When Your
Textbooks Just Aren't Making the Grade!

Great preparation for the SAT II and AP Courses

CAREE
PRES